Boater's Guide to
Lake Powell

Featuring **Hiking,** Camping, Geology, History & Archaeology

Michael R. Kelsey

Kelsey Publishing
456 E. 100 N.
Provo, Utah, USA, 84606
Tele. 801-373-3327

First Edition March 1989
Copyright ©1989, Michael R. Kelsey All Rights Reserved
Library of Congress Catalog Card Number 88-082307
ISBN 0-9605824-9-5

Distributors for the Kelsey Publishing
Please write to one of these companies when ordering any of Mike Kelsey's guide books.
A list of his titles are in the back of this book.

Primary Distributor
Wasatch Publishers, Inc., 4647 Idlewild Road, Salt Lake City, Utah, USA, 84124,
Tele. 801-278-3174.

Alpenbooks, P.O. Box 27344, Seattle, Washington, 98125, Tele. 206-672-9316
Bookpeople, 2929 Fifth Street, Berkeley, California, 94710, Tele. 227-1516
Canyon Country Publications, P. O. Box 963, Moab, Utah, 84532, Tele. 801-259-
6700
Gordon's Books, 2323 Delgany, Denver, Colorado, 80216, Tele. 303-296-1830
Many Feathers, 2626 West, Indian School Road, Phoenix, Arizona, 85012, Tele. 602-
266-1043
Nevada Publications, 4135 Badger Circle, Reno, Nevada, 89509, Tele. 702-747-0800
Pacific Pipeline, Inc., 19215 66th Avenue S., Kent, Washington, 98032-1171, Tele.
206-872-5523
Quality Books(Library Distributor), 918 Sherwood Drive, Lake Bluff, Illinois, 60044,
Tele.
Mountain 'n Air Books, 3704 1/2 Foothill Blvd., La Crescenta, California, 91214, Tele.
818-957-5338
Recreational Equipment, Inc.(R.E.I.), P.O. Box C-88126, Seattle, Washington,
98188, Tele. 800-426-4840(or check at any of their local stores).

For the **UK** and **Europe**, and the rest of the world contact:
CORDEE, 3a De Montfort Street, Leicester, England, UK, LE1 7HD, Tele. 0533-54379

All fotos by the author, unless otherwise stated.
All maps, charts, and cross sections drawn by the author.

Front Cover

Front Cover Fotos
1. Anasazi granary, Moqui Canyon
2. Camping scene, Padre Bay
3. Near Cottonwood Canyon, and Navajo Mountain
4. Sculptured narrows, Antelope Canyon

Back Cover

Back Cover Fotos
5. Kaibito Falls, Kaibito Creek, Chaol Canyon
6. Petroglyphs, big horn sheep, Chaol Canyon
7. End of inlet, Mountain Sheep Canyon
8. Sandstone Buttes, near mouth of Labyrinth Canyon
9. Rubber raft with motor, Cataract Canyon
10. Gunsight Spring, Gunsight Canyon

Table of Contents

Acknowledgments and the Author..4
Metric Conversion Table...5
Map Symbols and Abbreviations...6
Part I--Introduction and History..7
    The First Occupants 7   History of the Cattle Industry 11
    Spaniards and Trappers...................8   Glen Canyon & San Juan Gold Rush. 18
    The Mormons...............10   The Dam Builders 19
    River Exploration & John W. Powell...10   Sedimentation of Lake Powell..........20
Part II--Introduction to Boating, Hiking & Camping.....................22
    Marinas on Lake Powell..................22   Preserving Archaeology Sites..........36
    Other Launch Sites......................31   Insects and Pests........................36
    Weather and Climate.....................32   Drinking Water...........................37
    Hiking Season 35   Camping on Lake Powell 38
    Hiking Equipment 35
Part III--Geology, Maps and Odds and Ends.............................41
    Geology of Glen Canyon.................41   Odds and Ends of Information........48
    Maps of Lake Powell Country..........46   Reference Map of Hikes................49
Part IV--The Canyons 50
    1. Cataract, Imperial and Calf Canyons 50
    2. Gypsum, Palmer, Easter P., Clearwater & Bowdie Canyons & Ocean Pt. Hike...58
    3. Cove, Rockfall and Dark Canyons..................................66
    4. Freddies Cistern, Sheep, Narrow and Rock Canyons 72
    5. Dirty Devil River, North Wash,and Farley & White Canyons 76
    6. Trachyte and Swett Creeks 82
    7. Twomile, Fourmile, Scorup, Blue Notch and Red Canyons............86
    8. Ticaboo Creek and South Fork 90
    9. Sevenmile & Cedar Canyons,and Good Hope Bay.....................94
    10. Tapestry Wall Hike, Smith Fork and Warm Springs Canyon 100
    11. Knowles, Forgotten, Hansen and Crystal Springs Canyons 106
    12. North Gulch, Moqui & Stanton Canyons, and Bullfrog Bay 112
    13. Halls Creek & Bay, Waterpocket Fold Hikes and Lost Eden Canyon .118
    14. Lake & Annies Canyons and Schock & Gretchen Bar Trails & Lake Pagahrit..124
    15. Slickrock and Iceberg Canyons...................................132
    16. The Rincon and Rincon Overlook Hikes 136
    17. Long & Bowns Canyons and the Black Trail........................142
    18. Explorer, Fence and Cow Canyons.................................150
    19. Fortymile Gulch, Willow Creek and Bishop Canyon.................156
    20. Fiftymile Creek, Davis Gulch,and Clear & Indian Creek Canyons .160
    21. Ribbon & Cottonwood Canyons and Hole-in-the-Rock & Jackass Bh. Trails ...166
    22. Llewellyn Gulch & Reflection, Music Temple & Hidden Passage Canyons......174
    23. Mikes & Copper Canyons, Castle Creek and Johnies Hole & Nokai Dome 178
    24. Spencer Road, Williams Trail and Nokai Canyon...................184
    25. Great Bend Canyons and Neskahi & Piute Canyons..................190
    26. Deep, Desha , and Trail Canyons 196
    27. Wilson Creek Canyon 200
    28. Nasja, Bald Rock and Cha Canyons................................202
    29. Oak, Secret, Forbidding, Cliff & Rainbow Bridge Canyons 208
    30. Twilight and Anasazi Canyons 214
    31. Cascade, Driftwood, Balanced Rk & Dangling R. Canyons & Klondike Trail 216
    32. Cathedral and Mountain Sheep Canyons 224
    33. Wetherill and Dungeon Canyons 228
    34. Dry and Middle Rock Creeks 232
    35. Rock Creek, Woolsey Arch and Steer Canyon 236

36. West and Face Canyons 240
37. Last Chance, Croton, Little Valley & Friendship Canyons and Last C. Bay..... 246
38. Gunsight & Labyrinth Canyons and Padre Bay & Crossing of the Fathers...... 250
39. Navajo Creek & Chaol Canyon and the Dominguez & Escalante Trail 258
40. Warm Creek Bay, Crosby Canyon and the Spencer Coal Mines 266
41. Antelope Canyon 272
42. Wiregrass Canyon and Wahweap Bay 276
Further Reading and Information Sources **286**
Other Guide Books by the Author **288**

Acknowledgments

There must have been dozens of people who helped with information leading to the writing of this book, but the following people were most helpful. There were several people in the National Park Service who parted with advice and information. Archaeologist Chris Kincaid read the rough draft and made helpful suggestions. Paul Zaenger and Chuck Wood were helpful concerning hiking places and water quality. Ross Rice(NPS) and Max Jackson(Kane County Sheriff), informed the author of the wild horse roundup in Bowns Canyon. Jim Holland, Vic Viera, Kate Cannon and Karen Whitney reviewed the rough draft.

There were older stockmen in the local communities who helped to locate and gave a history, on some of the old cattle trails in the area. They include Riter Ekker of Hanksville; Leo Wilson and Vernon Griffin of Escalante; hunting guide and former BLM ranger Carl Mahon; John Scorup and Melvin Dalton of Monticello; Clarence Rogers of Blanding; and Edith Clinger of Orem.

In addition, the author spoke with two aging Navajo men about trails located on Navajo Nation lands. They were Kee B. Tso, who lives near the Kaibito Chapter House, and Owen Yazzie who lives just southeast of the butte named Leche-E Rock. Yazzie worked as a member of one of the Civilian Conservation Corps(CCC) crews which built trails in Navajo Canyon in the mid-1930's.

Stan Jones of Page correlated some information with the author, and his map of Lake Powell got the author started. There was no personal communication with C. Gregory Crampton of St. George, but his published research from the University of Utah in the late 1950's and early 1960's, was most helpful in locating many old stock trails and gave a history of Glen Canyon before the coming of Lake Powell.

There were several employees of the Del Webb Corporation(the concessionaire on Lake Powell) who looked at the rough draft. They were Steve Ward and Dave Neuburger. As this book goes to press, this company is being sold. The likely owner will be ARA Leisure Services.

As usual, my mother Venetta Kelsey, was instrumental in proof reading the manuscript and watching after the business while I was out boating and hiking on the lake.

The Author

The author experienced his earliest years of life in eastern Utah's Uinta Basin, namely around the town of Roosevelt. Then the family moved to Provo, where he attended Provo High School and later Brigham Young University, where he earned a B.S. degree in Sociology. Shortly thereafter he discovered that was the wrong subject, so he attended the University of Utah, where he received his Masters of Science degree in Geography, finishing that in June, 1970.

It was then that real life began, for on June 9, 1970, he put a pack on his back and started traveling for the first time. Since then he has traveled to 130 countries and island groups. All this wandering has resulted in several books written and published by him: *Climbers and Hikers Guide to the Worlds Mountains(Out of print--3rd Ed. due in 1990-91); Utah Mountaineering Guide, and the Best Canyon Hikes(2nd Ed.); China on Your Own and the Hiking Guide to China's Nine Sacred Mountains(3rd Ed.); Canyon Hiking Guide to the Colorado Plateau(2nd printing); Hiking Utah's San Rafael Swell; Hiking and Exploring Utah's Henry Mountains and Robbers Roost; Hiking and Exploring the Paria River; and Hiking and Climbing in the Great Basin National Park(Wheeler Peak, Nevada).*

Metric Conversion Table

1 Centimeter = .39 Inch	1 Mile = 1.609 Kilometers	1 Quart (US) = .946 Liter
1 Inch = 2.54 Centimeters	100 Miles = 161 Kilometers	1 Gallon (US) = 3.785 Liters
1 Meter = 39.37 Inches	100 Kilometers = 62 Miles	1 Acre = 0.405 Hectare
1 Foot = 0.3048 Meter	1 Liter = 1.056 Quarts (US)	1 Hectare = 2.471 Acres
1 Kilometer = 0.621 Mile		

METERS TO FEET (Meters x 3.2808 = Feet)

100 m = 328 ft.	2500 m = 8202 ft.	5000 m = 16404 ft.	7500 m = 24606 ft.
500 m = 1640 ft.	3000 m = 9842 ft.	5500 m = 18044 ft.	8000 m = 26246 ft.
1000 m = 3281 ft.	3500 m = 11483 ft.	6000 m = 19686 ft.	8500 m = 27887 ft.
1500 m = 4921 ft.	4000 m = 13124 ft.	6500 m = 21325 ft.	9000 m = 29527 ft.
2000 m = 6562 ft.	4500 m = 14764 ft.	7000 m = 22966 ft.	

FEET TO METERS (Feet ÷ 3.2808 = Meters)

1000 ft. = 305 m	9000 ft. = 2743 m	16000 ft. = 4877 m	23000 ft. = 7010 m
2000 ft. = 610 m	10000 ft. = 3048 m	17000 ft. = 5182 m	24000 ft. = 7315 m
3000 ft. = 914 m	11000 ft. = 3353 m	18000 ft. = 5486 m	25000 ft. = 7620 m
4000 ft. = 1219 m	12000 ft. = 3658 m	19000 ft. = 5791 m	26000 ft. = 7925 m
5000 ft. = 1524 m	13000 ft. = 3962 m	20000 ft. = 6096 m	27000 ft. = 8230 m
6000 ft. = 1829 m	14000 ft. = 4268 m	21000 ft. = 6401 m	28000 ft. = 8535 m
7000 ft. = 2134 m	15000 ft. = 4572 m	22000 ft. = 6706 m	29000 ft. = 8839 m
8000 ft. = 2438 m			30000 ft. = 9144 m

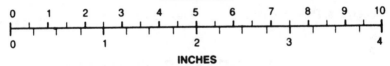

CENTIMETERS / INCHES

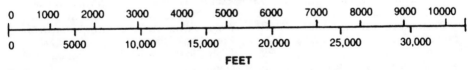

METERS / FEET

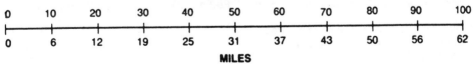

KILOMETERS / MILES

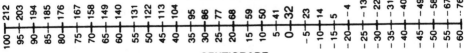

FAHRENHEIT / CENTIGRADE

5

MAP SYMBOLS

Building, Ranch or Cabin.............	▫	Trail...	‐‐‐
Lakeside Campsite......................	▲	Route, No Trail...........................	......
Towns or Communities...............	▫▫	Peak and Prominent Ridge...........	〜✕〜
Campground(Developed)	⅄	Stream or Creek.........................	〜
Visitor Center(NPS)	⅄	Dry Creek Bed	▬‐‐
Landing Strip..............................	✚	Waterfalls, Dry Falls..............	▬✈
State, US Highway..................	�995 🛡89	Canyon Rim, Escarpment...........	🗂
Road(Maintained)...................	▬ ▬ ▬	Lake, Colorado River...............	▨▨
Road(4WD or HCV)	⟋⟋⟋	Mine, Quarry, Adit, Prospect	⤣⤢
Mile Post Markers................ 1 2	⟋⟋	Spring....................................	○
Geology Cross Section...........	⌐⌐	Pass......................................	)(
Buoys........................M76(K122)	●	Natural Bridge, Arch or Cave..........	∩
Ruins, Petroglyphs, Pictographs....	●	Elevation in Meters.....................	1128

ABBREVIATIONS

Canyon	C.	Campgrounds............................	CG.
Lake..	L.	Campsites	C.S.
River..	R.	Mine	M.
Creek...	Ck.	Four Wheel Drive.......................	4WD
Peak..	Pk.	High Clearance Vehicle................	HCV
Waterfall, Dry Fall, Formation............	F.	Spring......................................	Sp.
Kilometer(s) .... km, kms		High Water Mark........................	HWM
Sandstone................................	S.S.	Pothole	PH.

Glen Canyon National Recreation Area .... GCNRA
United States Geological Survey... USGS
National Park Service.. NPS
Bureau of Land Management .... BLM
Miles(Kilometers) up lake from Glen Canyon Dam............................... M171(K274)
Miles(Kilometers) up lake from the mouth of the San Juan River................ M54(K86)

Part 1--Introduction

For several years now the author has considered writing some kind of guide book to Lake Powell, but it wasn't until he saw the visitation chart showing nearly 3 million people visited the Glen Canyon National Recreation Area in 1987, that the idea was really seriously considered. It seemed odd that an area so popular would be without a guide book of any kind.

The only problem was, he had never boated before in his life. This was the biggest challenge of the entire summer of 1988; going out on the second largest man-made lake in the United States alone, with new and untried equipment.

It was decided to buy an inflatable boat(rubber raft) because; it could be used later for river running, it would be very light weight, no trailer would be involved, and storage would be easier. An underpowered VW Rabbit diesel was instrumental in making the decision to buy an inflatable.

To go with the raft, a small 4 hp outboard was bought, and a small frame to make the motor mount more rigid was built. At times the speed of movement was sheer agony, but the 4 hp did well, and the author did most of the footwork for this book in a 3 month period, during the spring and early summer of 1988. Another month of footwork was completed in the fall of 1988.

The original idea for this book was that of a *hiking guide* only, since that's the author's specialty. But once on the lake for the first time, it was realized immediately that more was needed. First of all, some sections of the lake have no camping places whatsoever. The already available written material didn't cover camping very well, so it became necessary to include some kind of guide for this.

Since there were a number of Anasazi ruins in the canyons and below the lake, it was necessary to include something about these ancient ones. Many years after the Anasazi left this canyon country, in came fur trappers and explorers, then miners and cattlemen. All of these people left a mark on Glen Canyon, so it was thought something should be said about each, and their history. The last subject to be included was some kind of discussion on the unique geology of the canyon, which is after all, the heart of the reason everybody wants to go there. It's the scenery! Lake Powell has to be rated the best all around boating lake in this country and perhaps the world.

The First Occupants

We know little about the first peoples who may have lived in the canyons of the Colorado River. Studies made of the bottom layers of caves in the region reveal there were mammoth, bison, sloth, and camel inhabiting this region about 13,000 years ago. Just west of the Henry Mountains, in Cowboy Cave, dung from the above listed animals was found. Bechan Cave in Bowns Canyon revealed similar findings. Most researchers believe the reason these animals disappeared on this continent was over-hunting by man. Most believe man first appeared in North America about 20,000 to 15,000 years ago, but evidence that old has never been found in the Glen Canyon area.

In Cowboy Cave, the earliest sign of human existence(charcoal) was concluded to be about 8900 years old. In another layer, some clay figurines were found and dated to about 6700 to 6400 years ago. In each layer of that cave more evidence was found of human habitation, up until nearly the present.

Some of the more recent settlers to these canyons have been called the *Anasazi*. This is a Navajo word meaning, *The Ancient Ones*. They may have been in the canyons about 2000 years ago, but little is known of these early groups. The people we know so much about today are the ones who lived in the Four Corners area from about 900 AD until about 1300 AD. It's this last group of people who built the cliff dwellings seen in some of the canyons leading to Lake Powell.

The Anasazi have been divided into several groups. The ones in the area north of the San Juan River, but east of the Colorado River, are the Mesa Verde with the heart of their civilization at Mesa Verde in southwest Colorado. South of the San Juan and east of the Colorado, was inhabited by what we call the Kayenta Anasazi. In areas west of the Colorado River, and south of the Aquarius Plateau, were the Virgin Anasazi; and west of the river and north of the Boulder Mountains were the Fremonts, a totally different linguistic group of people.

The Anasazi, whose ancestors are now believed to be the Pueblo Indians of the southwest, developed into an agrarian society. They grew corn, beans, and squash, and ate wild fruits. They had domesticated turkeys and made permanent homes. They also did some hunting. The earliest Anasazi made baskets, but had no pottery. Later they did make fine pottery, some of which has been found in the former occupied areas.

The Fremonts, who may have been the forefathers of today's Utes and Piutes, were hunters and gathers. However, they borrowed ideas from the Anasazi, including some agriculture, but it was used

7

very little. The Fremonts left behind much less that is visible today than did the mostly cliff dwelling Anasazi. Both groups however did engage in rock art. They both made pictographs(painted images) and petroglyphs(pecked onto the rock), and some of these are visible in almost every canyon. Pictographs and especially petroglyphs, are almost always found on south facing boulders or walls, with lots of desert varnish; or in the case of pictographs, in caves or in protected places under overhangs.

Most of the cliff dwellings studied in this area date from about 1150 AD to 1300 AD. There is little or nothing dated from after that period, until more recently when Navajos, Piutes and Utes were in the same area. Why they left is still a mystery, but prominent ideas are; there was a long drought, or there was fighting with some hostile tribe. The author bought these ideas, until he saw Lake Canyon and the remains of Lake Pagahrit.

Briefly, this little lake at the head of Lake Canyon, was in an unused area until the white man came with his herds of cattle and his greed. Cattle were first introduced there in the 1880's, then in the mid-1890's there was a sustained drought, which forced many of the big cattle operators to leave the area. After a few years of overgrazing and trail making, the land couldn't handle it any longer. After three days of heavy rains, Lake Pagahrit burst it's natural dam on November 1, 1915. That resulted in the down cutting of the soil seen in the lower canyon today, and the lowering of the water table.

With lots of Anasazi people in the same canyons, the same erosional patterns could surely have taken place, with all the trails, disturbed ground, etc. Once erosion got started, it would have down-cut during periods of flash flooding to the point that water couldn't be used for irrigation and the water table would be much lower. Thus they had to leave. There are many other theories as to why they left as well.

The Spaniards and Trappers

During the years after about 1300 AD, not much is known of the Glen Canyon country until the Spaniards came in 1776, a void of almost 500 years. Surely there were occupants, but they were likely nomadic and left little or nothing but foot prints.

Some researchers believe the Navajo came into the region very late in time, about 1500 AD. The Navajo people are part of the Athabascan language group, and are not related to the Hopi and other Pueblo Indians of the American southwest. They migrated south from the Yukon region where others of the same tribe still reside(the Athabascan Tribe of the Yukon Territory). Navajos were in the canyon country, mostly to the south of the San Juan River, at the time the Spaniards first arrived.

A new era came to Glen Canyon with the Dominguez and Escalante Party. They were Catholic priests, who were out to find a new route to California from their home in Santa Fe, New Mexico. They went north through western Colorado, west to Utah Lake near Provo, then south to about Cedar City, approximately along the present-day I-15 Highway route. Because of various reason they decided to head home rather than complete the journey to California. Rather than backtrack, it was decided to look for a new short-cut route, so they headed east across southern Utah.

They ended up at the mouth of the Paria River, which in recent years has been known as Lee's Ferry. From there they headed northeast and crossed the Colorado River at a place now under the waters of Padre Bay, at the Crossing of the Fathers. That was on November 7, 1776. Then they headed south and east back to Santa Fe. Read more details under Map 38.

These two priests were the first white men to see the Colorado and the Glen Canyon area. Half a century later, and about the same time Mexico became independent(1821), a Mexican named Antonio Armijo took a trading party of 31 men across the Colorado at the Crossing of the Fathers, and later returned from California the same way. These people called the crossing, "El Vado de Los Padres". But it was so rugged and wild, another easier route was eventually opened further north near Moab, Utah. After that, the crossing became lost and was not re-discovered until the Powell Expeditions.

In the 1820's and 1830's, the Old Spanish Trail crossed the Colorado River at what would later be Moab; then the Green River where Green River town is today. From there it headed west, but north of the San Rafael Swell, up over Salina Canyon and on southwest to California.

After the Spaniards and Mexicans left the region, there were a few solitary travelers in the canyon, mostly the trappers. Little if any is known of these men, but one apparently put his graffiti on the walls of Cataract Canyon. That was Denis Julien, a French fur trapper, who must have passed that way by boat in 1836.

ANASAZI AND FREMONT INDIAN GROUPS

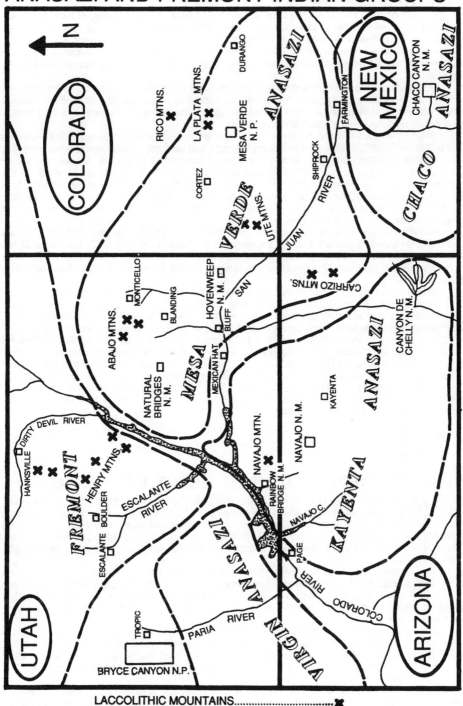

LACCOLITHIC MOUNTAINS.............................**✕**
NATIONAL MONUMENTS.............................**N. M.**

The Mormons

The next reported time any white man crossed the Colorado at the Crossing of the Fathers was on November 8, 1858. That was when Jacob Hamblin and 10 companions headed south to Hopi Land to preach to the Indians. On a subsequent trip, their luck ran out and one Mormon was killed near Moenkopi as the group rode toward the Colorado River. All in all, Hamblin and other missionaries made many trips across the river at this old Spanish crossing, which in Hamblin's day was referred to as the Ute Ford or Crossing.

In the mid and late 1860's, there were many crossings of the Colorado, mainly by Navajos, who raided Mormon settlements and drove cattle back across the river. Indians all over Utah were more or less at war with the Mormons for a time in the late 1860's. The reason for it all was that the Mormons were taking over the hunting grounds of the Indians.

All this fighting led to a war between the Navajo Nation and the United States. Kit Carson was sent to Arizona in 1863, with orders to destroy all crops and livestock. Their hogans were destroyed, fields burned, and they were hunted down, with many being killed by the US Cavalry. Finally the majority of the Navajos, about 8,000, were incarcerated at Fort Sumner in eastern New Mexico from 1864 through 1868. In Navajo history, this was known as the "Long Walk". Those who refused to be exiled, hid out in lonely canyons, or mixed with the Piutes. During this time period the Mormons withdrew from outlying areas, but the Navajos still raided and took cattle east across the Colorado along the Crossing of the Fathers route.

All traffic stopped using the Crossing of the Fathers route in the period after 1872-73. This was because of the opening of Lee's Ferry at the mouth of the Paria River by John D. Lee. John D. was sent to this lonely outpost by the Mormon Church because Federal lawmen were pursuing him for his involvement in the Mountain Meadows Massacre, which left 120 members of a Missouri wagon train dead.

Lee and part of his family had arrived at the Colorado River on December 23, 1871, and first used one of John W. Powell's boats as a ferry on January 18, 1872, to help some Navajos across the river. Later, a real ferry boat was built by a man named Heath, and was first launched on January 11, 1873. After the building of this ferry, the Crossing of the Fathers or Ute Ford simply was used no more.

Another group of Mormons was called in 1879 from the southern Utah communities of Parowan and Cedar City, to colonize the San Juan River Valley in the area of what is known today as Bluff. They could have used John D. Lee's boat at Lee's Ferry, or they could have headed north to Green River, then south to Moab, and on to the San Juan, but they chose to try a new shorter route instead. This is what we now call the Hole-in-the-Rock Trail. They thought they could make it in 6 weeks, but it took 6 months. This was the San Juan Mission Party, otherwise known as the Hole-in-the-Rock Expedition. Read more details under Map 21.

River Exploration and John W. Powell

On May 24, 1869, John Wesley Powell and nine other men got off the train in Green River, Wyoming, jumped into four little row boats and started one of the epic journeys of all time, a boat trip down the uncharted Green and Colorado Rivers. This was the first time it had been done. Surely others had seen parts of the river canyon, but he and his men saw it all. Actually, while in the Grand Canyon, three of his men abandoned the expedition, and while walking north to Kanab, were killed by Shivwits Indians.

A second journey resumed in May of 1871. The second trip was better organized and more for scientific study than the first, which was more a test of survival. This trip ended at Lee's Ferry, and Powell spent nearly a year doing survey work in southern Utah. Finally, they resumed the river expedition again at Lee's Ferry, and went as far as Kanab Creek in the middle of the Grand Canyon, then it was abandoned.

Because of his exploits on the Colorado, and other survey work in the region, the one-armed Powell ended up as head of the USGS, and the lake behind Glen Canyon Dam was named in his honor. Years after his expeditions, he published his report originally titled, *Canyons of the Colorado*. Later printings of the same book were called, *The Exploration of the Colorado River and it's Canyons*. This one is still in print, and is based mostly on his first trip down the Colorado.

On Powell's second expedition was a man named Frederick S. Dellenbaugh. He kept a good diary, which he later published. It's titled, *A Canyon Voyage*. In the canyons section of this book, are quotations from both of these men's diaries.

History of the Cattle Industry

The history of raising and herding cattle in the canyons leading into the Colorado River and the present Lake Powell, largely began with the early settlements founded by the Mormons. On the west side of the river it took until the 1880's before any one even got close to the river and the almost impenetrable canyons. Hanksville was first settled in 1882, but most of those people were farmers, with cattle ranching mostly a sideline. It must have been sometime in the late 1880's before they really got down into the canyons. By that time some ranches were being developed in the Henry Mountains south of Hanksville and others in the Robbers Roost area east of town. It was only then the lower winter ranges were fully utilized.

In 1887, Wise Cooper, John King and Mack Webb of the Fillmore area, took a herd of cattle to the east side of Boulder Mountain for the summer. Later on, they moved them down into the lower canyon country near the Colorado River to winter. This was likely the first time cattle had ranged so near the river on the west side. A little further to the southwest is the ranching community of Boulder. It was first settled by Amasa Lyman and his family in 1889. These original settlers were farmers.

Slowly but surely, others migrated into the region and settled places like Escalante(late 1870's) and Kanab, but these people were mostly farmers too and it took a while before they built up large herds of cattle. Also, in the beginning there was trouble with the various Indian tribes stealing their livestock, so this factor kept herds close to home. It appears to have been in the 1890's and near the turn of the century before Glen Canyon was really used much as a winter grazing area for cattle on the west side.

The east side of the Colorado River has quite a different history. All this country was later to become San Juan County, a region almost forgotten by Brigham Young in his early colonizing efforts. The Moab region, or Spanish Valley, was first settled(rather, attempted to be settled) by what was called the Elk Mountain Mission in 1855. They were Mormons sent there by the church. But it wasn't long afterwards that two members of the group were killed and three others wounded by Indians. The settlement and fort were abandoned, and the land returned to its rightful owners.

It wasn't until the late 1870's that any more whites attempted to settle this forgotten corner of the Utah Territory. These were scattered farmers and ranchers that generally speaking didn't have successful beginnings. One farmer was Peter Shirts, who built a cabin on lower Montezuma Creek, south of the Abajo Mountains near the San Juan River.

There were others in the Moab area and to the south of the La Sal Mountains. This included the Maxwells, Rays and McCartys in 1877. At about this same time, there were several individuals from the settlements of Mount Pleasant, Salina, and Manti areas of central Utah, who took small herds of cattle and built homes at what would be called La Sal and Coyote, just south of the La Sal Mountains. They wintered their cattle close to the Colorado, in what is today Canyonlands National Park, just northeast of the north end of Lake Powell.

The first successful effort to colonize any part of San Juan County by the Mormon Church was with the San Juan Mission, otherwise known as the Hole-in-the-Rock Expedition. This group from the Cedar City and Parowan areas arrived on the San Juan River at Bluff in April of 1880. They had begun with 1000 head of livestock, but fewer than that ended up at Bluff. However, they did stop at Lake Pagahrit along the way to rest their animals, and found it to be an excellent pasture. From that time on, the Bluff Mormons always had cattle grazing the Pagahrit country. Read the full story of their incredible journey under Map 21.

At about the same time Bluff was first settled(1880), a man named Wilson brought a number of cattle to Recapture Creek, due south of the Abajo Mountains and near the San Juan River. According to Day's thesis, his cattle soon spread over a large area, then in the early 1880's, he sold all or most of his stock to the L. C. or Lacy Cattle Company. The Lacy outfit ran stock from the area of Monticello south to the San Juan River. Later, the Lacy Company sold most of its holdings in the late 1890's to people outside the state, but many cattle were stolen by their own rustlin' wranglers.

The author believes this may be the Wilson who first ran livestock in the Wilson Mesa area, which includes Grey Mesa, Wilson Creek(originally called Sunshine Canyon), Cottonwood and Iceberg Canyons(for many years before Lake Powell days this drainage was called Wilson Canyon), and The Rincon. If indeed it's the same Wilson who left his name on so many geographic areas, it is perhaps he who first began to build some of the livestock trails down into the slickrock canyons between the Colorado and San Juan Rivers. According to old timer Clarence Rogers of Blanding, Wilson had a number of horses on Grey Mesa in the mid-1880's to about 1890, then he left the country.

At the same time period Bluff had its beginnings, a man from western Colorado named Joshua(Spud) Hudson discovered the Blue Mountains(now known as the Abajo Mtns.), which he said was virgin cattle country. He put stock there for the first time in 1880. This also appears to be the first time any non-Mormon had attempted to settle that region.

In 1883, a large outfit known as the Kansas and New Mexico Land and Cattle Company, owned by two English brothers named Harold and Ted Carlisle, began operations in southeastern Utah. They bought out the Hudson interests, and later became one of the biggest cattle companies in the United States. It appears they never did make it to the canyons close to the Colorado River, but instead ran cattle in the Abajo Mountains during the summer, and between the Abajos and the La Sal Mountains in winter. Their company headquarters was just north of present-day Monticello, at a place called Double Cabin.

Later the ranch headquarters was called Carlisle. They ran cattle until about 1898, then the drought forced them into selling most of their stock. When they sold the cattle, sheep were brought in as replacements. The Carlisle Ranch was sold to a group of Mormons, including some of the Redds, in 1911. From that point on, Charley Redd and some of his kinfolk, and others, ran cattle in the former Carlisle and Lacy or L. C. Cattle Company ranges.

In February of 1884, a big flood came down Cottonwood Canyon, and nearly wiped out the town of Bluff. As a result of plentiful rainfall that spring, a man from New Mexico brought a large flock of sheep into the country, and grazed them in the vicinity of Bluff. The Mormons became worried for fear their own livestock wouldn't have enough grass to eat, so they banned together and bought the entire flock. This community effort was known as the San Juan Co-op, which also ran the only store in town at that time. Later writers have called this the Bluff Pool.

In 1885, Charles H. Ogden and Jim Blood, who represented investors from Pittsburg, arrived in the Moab and La Sal region of San Juan County. They bought out all or most of the small cattle ranchers to form the Pittsburg Cattle Company. They wintered their stock to the west and in the lower canyons leading into the Colorado River, just to the northeast of the upper end of present-day Lake Powell. This is the east part of what is now Canyonlands National Park. The Pittsburg outfit lasted until just after 1900, when Cunningham, Carpenter and Prewer bought them out. Still later, these three sold out to the La Sal Livestock Company. This cattle company still exits today, but it's had many different owners over the years.

In 1885, a number of small cattlemen moved into the Indian Creek area, which drains the north slopes of the Abajo Mtns. Today(1989), this area belongs to one big outfit known as The Dugout, or Dugout Ranch. It got its name because some of the early settlers lived in dugouts. It's near Newspaper Rock and along the road leading to The Needles section of Canyonlands National Park. These stockmen used the Abajo Mountains as their summer range, and the canyons closer to Cataract Canyon of the Colorado as the winter range.

The first to settle Indian Creek was D. M. Cooper and Mel Turner. In 1887, John E. Brown settled in the same area and planted an orchard and began to raise hay. He was the first of the cattlemen in San Juan County to use hay or alfalfa for winter feed. In 1895, the Indian Creek Cattle Company or Dugout Ranch, was bought by David Goudelock. He lived there until 1918. It's believed by present day cowboys, that Goudelock was the one who built many of the stock trails in the region just east of Cataract Canyon.

On the other side of the mountain at Bluff, things weren't going so well. The Mormons were basically farmers, and they had hoped to create diversion dams and canals to divert water from the San Juan River to irrigate their farms. But this proved more difficult than they had imagined. The San Juan was prone to huge floods at times and very low water at other times. It also had a wide sandy bottom, which made it difficult to get river water out and onto their fields. Also, the spring flood of 1884 down Cottonwood Canyon, had wiped out many of their ditches and roads. In 1885, and on the verge of failure, they decided to expand and get into the cattle business. At that time, they were surrounded by an estimated 50,000 head of cattle belonging to *Gentile outfits* in San Juan County. Thus began a new era in the history of Bluff. In a years time it changed from a struggling farm village to a cooperative livestock enterprise, which made Bluff one of the richest towns in America, per capita.

The person who began to implement this change was Francis A. Hammond, who was appointed president of the Mormon San Juan Stake in 1885. According to Charles Peterson's story of *San Juan in Controversy*, it states; he[Hammond] was elected to the San Juan county court in the August election of 1885, thus giving him an important political position several months before he left his home in Huntsville[northern Utah].

After several months of planning, Hammond and the Mormons put together what was later known as the Bluff Pool(sometimes called the Mormon Pool), on January 16, 1886. According to L. H. Redd, in those days they just called it the San Juan Co-op. And since they grazed on the Elk Ridge to the north during the summer season, the livestock end of the business was called the Elk Cattle Company.

They put out an invitation to other Mormons, *to come immediately and help us stock up the range.*

BIG TIME CATTLE COMPANIES AND THEIR RANGES--1890

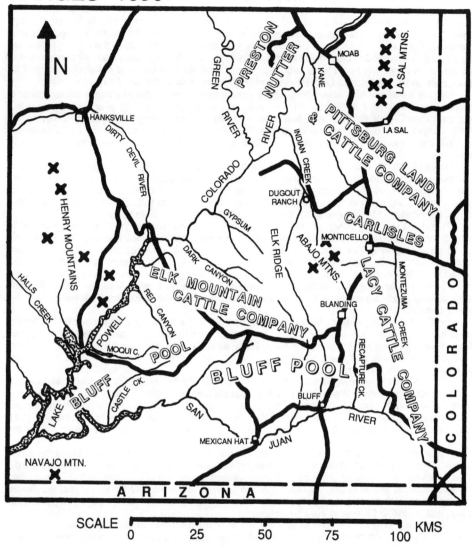

They also made friends with the Piute Indians who had camps high in the Abajo Mountains, which they claimed as exclusively theirs. This alignment effectively kept the *Gentile outfits* off the west slope of the Abajos, an area usually known as Elk Ridge or the Elk Mountains, an important summer range. The Mormons also filed for water rights and crossings, and used the Indians to their advantage. From that time on, until the Bluff Pool sold most of the stock to Al and Jim Scorup in 1898, they ran cattle in the area east of the Colorado, north of the San Juan, and west and southwest of the Abajos.

In 1888, the last of the large cattle companies arrived in San Juan County. A herd of 2000 Texas Longhorns under the foremanship of John Crosby, ended up in the southern end of Comb Wash(south of the Abajos). In Utah, this company took up the name Elk Mountain Cattle Company, with the brand

ELKM. They soon began herding their stock into White Canyon and to other canyons close to the Colorado River. Since their supply lines were so long and competition tough, they only lasted four or five years, then sold out to the Bluff Pool. Some local ranchers believe it was these Texans who may have built some of the first stock trails down into the canyons of the Colorado.

In 1891, enter two of the most important characters in the building up and development of stock ranges in the western half of San Juan County, and in the canyons leading directly into what is now Lake Powell. They were the Scorup brothers, Al and Jim. For more than half a century these two men dominated the scene. According to family members, Al was the one who did all the buying, selling and big deal making, while Jim did most of the range development, steer wrestling and cow punchin' out on the range. It very likely could have been the Scorup Brothers who built and developed many of the stock trails on the east side of Lake Powell, and on the north side of the San Juan Arm.

Most of the information about the Scorups, comes from a book written by Stena Scorup, sister of the two brothers, titled *J. A. Scorup: A Utah Cattleman.* As the story goes, 19 year old Al made a deal with cattleman Claude Sanford, who had about 150 head of Texas Longhorns grazing somewhere in White Canyon. The deal agreed upon was that Scorup was to get a third of the calves if he would just go down there, round them up, and bring them back to Salina(in central Utah), where the Scorup family lived.

So on March 20, 1891, Al left home alone with two horses, two quilts, some grub, and a $5 bill in his pocket. He rode to the Colorado River, swam across, and began to look for Sanford's cattle. This was no easy task, as the Longhorns were wild as buckskins, and soon his grub stake was about gone. He sold one steer to some prospectors along the Colorado for $20, then bought a sack of flour from Cass Hite for $11. The rest of the twenty went for salt pork and pinto beans.

This didn't last long either, so instead of heading home, he shoved the Longhorns into a side canyon and headed east, getting a job with the Elk Mountain Cattle Company driving 350 steers from Elk Ridge to Ridgeway, Colorado, a distance of 500 kms. On that drive, which put $75 in his pocket, he made friends with several Bluff cowboys. He was then talked into going back to Bluff, where he stayed in the Bayles Hotel, and had a chance to meet the local girls. One of the daughters of the hotel owner, who was working as a cook, later became his wife. In later years Al recalled that *Bluff girls were cowboy shy[most cowboys were gentiles], and they along with their parents were dyed-in-the-wool Mormons.*

He didn't stay long in Bluff, but did get acquainted with the folks there, which helped him land a job a few years later. On his way back to White Canyon and Sanford's cattle, he met five armed Texans, wrangling for the Elk Mountain outfit. They were tough hombres and they told Al, *see here, youngster, we've scattered your cattle and we mean to use all this feed for our own stuff. You'd better go way back where you came from.*

So Al moved on quickly, but called in on prospector Charley Fry(of Fry Canyon), who he had made friends with while in White Canyon earlier that season. Fry said he'd look after the Longhorns, while Scorup headed back to Salina for help. Upon arriving home, he talked his father, brother Jim, and the Hugentoblers, to go back with him. When they did move out, which was in November of 1891, they took with them 150 head of their own family cattle, apparently to leave on the east side of the river.

When they reached the Dandy Crossing at Hite, they had a hell of a time getting the cattle across. With the river high at that moment, they enlisted the help of several miners, and with the aid of Cass Hite's rowboat, finally got the herd across. When they arrived at the camp of the Texans, they were surprised to see Al return, but didn't give the Scorups any trouble. As it turned out, the Texans had rounded up Sanford's Longhorns and were on their way out of the country. When they finally did leave, that left White Canyon to the Scorup herd.

The Scorup brothers decided to stay the winter with big dreams of building up their own herd. During that winter, and for many years afterwards, they stayed in alcove caves in the canyons, one of which was near Collins Spring, in the middle part of Grand Gulch. They lived on sourdough, beans, dried fruit, and venison.

After a couple of years of wrangling and competing for range with the Bluff Pool, which had moved into White Canyon when the Texans and the Elk Mountain Cattle Company moved out, they began to feel the effects of the drought for the first time. During the winter of 1893-94, the Scorups lost 60% of their small herd, and the Bluff Pool lost half of theirs. In the spring, the Pool rounded up 600 head and left White Canyon to the Scorups. That year was the beginning of a drought period, which lasted several years. This extended drought was one reason for the big cattle operators leaving San Juan County in the late 1890's.

Not long after that, the Bluff Pool hired Al to be their foreman, paying him $37.50 a month. Brother Jim stayed with their own little herd. Later in the fall of 1894, Al moved part of the Bluff herd to Denver, where they were sold for $13 a head. Upon returning to Utah, he headed for Salt Lake City, where he and Emma Bayles were married in January, 1895.

Later, in the winter of 1895-96, Al made a contract with the Bluff Pool to gather wild cattle from the area west of Bluff, and near the upper end of the San Juan Arm of Lake Powell. He was to get $5 a head. Al used some of the young buckaroos from town, and gathered 2000 head. That translated into $10,000, which was enough to get the Scorup Brothers back in the cattle business.

Al worked for the Bluff Pool until 1898. That's when it collapsed, which was due in part to the drought. The Scorups then bought out most of the Co-op and had all of the area between the San Juan, the Colorado, and the Abajos Mountains as their range, with no competition. They summered their stock on Elk Ridge and the Abajos, and wintered them in White Canyon and other drainages to the south, such as Red, Cedar, Knowles, Moqui, Lake, The Rincon, Cottonwood, Wilson Creek, San Juan, Castle Creek and Mikes Canyons.

BIG TIME CATTLE COMPANIES AND THEIR RANGES--1900

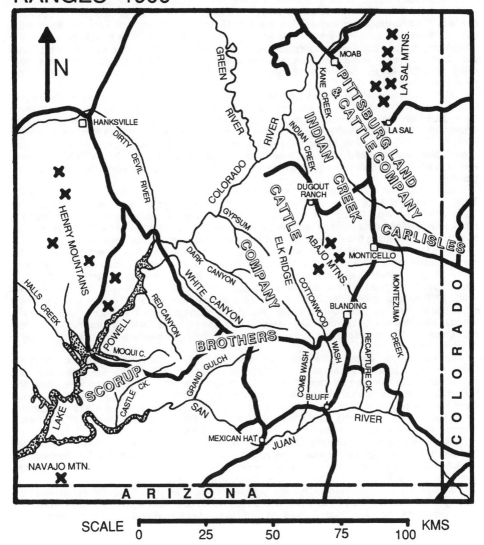

During this period of time there were lots of wild horses out on the range, possibly left-overs from the Wilson herd which had been on Wilson and Grey Mesas. They were eating grass the cattle needed, so they were eliminated when ever possible. Al later stated that on one roundup or hunt, they shot 700 head of horses.

Throughout the years, the Scorups had some experiences worth telling. In the winter of 1900-1901, Jim Scorup and cowhand Henry Knowles ran into members of the Wild Bunch camping along the Colorado near Dandy Crossing. They surprised each other and everyone drew their revolvers, but put them away moments later. Jim later stated that Butch Cassidy himself actually pointed his six-shooter at Henry, but neither side wanted any trouble(This same Henry Knowles, along with his brother, once ran cattle on Mancos Mesa east of Good Hope Bay, beginning some time around 1890. They were a small outfit and the first to be on the Mancos. They are also the ones credited with building the stock trail down into, and the naming of, Knowles Canyon).

Another time, they went to Ephraim(central Utah), and bought 30 pure-breed Hereford bulls to increase the quality of their herd. When they got those stubborn critters to Dandy Crossing, they had to use Cass Hite's rowboat again to take the bulls across, one at a time. That was in December, and not a pleasant undertaking.

In 1908, Jim finally got off the range long enough to get married. That was to Elmina Humphreys, a Salina school teacher. In the years after the turn of the century things went well for the Scorup Brothers outfit. Their herd increased, and prices remained good. They built up the herd to thousands of head. Their headquarters was at Bluff, but in 1917, the brothers began to seek an alternate life style. One reason for this was the death of Jim's wife Elmina. This forced Jim to want to live closer to his four children, one boy and three girls. So while Al moved his family to Provo so their six girls could get a better education, Jim moved back to Salina, where they had other livestock interests at a place called Lost Creek. In March of 1918, all the Bluff holdings were sold for a total of $291,700. Everything seemed OK. But,...

Al Scorup had developed into a big time cattleman and dreamer, and wanted more challenges. Less than a month after selling the herd, he headed for Moab where he met the Somerville brothers, Bill and Andrew. They discussed the purchase of the Indian Creek Cattle Company, owned by David Goudelock. Goudelock, had moved to Indian Creek in 1895, and had built it into a first class operation. In the years since, this same ranch became known as The Dugout, or the Dugout Ranch. John Scorup, grandson of Jim Scorup, now living in Monticello and working for the BLM, believes it was Goudelock who first built and used the old stock trails leading down into Gypsum and Dark Canyons.

As it turned out, Al Scorup(without telling his brother Jim), along with the Somervilles and Joe Titus, paid a total of $426,000 for the Dugout Ranch. The new company was to be called the Scorup-Somerville Corporation. Al looked out for the Indian Creek holdings, while Jim stayed on in Salina to care for that end of the business. Their new range included the north slopes of the Abajos in summer, and the canyons leading into Cataract Canyon to the west and northwest as winter range.

After this purchase, the Scorup-Somerville outfit went through good years and bad. By far the worst disasters came in the winter of 1919-20. That's when Al really started getting old. To begin with, in mid-winter it snowed heavily and they had nearly a meter of snow on the ground. The stock couldn't get at the grass. There was no hay to buy either. Everyone suffered. The company lost nearly 2000 head of cattle alone; 300 in the feed lot. Al paid a trapper $1.50 apiece to skin as many carcasses as possible, then sold the hides. And if this wasn't enough, in February, 1920, Al got a telegram from Salina, saying brother Jim was ill. By the time he got to Salina, Jim had died. Jim's four children ended up being raised by their grandmother Humphreys, and in the end got almost nothing of an inheritance.

Because of that winter, many stockmen folded, but Scorup got through. Then finally in the 1920's the cattle prices roses steadily, and things got better. In 1926, Scorup, the Somervilles, and Jacob Adams(the man Al sold most of their Bluff holdings to in 1918), combined their stock and ranges, to create the Scorup & Somerville Cattle Company. This new and bigger outfit held grazing rights from the canyon country east of Moab, south to the San Juan River. It included all the canyons on the east side of present-day Lake Powell and Cataract Canyon. It covered nearly 800,000 square hectares, or about 2 million square acres, all west of the Abajo Mountains.

As the years passed, Al Scorup continued to ride with the cowboys, at least during roundup and branding times. He stayed in the saddle until he was nearly 80 years of age, and until he had a stroke. Not long after that, and while in a wheelchair, he passed the reins of the S & S Cattle Company to his son-in-law, Harve Williams. He died soon after, on October 5, 1959.

In 1965, the Scorup & Somerville Cattle Company came to an end. The entire outfit was sold to Charley Redd of La Sal, after Veda Williams(Al's oldest daughter) had it legally for a two week period. A few years later, Redd divided his holdings and sold part of it to Ken Schmidt of Colorado, while

BIG TIME CATTLE COMPANIES AND THEIR RANGES--1930

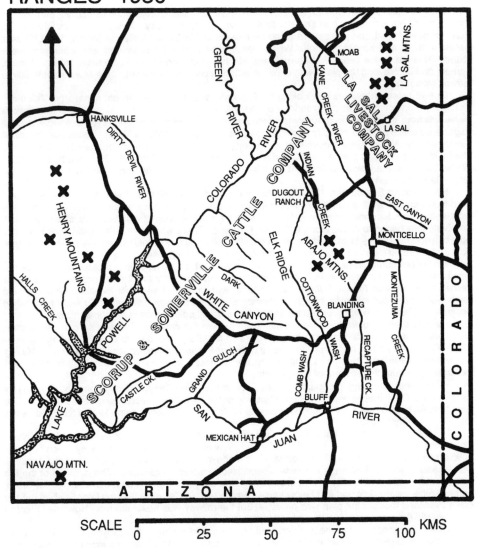

giving the other part to his son Robert Redd.

Robert still owns the Dugout Ranch part of the original spread. At a later date, sometime in the mid-1970's, Schmidt sold most of his stock and grazing rights to Melvin Dalton of Monticello. Another part, in White Canyon and the Woodenshoes(north of Natural Bridges N. M.) country at the head of Dark Canyon, went to Cloyd and Sandy Johnson. And that's how it stands in 1989. The division line between the Dugout Ranch range and that of Dalton's, is Dark Canyon. Dalton now grazes cattle as far south as the San Juan River Arm of the lake. They are his cattle you may see in Knowles, Cottonwood, Wilson Creek, San Juan, and Castle Creek Canyons. Any cow you may see on the eastern rim of Cataract Canyon belongs to the Dugout Ranch.

The Glen Canyon & San Juan River Gold Rush

The gold rush in Glen Canyon and along the San Juan River started when wandering prospectors tried to figure out where the Navajo's got all the silver for their jewelry. Two prospectors who may or may not have found that place were killed by Indians in Monument Valley in March, 1880. It was James Merrick and Ernest Mitchell. When their bodies were later examined, silver samples were found. This led to the belief that Merrick and Mitchell had found the Navajo silver mine. Rumors spread, and before long the place was crawling with prospectors, all the way from Monument Valley to Navajo Mountain.

One of those old miners out looking for Eldorado was Cass Hite, an old miner from Telluride, Colorado. According to David Lavender, *he'd got into some sort of trouble that recommended speedy departure* from the Colorado mountains. *Monument Valley seemed a good place to lie low, and he might even utilize his time trying to find Pish-la-ki*(the Merrick and Mitchell Mine). Somehow Hite made friends with the Navajo Chief Hoskaninni, even living with him in his hogan for one year. In the end the chief told him there was gold in Glen Canyon. Cass took off, crossed the San Juan and headed down White Canyon to the Colorado River, at what later became Hite, or Hite Ferry. Hite himself called the place Dandy Crossing.

He arrived in September, 1883, and did indeed find gold, although it was a very fine dust and hard to separate from the sands. At first Hite prospected for gold, but it was slim pickins. When the Hole-in-the-Rock Mormons found out this was a better route between the settlements of western Utah and Bluff, they began to use it, along with Halls Crossing. That's when Hite built a small rock store and post office(in his name) to catch their business. According to Lavender, two miners even built a row boat and operated it on call. Mail and supplies came in from Hanksville once a week.

Slowly but surely, Hite collected a pouch of gold dust, by doing a little prospecting and by his small business. *He showed it around now and then, and suddenly the rumor spread that he had a secret mine. He was followed, threatened, bribed, and cajoled to reveal its location. Of course the mine didn't exist, but when he said so it was believed that he was being sly. To keep from being pestered to death, he finally touched off one of the weirdest gold rushes in American history.*

He said that the gold came from riffles farther down the canyon. The tale spread like wildfire. Hundreds of miners rushed into the grim gorge, and tore it's gravel bars to pieces. Eventually even staid Eastern capital fell prey to the excitement and organized the Hoskaninni Mining Company(Lavender). Hite then settled into the business of keeping his small store alive and extracted gold from the pockets of prospectors.

From Dandy Crossing, prospectors spread out all over Glen Canyon. Entry points other than Hite were at Halls Crossing, Hole-in-the-Rock, Crossing of the Fathers(Ute Ford), and at Lee's Ferry. The San Juan River also had a gold rush, beginning is 1892-93, but it was the same kind of fine gold as was found in Glen Canyon.

In 1889, a group of men under the guidance of Frank M. Brown reached the mouth of North Wash, just across the lake from present-day Hite Marina. He was the president of a company which hoped to build a railroad from Colorado to California, via the canyon of the Colorado River. His chief engineer was Robert Brewster Stanton, a man who specialized in mountain railways. The purpose of the trip was to determine the feasibility of a railway through the canyon. That trip ended in disaster; for Brown and two others were drowned just below Lee's Ferry in Marble Canyon. Stanton later finished the trip down river and thought the plan was possible, but the railway was never started. However, Stanton remembered the placer mining activity in Glen Canyon.

Late in the century, after most miners had given up gold mining in the canyon, Stanton returned as the chief engineer and founder of the Hoskaninni Company. With investors money, he re-claimed all of Glen Canyon, from North Wash down to Lee's Ferry, with 145 new claims. This was in 1898-99. After that they were required to make improvements on the claims to keep them valid. Crews were sent throughout the canyon to make roads and trails and make it appear like things were really happening.

In the mean time, a dredge was being built and shipped from Chicago by rail. From Green River, Utah, it was loaded onto wagons and hauled to the river at Stanton Canyon(just east of Bullfrog Marina) and to nearby Camp Stone, named after the company president. The assembly began in 1900, and by early 1901, the dredge was in operation. It worked only for a short time, then shut down, a total failure. It simply couldn't separate the fine gold dust from the sands. After that, things were pretty quiet along the river for a while, as one colorful chapter in the history of Glen Canyon ended.

But not long after one chapter ended, another was about to begin. The lead character in the new drama was Charles H. Spencer. His career began on the San Juan River at about the turn of the century. Not much is known about his early days, but the first we hear of him was at Williams Bar, otherwise known as Williamsburg, just up stream or east of the mouth of Copper Canyon. Spencer apparently built a little red rock cabin, near where a boiler and other equipment was found years later. That was in 1908.

He later discovered the Wingate Sandstone held small quantities of gold and silver, so after he got investors interested, he moved operations down river. There he set up Camp Ibex, otherwise known as Spencer Camp, under the Wingate Cliffs. They put their rock crusher to work in June, 1909, then again the following winter. But it turned out, they had a hard time getting the gold out of the sandstone, so it ended in failure.

Next stop for big-time dreamer Spencer was Lee's Ferry. He became the head engineer for the American Placer Corporation, which re-filed on claims in the area, as well as around Pahreah, up the Paria River in Utah. Their plans were to use a boiler to create steam to run a sluicing operation and attempt to separate gold from the Chinle Formation clay beds. They thought if you could get coal from mines in upper Warm Creek down to Lee's Ferry, they could run the operation, and surely then could get at the gold. But after several attempts to use two different steam boats and a barge on the river to get coal to the Ferry, it became apparent they still couldn't get the gold out of the Chinle clays. After the venture at Lee's Ferry, Spencer tried once again at Pahreah, Utah, but had the same results.

After the big-time promoters left the canyon, things became very quiet until the 1930's and the Depression days. Then there was another flurry of activity in and around the canyon, but it didn't amount to much. There was another period of exploration as well after World War II and in the 1950's. Those were the uranium boom days. Anywhere on the Colorado Plateau where the Chinle Formation is exposed, is where bulldozers went to look for uranium deposits. The Chinle forms a talus slope, then usually a bench just below the big Wingate Sandstone walls. There are several areas around the lake where you can still see mining exploration tracks, including the areas southwest of Hite, around The Rincon, and in the upper San Juan River Arm.

Over the years, and at a very slow rate, interest gradually shifted from mining or prospecting, to recreation. The first boat load of people said to have gone down the river just for the fun of it, was in 1909. That's when Julius Stone, the big loser in the Hoskaninni Company and Stanton Dredge scheme, and Nathaniel Galloway as guide, rafted through the canyons from Green River, Wyoming, to Needles, California. In 1911, Ellsworth and Kolb, fotographed the canyons using Dellenbaugh's book, Canyon Voyage, as a guide.

After World War II, and with the coming of inflatable rafts, there was renewed interest in the canyons. Bert Loper and Norman D. Nevills were a couple of the more prominent river guides, and David E. Rust was the one who began commercial tours in Glen Canyon. Just about the time river runners were getting in the water, in came the dam builders, which changed the character of recreation in the Glen Canyon area forever.

The Dam Builders

In 1921, the U.S. Geological Survey and the Southern California Edison Company sponsored a joint effort to map the Colorado River from the confluence of the Green and the Colorado Rivers to Lee's Ferry, and the San Juan River. The next year the first really good maps of the river were released. This coincided with a big conference between all the states bordering the Colorado River Basin. It had to do with water allocations and distribution, as well as flood control and hydroelectricity.

The result was the Colorado River Pact. It separated the river into the upper and lower basins. The upper basin states included Utah, Colorado, New Mexico, and Wyoming. The lower basin states were Nevada, Arizona and California. The dividing line was at Lee's Ferry. The flow of the Colorado River would be divided there. A certain percentage of the annual flow was to pass Lee's Ferry in order for the upper basin states to fulfill their obligation to the lower basin states. The only way that could be accomplished would be to erect a series of dams up stream so spring floods and heavy runoff during above average water years could be stored and released during drier periods. This was the real beginning of the Glen Canyon Dam project.

By 1952, the Bureau of Reclamation had completed a master plan for water development in the upper basin states. After much debate, this master plan was passed by Congress on April 11, 1956. The law authorized four large dams to be built above Lee's Ferry. The first one started was the Glen Canyon Dam, located just south of the Utah-Arizona state line, and about 24 kms up from the mouth of the Paria River.

The actual construction, or at least preliminary work, began on October 1, 1956. Tunnels were blasted and the river diverted into these diversions on February 11, 1959. The very first concrete for the dam was poured on June 17, 1960; the last bucket poured was on September 13, 1963.

The thickness of the dam at bedrock is 91 meters, while the thickness at the crest is about 8 meters. The height of the dam above bedrock is 216 meters, while it is 179 meters above the Colorado River.

When the reservoir is completely full, the elevation is to be set at 1128 meters. When full, the lake is 298 kms long, with a shore line of about 3136 kms. The water first started backing up in the new lake on March 13, 1963, and it took until June 22, 1980, to first reach the high water mark(HWM) of 1128 meters. However, on July 14, 1983, the lake reached it's all time high point of 1130 meters. This was due to the rapid and heavy runoff after a winter of unusually deep snows all over the upper basin. That historic high level was only two meters below the crest of the dam.

The dam has eight hydroelectric generators, the first of which began to operate on September 4, 1964. By February 28, 1966, all eight were in operation. For those interested in touring the dam, go to the Carl Hayden Visitor Center just west of the Glen Canyon Bridge. There are self guided tours going down into the dam, plus park rangers who interpret the scene and sell books and maps. It was on October 27, 1972, that the region around Lake Powell was established as the Glen Canyon National Recreation Area. It is now administered by the National Park Service.

Over the years, and as Lake Powell has grown in size, it has also grown in popularity. It seems that through Lake Powell the nation has recently discovered the wonders of the Colorado Plateau. Below is a chart showing the visitations to the Glen Canyon National Recreation Area. Keep in mind that the GCNRA covers all the lake at the HWM and bordering areas, and down river from the Glen Canyon Dam to include Lee's Ferry. On lands bordering the Navajo Nation, the GCNRA extends up to the 1134 meter mark(that's 6 meters, or 20 feet above the HWM). The visitation figures include Lee's Ferry, but not traffic going across the bridge on Highway 89A.

Total Visits to the Glen Canyon National Recreation Area

1962 9,282	1971 687,721	1980 1,646,968
1963 44,285	1972 970,922	1981 1,820,163
1964 196,422	1973 1,209,116	1982 1,826,572
1965 303,548	1974 1,159,383	1983 1,975,273
1966 359,659	1975 1,139,275	1984 2,052,642
1967 590,037	1976 1,061,716	1985 2,160,542
1968 654,505	1977 2,127,419	1986 2,484,024
1969 781,250	1978 2,211,818	1987 2,883,412
1970 788,482	1979 1,733,282	1988 3,500,000

Of all the entry points to Lake Powell, or rather the GCNRA, Wahweap is the busiest, followed by Bullfrog, Lee's Ferry(which is the entry point for rafting down the Grand Canyon), Hite, Halls Crossing, and finally the new San Juan Marina. The 1988 figure of 3.5 million is an estimate. This estimate was made in mid-December of 1988.

Sedimentation and the Filling Up of Lake Powell

For those who have wondered how long it will take for Lake Powell to fill up with sediment, here is some of the latest information. The Bureau of Reclamation(BOR) recently released one of its studies titled, **Lake Powell 1986 Sedimentation Study Report.** Here is a brief summary of that report and some conclusions drawn by one employee of the National Park Service.

It was found that in recent years, the amount of sediment being carried downstream and into the lake, is less than what was recorded in the Colorado River and other tributaries earlier this century. Several reasons were sited for this change. First, erosion has been reduced, in part at least, by reduced grazing of livestock, and by better range management. Second, new upstream reservoirs have begun to trap small amounts of sediment.

Because less sediment is entering the lake, new figures were calculated. The BOR now puts the annual amount of sediment entering the lake at 35,000 acre-feet/year. The original carrying capacity of Lake Powell was set at 27,000,000 acre-feet. By simple division, this means it will take 771 years for the lake to fill to capacity(to the HWM). In coming up with these figures, they may or may not be taking into account the fact that new sediment entering the lake will settle upon older layers, causing compression of the old. If all factors remain constant, the lake will fill up to the HWM in 771 years, if settling and compression are not taken into account.

As you think of these figures, here are a couple of things to keep in mind. As the lake gets close to being filled, muddy water will begin to pass through the penstocks, instead of dropping its sediment behind the dam. Also keep in mind, that the penstocks are 15 meters(50 feet) below the HWM, and 50% of the lakes water storage capacity is in the top 15 meters of the reservoir. When that point is reached, then the ability to generate electric power will diminish, but there will still be some ability to store heavy winter runoff, and at least some water around for boating and other forms of recreation.

It's likely impossible for the lake to fill to capacity with sediments. It seems that at sometime in the distance future, the upper end of the lake will end up being one big mud flat, with the Colorado and San Juan Rivers meandering down the middle. But closer to the dam, there should always be some of the lake remaining. How much is unclear. At that point in time most of the functions for which the dam was originally built, will have run their course.

Looking across the lake at the mouth of Smith Fork, with Mt. Ellsworth in the background.

Part II--Introduction to Boating, Hiking and Camping

Marinas on Lake Powell

Wahweap Wahweap Marina, just south of the Utah-Arizona line, is the most popular and busiest entry point on the lake. It's located just a few kms north of the dam, and 10 kms northwest of Page, Arizona. The main commercial enterprise at Wahweap is operated by the Del Webb Corporation(As this book goes to print, Del Webb is about to be sold to the ARA Leisure Services. The change will take place in early 1989). These facilities include a lodge, with dining room, gift shop, lounge and swimming pool. The lodge is headquarters for scheduled and charter lake cruise boats. Most popular are the daily boats heading for Rainbow Bridge.

Near the lodge is a cement boat launching ramp, a fuel dock with regular or 50 to 1 gas(pre-mixed), and diesel, a floating dock and store, another shore-side store, a boat repair shop, long and short term parking, and a gas station for automobiles. They also provide boat rentals, a sports store with fishing and boating supplies and boat storage facilities. These are all operated by the Del Webb Corp., P.O. Box 1597, Page, Arizona, 86040, tele. 602-645-2433.

In addition, there is a National Park Service ranger station and visitor center(tele 602-645-8883). Just northwest of the Wahweap operation is the State Line launch ramp, boat pump-out facilities, swimming beach, picnic site, fish cleaning station, and a large campground(with space for late arrivals). Informed sources say that boat rental and repairs, plus food service will be moved to the State Line ramp area in the next couple of years.

Tourist cruise boats at Wahweap Marina. Boats like the one on the right take tourists to Rainbow Bridge.

WAHWEAP MARINA AND AREA MAP

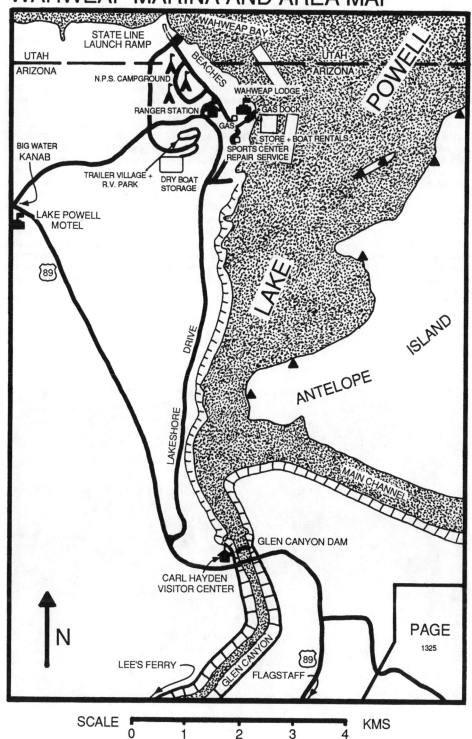

SCALE 0 1 2 3 4 KMS

Dangling Rope Marina This is the only marina on the lake with boater access only. There are no roads to this one, which is located about 41 miles(66 kms) from the dam, about halfway up Dangling Rope Inlet, and almost due south of the end of Kaiparowits Plateau. It's also on the route to Rainbow Bridge.

Dangling Rope is a floating marina which has a small store, equipped with basic food and camping items(including ice), a snack bar with ice cream, a covered picnic area with tables, garbage disposal bins, and a small NPS ranger station(which isn't open very often?). Just down the ramp from this part is the fuel dock, which sells regular and 50 to 1 gas and oil. They also have a repair and maintenance shop, boat pumpout, drinking and flushing water facilities, and a cold water tap. They have a telefone where calls can be made via satellite(long distance calls only!). You can post letters from this marina, but they will be post marked Page, Arizona.

One odd thing about this place is that although it's located in Utah, they still use Arizona time. During the winter months, these two times are the same, but when the daylight savings time period rolls around, Arizona does not participate. The Navajo Nation uses daylight savings time, as does Utah and everywhere else in the west. In the summer season, the store and gas station are open from 7 am until 7 pm, Arizona time. The ice cream window is open from 8 am until 5:30 pm, Arizona time. The busiest times for the marina are from about 10 am to 5 pm, Arizona time. One of the main reasons they prefer to use Arizona time, is that Page and Wahweap use it, so for them it's less confusing to stay on the same clock as the company headquarters, which is the Del Webb Corp. Also, most of the visitors to Dangling Rope begin at Wahweap, and are already on Arizona time.

Food prices at Dangling Rope are about double what you would pay in the cheapest supermarkets in northern Utah(which have the lowest prices in the USA). Dangling Rope gets all it's supplies from Wahweap, and is regularly serviced by barge carrying container units. The garbage is hauled out by barge in trailers, which are hooked onto truck tractors at Wahweap and taken to a disposal site. Gasoline is brought in daily in a large Chevron gas boat. This marina is open the year-round.

Dangling Rope Marina. Store on the left, NPS ranger station to the right.

Floating gas pumps at Dangling Rope Marina, Dangling Rope Canyon.

Garbage containers on a barge at Dangling Rope Marina.

Bullfrog Marina Most boaters from Utah end up at Bullfrog Marina, located due south of Hanksville and the Henry Mountains, and in about the middle of the lake. It's the second busiest port on the lake. At Bullfrog, you will find a motel with dining room, a gasoline station which performs minor repairs, and a curio shop. There is a dock-side store with all the basics, including fishing tackle, food, drinks, and other supplies. Nearby is a fuel dock, which sells regular and 50 to 1 gas, and diesel fuel. You can rent houseboats or small fishing boats, or join group tours of the lake. These facilities all belong to the main concessionaire on the lake, the Del Webb Corp. Their Bullfrog mailing address is Hanksville, Utah, 84734. You can call tele. 801-684-2278

In the public housing section is a small grocery store, as well as an RV park, a small campground and a day-use picnic site. The National Park Service has a small visitor center along with the district office(801-684-2212). There is a public cement boat launch ramp, with drinking and flushing water, restrooms and a fish cleaning station.

Bullfrog is also the terminal for the ferry boat, the **John Atlantic Burr.** This boat is 30 meters long and 13 meters wide. It has two 8V-71 Detroit diesel engines, and a 9450 liter diesel fuel tank. It will hold 8 cars and two buses, and a maximum of 150 passengers.

The boat was designed by the Alexander Love and Co., from Victoria, British Columbia, but was constructed by Mark Steel Co., Salt Lake City, Utah. The ferry is named after John Atlantic Burr, a pioneer Utah rancher born in 1846 aboard a ship somewhere in the Atlantic Ocean. Funding for this venture was the Utah Department of Transportation. They paid for the design, construction and transportation of the boat to the lake. The ferry boat launch facilities were provided by the NPS, and it is operated by the Del Webb Corporation.

The ferry runs between Bullfrog and Halls Crossing, a distance of about 5 kms, which takes about 25 minutes. Here's a price list as of 1988: for foot passengers, $2 for adults, and $1 for children. Those over 65 or under 5 years of age travel free. For vehicles(the price includes vehicle, driver and passengers); cars, small vans, and pickups(with or without campers), $9. Motorhomes, $15, and buses, $30.

The ferry begins and ends at Halls Crossing. In the summer season, which is May 15 through October 15, the first departure is at 8 am. The next departure is at 9 am, from Bullfrog. This schedule continues at one hour intervals throughout the day until the final departure from Bullfrog at 7 pm. In the winter months, from October 16 until May 14, it has exactly the same schedule, beginning at 8 am and runs at one hours intervals, except the last departure from Bullfrog is at 3 pm. Unless there is a shut down for repairs, this ferry runs year-round. If it should shut down for any reason, you will see the closure notice stated clearly on the big signs as you turn off Highway 95 and onto Highway 276, at both ends of this paved highway.

Ferry boat John Atlantic Burr, at the terminal at Halls Crossing Marina. Henry Mountains in the background.

BULLFROG & HALLS CROSSING MARINAS

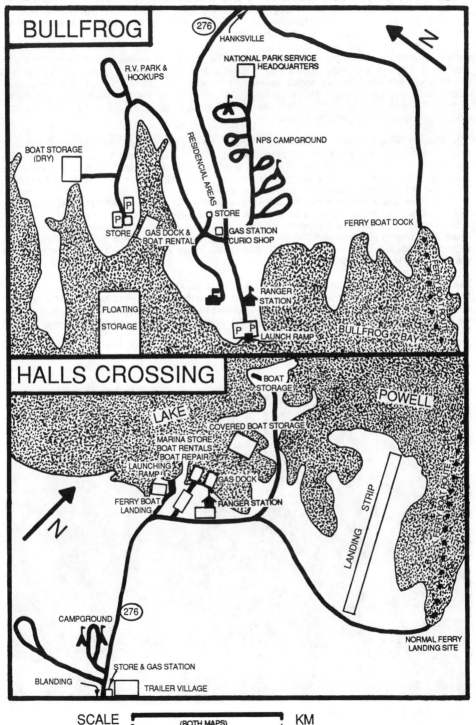

BULLFROG

(276) HANKSVILLE

NATIONAL PARK SERVICE HEADQUARTERS

R.V. PARK & HOOKUPS

RESIDENCIAL AREAS

NPS CAMPGROUND

BOAT STORAGE (DRY)

P P
STORE
GAS DOCK & BOAT RENTAL

STORE

GAS STATION CURIO SHOP

FERRY BOAT DOCK

FLOATING STORAGE

RANGER STATION

P P LAUNCH RAMP

BULLFROG BAY

FERRY BOAT ROUTE

HALLS CROSSING

BOAT STORAGE

POWELL

LAKE

COVERED BOAT STORAGE

MARINA STORE
BOAT RENTALS
BOAT REPAIR

LAUNCHING RAMP

GAS DOCK

FERRY BOAT LANDING

RANGER STATION

LANDING STRIP

FERRY BOAT ROUTE

(276)

CAMPGROUND

BLANDING

STORE & GAS STATION

TRAILER VILLAGE

NORMAL FERRY LANDING SITE

SCALE 0 (BOTH MAPS) 1 KM

Halls Crossing Marina This marina is just across the main channel from Bullfrog Bay, and about 5 kms across the lake from Bullfrog Marina. It's at about the half-way point along Highway 276, the paved road that makes a loop to the south from Highway 95. One part of this road ends at Bullfrog, the other at Halls Crossing. The ferry boat, the John Atlantic Burr, completes the loop across the lake. See Bullfrog Marina for ferry boat information.

At Halls Crossing you will find a campground, a pump-out station, trailer village, mobile home rentals, boat storage and a gas station and garage. The marina has a floating boat house with repair facilities, and fishing and house boats for rent. It has a dock store, with food items, fishing tackle and other boater's supplies. The fuel dock supplies regular and 50 to 1 gas, and diesel fuel, which is open during most daylight hours. These facilities are operated by the Del Webb Corp., (mailing address)Blanding, Utah, 84511; tele 801-684-2261. The National Park Service maintains a district office and a visitor center, tele. 801-684-2270.

Hite Marina Hite Marina is located at the upper end of Lake Powell, about half way between Blanding and Hanksville, and just south of Highway 95. This marina is about 8 kms north of where the old Hite town and ferry were located. At Hite is a small store with all the basic needs for fishermen and campers. Included with the store is a gas station, which doesn't carry diesel(but it's at the fuel dock). This is like the standard convenient stores in your home town.

On the lake is a floating dock with another small store, with regular and 50 to 1 gas, and diesel fuel. You can rent boats, including houseboats. There is also boat storage. Nearby is a cement public launching ramp and a campground without water. At the launch ramp are toilets and water. There is no charge for camping. The concessionaire is again the Del Webb Corp., with the mailing address Hanksville, Utah, 84734, tele. 801-684-2278. There is also a NPS ranger station, but it seems there is seldom anyone there.

San Juan Marina This is the only marina located on Navajo Nation lands and along the San Juan River Arm of the lake. San Juan Marina is located at the mouth of Piute Farms Wash near the upper, or east end, of the inlet. To get there, drive into Monument Valley. At the major cross roads just north of the Utah-Arizona line, turn west from Highway 163 and head in the direction of Gouldings Trading Post.

On board the ferry running between Bullfrog and Halls Crossing Marinas.

HITE AND SAN JUAN MARINAS

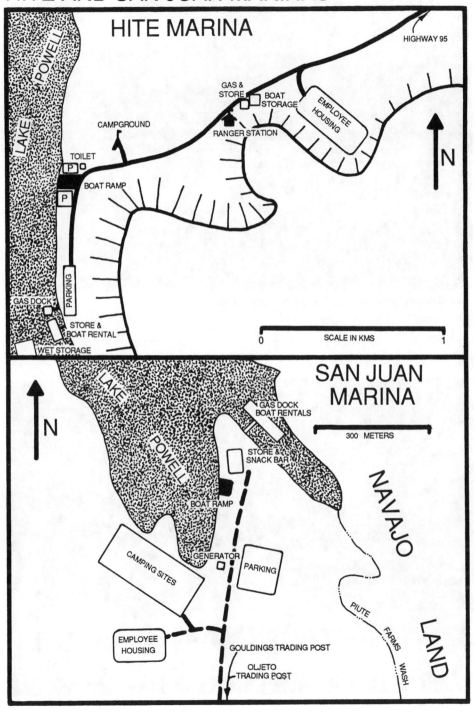

HITE MARINA

HIGHWAY 95

GAS & STORE

BOAT STORAGE

EMPLOYEE HOUSING

CAMPGROUND

RANGER STATION

N

TOILET
P

BOAT RAMP

P

PARKING

GAS DOCK

STORE & BOAT RENTAL

WET STORAGE

LAKE POWELL

SCALE IN KMS
0   1

SAN JUAN MARINA

N

LAKE

POWELL

GAS DOCK
BOAT RENTALS

300   METERS

STORE & SNACK BAR

BOAT RAMP

NAVAJO

CAMPING SITES

GENERATOR

PARKING

LAND

PIUTE

FARMS

EMPLOYEE HOUSING

GOULDINGS TRADING POST

OLJETO TRADING POST

WASH

Halls Crossing Marina with the Henry Mountains in the background.

Hite Marina, located at the northern end of Lake Powell.

From Gouldings, turn west at the sign, and drive on the paved road toward Oljeto skirting around to the north of a mesa. After a few kms, you'll turn due west, and onto an improved gravel road. This road gradually veers to the north, then runs down Piute Farms Wash to the lake and marina. The distance from Highway 163 to the marina is about 50 kms. The graveled section of the route is about 30 kms. Even though it's not paved, it is for the most part, an all-weather type road.

At the marina is employee housing, a resident NPS ranger(living and working), and a primitive type campground. The marina itself has a small store with all the basic food and fishing supplies, plus a cement launching ramp. Next door is a fuel dock with regular or 50 to 1 gas, and boat rentals including houseboats.

There are a couple of discouraging things about the San Juan Marina, as of 1988. One is, you travel a gravel road for part of the way; but it's really not that bad, just a little dusty at times. It's maintained regularly, and is basically an all-weather road. Also, the lake is quickly silting up and the water in the area of the marina is a little cloudy all the time, but more so during the spring runoff period. You only have to go 3 or 4 kms to the northeast to find mud flats or very shallow water.

The San Juan Marina is run by Utah Navajo Industries out of Blanding, Utah, a corporation which has a lumber and clothing industry, and other projects besides this marina. This tribal company always wanted to locate the operation at the bottom end of Copper Canyon, about 16 kms west, or down-lake from the present-day site. That would be in an area which always has clear water, and it would take a couple of centuries or more to be silted up.

The problem was, it would have taken a large sum of money to build a good road and bridges to that site. They couldn't get the loans from banks or the Navajo Government at Window Rock, so they were forced to locate at a less desirable site, which required no money spent on road building. Since there was already a pretty good road to Piute Farms, they decided to build a temporary facility there.

So the plan goes like this. If the Utah Navajo Industries can turn a profit and prove to the government in Window Rock they can run a good tight ship, then they will be loaned the money needed to build a good road down Copper Canyon. Then they will move the marina lock, stock and barrel to the new site. The hope is, by about 1990 they can make the move, as the operation appears to be a success. The telefone number of the Blanding headquarters is 1-801-678-2217.

Other than these minor setbacks, this marina is a pleasant place to visit, with prices which seem a little lower than at other marinas. It's in a slightly more primitive location, but it's also a lot quieter, and has a definite Navajo atmosphere; which is far different from the hustle and bustle of the other marinas, especially Wahweap.

Other Launch Sites

Just to the west of Wahweap Marina is **Lone Rock Beach.** You can get there from Highway 89, and from between the state line and mile post 1, on the Utah side. It's about 3 kms of gravel road to the beach, which has toilets, but no drinking water. It's a great sandy beach, where you can camp or park right at the shore line. You can also launch a boat at Lone Rock. For some, one disadvantage would be, this is the only area in the GCNRA where ORV's are allowed. They do make a hell-of-a-racket on busy weekends. Please haul out all of your own garbage.

Just north of Bullfrog, as you're about to drop down over the hill to the marina, you will see a dirt road turning off to the left, or east. This road takes you down to what's left of **Stanton Canyon**. At the end of the road, you can wander about and pick the camping place of your choice. There are a couple of toilets, but they are a long way from some of the campsites. It's possible to launch there, but it will depend on lake levels. Usually you can get a boat in OK. The camping is free, but a little primitive; which suits some people just fine. There's no garbage pickup, so haul out everything you take in.

Another vehicle access point to the lake is in the **Upper Bullfrog Bay.** About 10 kms north of the boat ramp on Bullfrog, is the beginning of the Bullfrog-Notom Road. It runs north along the Waterpocket Fold to Highway 14, just east of the headquarters of Capitol Reef National Park. About half way along this road, it is intersected by the Burr Trail Road, which connects it to Boulder and Escalante. Because of this connection, some refer to this entire road as the Burr Trail Road. From the beginning of the Bullfrog-Notom Road, drive between 5 and 10 kms, to find one of several places to turn off to the left to reach the lake. There are several sandy campsites along the upper end of the bay. One site has two pit toilets, but no one to collect garbage but you.

Just north of Hite on the west side of the Dirty Devil River Bridge, is another primitive camping and boat launching area next to the highway and at the mouth of the **Dirty Devil River.** This site is almost under the Wingate cliffs to the west. There are no toilets or drinking water and no garbage collection, so take the proper steps to leave a tidy camp. This place has, or rather it did have, lots of driftwood lying about. Another place to camp for free.

Drive due south from the turnoff to Hite Marina(which is between mile posts 48 and 49), to mile post 53 on Highway 95. Then turn west and after about 3 kms on an improved gravel road, you'll arrive at the lake at **Farley Canyon.** This is another primitive camping area with toilets, but no running water or garbage collection. You can camp for free and launch a boat.

Just around the corner from the Farley Canyon turnoff, is one of two improved dirt roads heading south off the highway to campsites along the upper **White Canyon Inlet.** The first entry place is on the west side, and although you can camp there, you can't launch a boat. If you have a boat to launch, drive a bit further east, between mile posts 54 and 55, and turn south at the sign pointing out White Canyon. From the highway, it's about 4 kms to the lake, whereas it's about 3 kms via the west side road. Along the east side of the upper end of White Canyon Inlet, is a long beach area where you can camp and launch a boat.

Weather and Climate of Lake Powell

One of the nicer things to say about Lake Powell is that it almost always has good weather. This is especially true in summer and fall. As you can see in the climographs below, it does have some warm temperatures in summer, and occasionally cold days in winter, but because it's the lowest elevation in the area, the winters are usually rather mild. It's a dry desert type region, so sun and good weather are the rule; bad weather the exception. The normal boating season is from about mid-March through about early or mid-November. Each year is a little different.

Winter The northern end of the lake, such as in Cataract and Narrow Canyons, will freeze over in some places, but it's never heavy ice. The reason it's colder and subject to some freezing there is that it's further north and the lake is confined to a deep, shaded, narrow canyon where temperature inversions are more common. The rest of the lake is more open and not subject to such temperature extremes.

There are some boaters out on the lake in winter, but usually on the southern end. In dry weather spells, the days are calm and rather pleasant, and hiking can be invigorating. The nights are normally crispy with cold weather bedding and clothing being a must. In bad weather, it'll be a miserable trip, but good weather is more the norm in this desert landscape. Generally speaking, the time period which is the coldest and most uncomfortable will be from about December 1, until mid-February. This is a period of time when you'll have very short days and long nights, so take plenty of candles or other ways to light the night.

Spring Spring is a pleasant time to visit Lake Powell, especially for hiking and/or fishing. The water is far too cold to do any swimming, but some people try water skiing with wet suits. The days are usually nice and the nights aren't so cold, but spring time does bring more windy conditions than at any other season. Another nice thing about spring, the days are longer and nights shorter than in winter or in fall. For example, April 21, has the same amount of daylight as does August 21. Late in the fall, such as in October, the nights are becoming very long.

Summer Summers are very enjoyable. The mornings are usually calm, but there are often breezes in the afternoon. Evenings are again calm. By about early June the water temperatures are getting warm enough for swimming and water skiing. In the middle of summer there are some really hot days, but it seems cooler right on the water, and you can always jump in and cool off. In the afternoons, you can expect some clouds to build up, but if there are showers, they don't last long. Strong gusty winds always accompany thunder storms, so remain alert if you're in a small boat.

Fall In some ways, fall is similar to the spring season temperature wise, but the days are getting very short, the nights long. Camping and fishing are usually good. There are cold fronts going through the area in fall too, but usually not as often as in spring. When bad weather comes, it usually doesn't last long. In bays or canyons which have gamble oak or cottonwood trees, the fall colors make for great fotography. Mid to late October through the first week or so of November is the best time to get color fotos.

Climographs on Lake Powell Weather

Below are climographs from three different weather stations near the lake. They are Hite Marina in the north, Bullfrog Marina, in about the middle(both in Utah), and Page, Arizona, at the southern end. Each is either on the lake, or very near the shore line.

The figures in the tables below are all in metric. You can refer to the Metric Conversion Table on page 5, for help in converting. Keep in mind that 0 degrees Centigrade is equal to 32 degrees Fahrenheit; 10 C is equal to 50 F; 20 C is 68 F; 30 C is 86 F; and 38 C is 100 F. Also, 0 degrees F is about -18 C. For every 10 degree of change on the Centigrade scale, the Fahrenheit thermometer changes 18 degrees. To convert, the author took the temperature in F, then -32, and multiplied that by .555. That equals C. Precipitation is shown in centimeters(cms). To convert, multiply inches by 2.54, which gives precip in cms. So one inch is about 2 1/2 cms.

Hite Marina, 1158 meters elevation, from 1949-1986(the earlier figures could only have come from Hite Ferry, formerly located on the Colorado River. Since about the mid-1960's, they would have come from the present-day marina site).

Month	Max(C) Average	Max(C) Record	Min(C) Average	Min(C) Record	Precip Av(Cms)
January	8.1	19.4	-3.1	-18.9	1.47
February	11.9	23.9	-0.8	-17.8	.79
March	16.7	28.3	2.9	-11.1	1.45
April	22.3	35.5	7.4	-6.7	1.14
May	27.9	39.4	12.9	-0.6	1.04
June	34.1	44.4	18.2	1.7	.61
July	37.2	43.3	22.4	7.2	1.45
August	35.9	42.7	21.4	12.2	1.35
September	31.5	41.1	16.2	3.3	1.68
October	23.3	37.2	9.1	-2.2	2.62
November	14.8	25.5	2.5	-8.9	1.68
December	8.8	20.6	-1.9	-14.4	1.14
Annual	**23.0**	**44.4**	**9.1**	**-18.9**	**16.41**

Bullfrog Marina 1165 meters elevation, 1967-1986

Month	Max(C) Average	Max(C) Record	Min(C) Average	Min(C) Record	Precip Av(cms)
January	7.2	19.4	-4.1	-16.1	1.37
February	11.4	22.2	-1.0	-14.4	.91
March	16.5	28.3	2.8	-9.4	1.83
April	21.5	32.2	6.4	-6.1	.58
May	27.8	37.2	11.8	0.6	1.17
June	34.1	43.3	17.1	5.6	.46
July	37.3	43.3	21.2	12.2	1.14
August	35.8	41.6	20.2	7.8	1.07
September	30.7	38.3	15.0	6.7	1.50
October	22.4	33.3	7.9	-3.9	2.64
November	14.3	25.5	2.0	-10.4	1.70
December	8.3	20.5	-2.9	-15.0	1.35
Annual	**22.4**	**43.3**	**8.2**	**-16.1**	**15.72**

Page, Arizona, Elevation 1335 meters. Based on a 25 year average?

Month	Max(C) Average	Max(C) Record	Min(C) Average	Min(C) Record	Precip Av(cms)
January	5.5	17.8	-4.4	-23.9	1.19
February	10.5	20.5	-1.0	-13.3	1.09
March	14.4	27.8	2.2	-7.8	1.85
April	20.0	32.2	6.1	-3.9	.86
May	26.6	36.1	11.7	-.5	1.09
June	32.7	46.1	16.7	5.5	.51
July	36.1	42.2	20.5	13.3	1.19
August	34.4	41.1	19.5	7.8	1.70
September	29.4	37.7	14.4	4.4	1.37
October	21.6	33.9	8.3	-4.4	1.92
November	12.8	23.3	1.7	-8.9	1.50
December	7.8	19.4	-2.8	-17.2	1.30
Annual	**21.0**	**46.1**	**7.7**	**-23.9**	**15.60**

Surface Temperature
of Lake Powell Water(Centigrade)

January	7.8	July	25.5
February	7.8	August	26.1
March	?12.2	September	23.3
April	?12.2	October	19.4
May	17.8	November	16.1
June	21.6	December	10.5

(National Park Service Data)

Cataract Canyon, in the north end of the lake.

Hiking Season Around Lake Powell

The hiking season on Lake Powell can be any time, but the very best months are from about late March until the end of May, and again from about late September until the first week in November. These are the best times because of the temperatures. It's not too hot, and it's generally not so cold that you have to bundle up in heavy clothes. During this time period you will often start out in the mornings with long pants and a long sleeved shirt, or maybe a light jacket; but later in the day, you can usually be in shorts and T shirt.

There are times during winter when you find very nice weather, but nights are cold and very long. Special care and equipment are needed for the hardy souls who venture out in winter.

Sometimes the period from late May through mid-June can be pleasant too, but it starts to get really hot in June. Generally speaking, hiking from Memorial Day(end of May) until Labor Day(first Monday in September) is a little unpleasant and on the hot side. But the author was hiking for about two months during the three month period from mid-April until mid-July, and managed. On one of those days, the temperature in Hanksville was 43 degrees C.(110 F.)! It was the hottest June and July in history, but he hiked in it and so can you; just plan to drink lots of water, and jump in the lake occasionally with your clothes on. September can be warm too, but it's usually a pretty good month for hiking.

Hiking Equipment

There will be two kinds of hikers reading this book. First, the serious hiker, the one who goes to the lake with the intention of walking. Others will be fishermen, water skiers, or just boaters out camping and soaking up rays with family and friends. For those unfamiliar with hiking, here is a list of items or equipment the *professional hiker* takes out on an average half day trek up one of the canyons from Lake Powell.

Most of the hikes in this book are into canyons, where the walking generally isn't too difficult and the way isn't too rugged. For the most part, a pair of running shoes is the very best. They are light weight and comfortable, and you'll never get blisters. If you take an older pair, you won't feel bad if they get wet while wading in a stream. Many canyons have small streams and wading is a must in some. Some kind of rubber and canvas shoe would be ideal as a *wader*.

On other hikes you'll be climbing up to canyon rims; for example, to the top of the Kaiparowits Plateau. For this type of climbing, a pair of rugged leather boots would be best. Under each hike in this book, is a brief statement as to which type of boots or shoes would be best for that particular walk or trek.

Because most people visiting the lake will do so in warmer weather, shorts or cut-off's of some kind are generally preferred to long pants. However, in the spring and fall months, you will surely want long pants for early mornings and evenings in camp. A pair of loose fitting shorts with zippered or buttoned pockets are best.

In the summer months, the best shirt to have is a plain cotton T shirt, or one that's made from a 50/50 blend of cotton and polyester. In the spring or fall season, you'll want a long sleeved shirt at times. Any kind will do, but one with pockets is best. The author usually has a flannel shirt, plus a sweat shirt with hood, if it's extra cool.

For those of us with light colored skin and hair, some kind of hat is required to prevent skin cancer. The big cowboy hats work fine, but they're not so good in the wind. The author has taken an adjustable baseball cap, cut the top out, and sewn a kind of *cancer curtain* around the sides and back; similar to the French Foreign Legion caps seen in the movies. This keeps the sun off the vital parts of the face and neck. You might also consider taking a sun screen for the hands and arms, especially if you don't have the time to get a tan the slow and safe way. It's the repeated sun burning of the skin which eventually causes skin cancer.

The serious hiker will take and use a small day pack. These come in various sizes, but must be large enough for the following items: a one liter water bottle, a light lunch, an extra camera lens, and in the cooler seasons, a pair of long pants and long sleeved shirt or jacket. In a small pack pocket, the author always has a short nylon cord, bandaids, extra pens, small notebook, a compass, map, toilet paper and perhaps sun glasses.

In his pants pockets, he carries chapstick(lip baum), nylon wallet(tied to the belt), and pocket knife. A camera is a must for most people visiting Lake Powell, along with extra film and lenses. A lightweight walking stick is good in some places, especially if you're in a stream valley and wading over slick rocks or into deep holes. The author uses one made from a shower curtain rod. One end was cut off, then welded together to form a "T"; which is used mostly with a camera clamp, and as a camera stand. A camera stand of some kind is good in the deep, dark canyons, of which there are many in this country.

Originally, the author thought there would also be some longer two or three day hikes in this book, but as it turned out, almost all are of the half day, or day variety. In a few canyons you could backpack in for a night or two in order to see it all, but overnight hiking is seldom done by boaters.

Preserving Archaeology Sites

In the side canyons leading to Lake Powell, there are many ancient cultural sites such as Anasazi or Fremont cliff dwellings, petroglyph and pictograph panels, and flint sites. Sometimes these are visible from the lake as you boat up the canyon inlets, but to find most you'll have to get out and hike and hunt for them. The author has marked some he found on the hiking maps.

However, if too many people visit these sites, damage will occur; not so much by vandals or pot hunters, but by simply careless visitors. It's highly unlikely you will ever discover any ruins which have not already been recorded and studied. And it is true that the simple cliff dwellings you will see will surely never contribute anything more to our present understanding of the Anasazi people. But regardless of how simple the sites may be, it's important to prevent any further damage to them and make as little impact as possible. Many more interested people will follow in your footsteps.

Here's a list of things you can do to help preserve these Anasazi ruins. First, don't allow children to climb onto the walls or any part of the structure. Some may seem solid, but in time all walls will tumble down. Why not stand back and look, take pictures, and leave it as is for the next visitor. Second, if the ruins are under an overhang approachable via a talus slope, try to get there from the side instead of scrambling straight up the talus. Undercutting ruins is a big problem for some lake side sites and most damage occurs simply by thoughtless individuals.

Third, if mother nature calls and you have to use the toilet, please don't do it in or near the ruins. Defecate as far from these sites as possible, and bury it. And fourth, keep in mind it is against Federal law to damage any ancient artifacts. Part of the Federal law states, *No person may excavate, remove, damage, or otherwise alter or deface any archaeological resource located on public lands or Indian lands unless such activity is pursuant to a permit issued.....* What this is saying is, picking up a potsherd or corn cob and taking it home is illegal. As is putting your initials on a wall next to some petroglyphs. And one last reminder, the NPS archaeologists ask visitors to report any significant finds to them at any ranger station or the park headquarters at Page, Arizona.

Insects and Pests

Here's some good news! There are very few insects of any kind to bother you while you're on the lake as a boater, fisherman, or hiker. In most boating places, one might expect to find **mosquitos** on or around large bodies of water, but not so with Lake Powell. First, it's a dry desert land, and there aren't many places for them to breed and reproduce. In other words, there are few if any swampy places. Also, much of the shore line is solid rock, commonly known as slickrock. Mosquitos simply can't survive in such an environment.

In the canyons, it's much the same way, but there are small streams and lush vegetation in many. If you walk into these areas in the day time only, you won't see any mosquitos; but if you were to camp in the same areas, you might. The variety of mosquitos in this region only come out at night, so if you're camping on the lake, but away from streams or lush vegetation, you'll find few if any of these insects. The only mosquitos the author remembers on Lake Powell, was while setting up his tent one evening, right where Lake Creek entered the inlet. The next morning, there were none.

Other insects you may encounter are tiny **gnats,** or midges. These sometimes get in your hair and bite hard, although they are very small. On one occasion, the author was camping next to his car near the lake at the head of White Canyon Inlet, and was nearly eaten alive. However, there was no wind that afternoon and he must have just been in the wrong spot, because he has seldom encountered these gnats at any other time. These pests seem to occupy a niche a way from the lake, so in most cases won't bother boaters. One NPS employee told the author they generally disappear around the middle of July or when the monsoon season sets in.

The common **house fly** is something the author almost never saw, or was annoyed by. The only time you may see flies, is if you arrive at a camping place which is often used, and if others before you have left food scraps around. Another place the author saw small flies, which resembled the Australian bush fly, was at the mouths of several canyons on the Navajo Nation lands. There you may see semi-wild Navajo donkeys hanging around the shore line. In these cases with all the dung piles around, expect to encounter more flies. Other than in those places, flies don't seem to exist.

Another pest you may encounter is the big gray **horse fly.** It's likely you'll never see these unless you go hiking, then you may find them flying around your bare legs and biting hard. However, these horse flies seem to be found only in dry washes, which have an occasional seep or enough moisture to grow tamarisks. Up and away from the tamarisks, the horse fly doesn't exist.

The author once docked at the HWM at the very end of the inlet to Bowns Canyon. He then hiked up canyon for about half a day. When he returned to the boat, he noticed several **ravens**(there are apparently very few crows on Lake Powell according the someone at the NPS) flying around making lots of noise. He soon discovered they had raided the boat and had gobbled up three loaves of bread and a small sack of raisins. The bread had been in a bucket under a seat and out of the sun. On later trips, he put the bread in places under a large and heavy backpack, and there were no more problems with ravens.

One last pest. On several occasions, the author found **mice** in his boat. This was always after it had been tied up against an embankment overnight, which either allowed them to hop right in, or they may have climbed up the rope to enter. They ate into bread sacks, and other packages made of plastic or paper. After a bad experience or two, all food was put into containers such as plastic buckets or Tupperware, and that ended the problem. For most people, it's likely mice won't be able to get into the boat. However, at night they can get into food that's placed around your tent if it's not carefully packaged. Just place your food in tight containers, and you'll have no problem.

Drinking Water

For the most part, drinking water isn't a problem on Lake Powell, because everyone takes enough in their boat to sustain them for the duration of the trip. However, there are times when you may have to replenish your supplies. The best place to do this is right at a spring where it comes out of the ground.

There are small streams or springs in almost every canyon entering the lake, and many would be reasonably safe to drink from. However, many streams have beaver, which seem to migrate from one canyon to another, looking for fresh food supplies. When you see fresh sign of beaver, then it's best not to drink from the stream. Instead head up canyon to the spring source if possible.

In the days before Lake Powell, there were cattle roaming most parts of this wide open range; but today, there are only a handful of canyons where cattle can enter and muddy up a stream or spring. When you see fresh sign of cattle, also beware of the water

On every hike the author made, he started out with one liter of culinary water, but in most canyons he found some kind of spring or stream, and in almost every case, sampled that water. He never got sick. In summer heat, you may have to take two liters of water on some hikes, or plan to drink from springs or streams In the description of each canyon, there is a short discussion on where you can find safe drinking water.

One problem many people have is, they have had very little experience when it comes to deciding what is good safe water and what is bad. Without that experience it's difficult to make such a determination. This is the reason the US Public Health Service tells the National Park Service to insist that all outdoorsmen treat, filter or boil all surface water. There are many water sources on or near Lake Powell, which are perfectly safe to drink, but some people haven't the experience-- therefore the common sense, to decide what is drinkable and what is not. Another reason why the

NPS tells everyone to drink only treated, filtered or boiled water, is to save themselves from lawsuits.
Lake water is another possible source, and believe it or not, it's some of the safest around. An un-named source told the author about lake water samples taken by the NPS. Samples taken near marinas, beaches, and other crowded campsites, nearly always showed some kind of pollution, and were considered unfit to drink. Samples taken near the shore line next to Navajo Nation lands, and where livestock graze near the lake, also showed pollution, but giardia apparently has never been found. Samples taken out in the main channel and away from congested areas, usually didn't pass rigid public health standards, but never has anything been found that would make a person sick. Keep in mind federal drinking water standards are probably the highest in the world.

On one fuel stop at Dangling Rope Marina, the author mistakenly filled his jugs with water coming from the tap marked *flushing water*. This water is pumped right out of the lake without treatment. He drank that water for 5 days, until he returned to the same dock to find the mistake. But there were no ill effects. Another boater told of running out of water and instead of boiling some to drink, they just took it from the main channel and drank it as it was. No one suffered. If you do run out of water, and have to take some from the lake, be sure to take it from the main channel and away from livestock areas or popular campsites. It's best to do something with the water before drinking, but the chances are good you'll go on living anyway even if you don't.

Camping on Lake Powell

National Park Service Campgrounds

Most of the following are quotations from a National Park Service hand-out on camping. The National Park Service in the Glen Canyon National Recreation Area, operates developed campgrounds at Wahweap, Lee's Ferry, Bullfrog and Hall's Crossing. These four campgrounds are operated on a first-come, first-served basis with a self-registration station located at the entrance to each. There is an undeveloped, designated camping area at Hite, which does not require registration (or a fee).

Camping in developed campgrounds in Glen Canyon National Recreation Area is limited to 8 people or two vehicles per site for up to 14 days per visit. Group sites are available for larger groups in some areas. For more information regarding the NPS campgrounds, please refer to the chart below.

The National Park Service requests that visitors be aware of and adhere to the regulations governing the use of the developed campgrounds.

Regulations:
1. Fires are permitted in fire grates only, not on the ground.
2. Quiet hours are between 10 pm and 6 am.
3. Pets must be leashed and under control at all times.
4. Use of fireworks and firearms is prohibited.
5. Trash and waste refuse must be disposed of in the provided receptacle.

Facilities at National Park Service Developed Campgrounds

	# of Sites	Camping Fee	Camping Limit (Days)	Open All Year	Self-Registration	Reservations	Overflow Loop	Group Camping Area (Reservation Only)	Dump Station	Restrooms	Running Water	Showers	Hookups	Picnic Tables	Grill/Fire Grate
Wahweap	189	$6	14	yes	yes	no	yes	yes	yes	yes	yes	**	no	yes	yes
Bullfrog	87	$6	14	yes	yes	no	yes	no	yes	yes	yes	**	no	yes	yes
H. Crossing	65	$6	14	yes	yes	no	no	no	yes	yes	yes	yes	no	yes	yes
Hite	12	no	14	yes	n/a	no	no	no	*	*	*	no	no	yes	no
Lee's Ferry	54	$6	14	yes	yes	no	no	no	yes	yes	yes	no	no	yes	yes

* A dump station, restrooms, and running water are available at Hite Marina, but are not located in the designated camping area.
** Public shower facilities are available from the concessioner, but not the NPS campground. There is a primitive camping area at the San Juan Marina. A no fee area.

Camping at the Concessioner's Campgrounds

At Wahweap, Bullfrog and Hall's Crossing Marinas, campsites with utility hookups suitable for RV's are available through the concessioner. Registration for these RV sites is through the concession operation at each marina.

During the busy summer months advance reservations are recommended. For advance reservations, call Del Webb toll free at 1-800-528-6154. For reservations seven days in advance or less, call the numbers below.

	# of Sites	Camping Fee	Reservation	Open Year-Round	Water Hookups	Elec. Hookups	Sewage Hookups	Tent Sites	Shower	Laundry	For More Information
Wahweap	143	*	yes	yes	yes	yes	yes	yes	yes	yes	(602) 645-2433
Bullfrog	23	*	yes	yes	yes	yes	yes	no	yes	**	(801) 684-2233
H. Crossing	32	*	yes	yes	yes	yes	no	yes	yes		(801) 684-2261
Hite		No RV camping facilities with hookups are available.									
Lee's Ferry		No RV camping facilities with hookups are available.									

* Fees vary depending on season and hookup services required.
** Laundry facilities are provided at Bullfrog Marina and are located a short distance from the RV park.

Lakeshore and Boat Camping

Many visitors to Lake Powell enjoy the peace and solitude of camping on the lakeshore. Boats may be launched from public launch ramps at any of the marinas. Camping is permitted anywhere on the lake outside of a one mile(1 1/2 kms) zone around developed areas. Camping is prohibited in Rainbow Bridge National Monument.

When camping on the lake, the National Park Service requests that all campfires be built below the high water mark(HWM) and in existing fire rings if possible. Boat out all trash and discard in receptacles provided at each marina. No trash may be left on the shore or thrown in the lake, and burying trash is not an acceptable method of disposal. Garbage bags may be obtained free of charge from ranger stations at any marina.

Some lakeshore camping areas can be accessed by vehicle. These include: Lone Rock, near Wahweap; Stanton Creek(Canyon) and Upper Bullfrog Bay in the Bullfrog area; and Farley Canyon, White Canyon and the Dirty Devil sites near Hite. There is no fee or registration required for camping in these areas. Please take out all you take in. Vault toilets are located in these areas(not White Canyon or the Dirty Devil sites). Like most other water sources, Lake Powell's water must be boiled or treated with chemicals prior to drinking(NPS).

Disposal of human waste is best accomplished through the use of a portable toilet system. Dump stations are located in all developed campgrounds and floating dump stations for boats are located at all marinas. For those who lack the portable system, human waste should be buried at a depth greater than 6 inches(15 cms). Federal regulations require the site to be over 100 ft.(30 meters) from a water source. This means the site must be 100 ft.(30 meters) from the high water mark(HWM) of 3700 feet(1128 meters).

Tips on Camping, Boating and Other Needed Equipment

For those who will be going out on the lake and camping for the first time, here are some things you should take. First and perhaps most important, is a **shovel**. With a shovel you can level a tent site. You'll sleep much better if you bed down on a flat spot. You can also bury human waste with the shovel.

In order to tie your boat down securely, take at least **two long ropes** of about 20 meters(60 ft.). Long ones are important, because sometimes it's hard to find a place to tie down. In sandy beach type areas, it is sometimes helpful to have a *metal stake* or pole you can pound in the ground, and tie your boat to. In slickrock areas, it's sometimes best to have a couple of *anchors* which you can place into cracks in the rock to hold your boat away from the rocky shore line.

If your tent has stakes, a *hammer* is sometimes a lot easier to use than a rock for driving the stakes. In slickrock areas, many people are now using the new little pop or dome tents, which can be used without stakes. Many people also take *plastic tarps.* These can cover equipment or the boat, and with several poles and ropes, can make a nice shade canopy. In the heat of summer, this is nice to have during the middle of the day.

If you plan to go out on an extended trip where there'll be no ice, remove the lid of your **ice chest,** put a small amount of water in the bottom, then cover everything with a wet towel. The water in the bottom will keep the towel wet, and the very low humidity of Lake Powell air will evaporative rapidly, keeping everything cool. Keep the cooler in the shade and exposed to a breeze if possible.

Another handy thing to take along is a **radio.** It will not only keep you informed to the news of the outside world, but will keep you updated on the latest weather forecasts. During the spring and fall season this is important, because it's at these times storms can come in with very little warning. Spring time storms usually bring strong winds. On one occasion, the author had to sit tight for nearly one full day(about 20 hours) before he could get back out on the lake in this little inflatable boat.

Here's the situation on the **boundaries of the GCNRA** as it relates to the lands of the **Navajo Nation.** If you're boating and camping in areas on the south side of the lake between Wahweap and the mouth of the San Juan River Arm, and on the south side of the San Juan Arm itself, you'll be on the Navajo Nation side of the lake. However, the line between the recreation area and the Navajo land is set at 1134 meters or 3720 feet. This means the boundary is 6 meters above the HWM(1128). So, when you camp anywhere near the lake, you're within the boundaries of the GCNRA. However, no one will arrest you if you hike up canyon onto Navajo lands to the south.

When looking for a campsite, it's usually best to head for a canyon inlet instead of picking a spot along the main channel. The reason is, if it becomes winding during your stay, there will be much calmer waters in the inlets. Along the main channel you can be bothered by wind or boater-made waves, which can do damage to your boat.

And last, if you're going out for an extended camping trip, be sure to have lots of **jugs,** or some kind of containers to carry a plentiful supply of drinking water. That way you can get by without having to take the time to hunt for a safe place to stock up.

Camping scene in the inlet of Oak Canyon.

Part III--Geology, Maps, and Odds and Ends

The Geology of Glen Canyon and the Lake Powell Country

Understanding the geology of Glen Canyon and the surrounding country presents a challenge to geologists and amateurs alike. The layering of the rock and the effects of erosion, although easily seen, are not always easily explained.

Most of the exposed rock surrounding Lake Powell is sedimentary in nature. Laid down millions of years ago during an age when shallow seas repeatedly invaded and retreated from the area, the layers vary greatly. Some of the deposits are actual sea sediment like limestone, some are wind-blown shore deposits, and some are silt from sluggish streams. Others, such as the thick sandstone beds in the Cedar Mesa, Entrada, Navajo, and Wingate Sandstones were originally sandy deserts like the Sahara. Whatever the source, these deposits, compacted by the weight of new deposits laid on top, hardened into the rocks we see and know today. The different layers, varying in degree of hardness, erode at different rates. This differential erosion has created the spectacular scenery we see today in the Glen Canyon and Lake Powell areas.

Here's a quick rundown on how each type of sedimentary rock was formed. The rock type which dominates all others around Lake Powell is **sandstone.** This rock began as a sea of sand, like much of the Sahara Desert is today. Then the land likely sank and was covered by shallow seas which deposited other sediments on top. The sand froze in place, and with time the grains were cemented together to form sandstone. Later the land rose, and erosion began to take place, leaving the spires, buttes and mesas we see today on the Colorado Plateau.

Next to sandstone, the rock type seen most often is **limestone.** All limestone was formed at the bottom of an ocean. After a period of sedimentation, the sea floor was raised along with other layers which formed over the limestone. Still later, the land rose higher, then began the process of erosion. This is the stage we see today on Lake Powell. Limestone always has a gray color and is composed of the remains of marine shell fish which sank to the sea floor and decayed. It almost always has many marine fossils, and because of its high content of lime, this is the rock from which cement is derived.

Another important sedimentary rock commonly found in the cliffs and mesas of Lake Powell country is **mudstone.** The history of mudstone began around the shore lines of fresh water lakes or shallow seas, and at or near the mouths of rivers which were heavily ladened with mud. The present-day delta of the Mississippi River will probably end up as a type of mudstone--perhaps 100-200 million years from now. You will recognize mudstone by its brown color and fine texture. Another rock that's very similar to mudstone, is **siltstone.** This one is also a very fine textured stone, but it can come in different colors.

Another common sedimentary rock found in the southwestern corner of Lake Powell country is **shale.** Shale is seen as thin layers of rock which often appear as clay beds. It is often gray in color, but thin beds of red shale are common. Shale is formed from fine sediments settling to the bottoms of fresh water lakes. Each layer of the shale would likely indicated one year's muddy sedimentation of the heavy spring runoff. Shale which is put under heat and pressure, evolve into *slate.*

Not all of the rock in the area is sedimentary. **Igneous rock** exists in the form of laccolithic mountains, such as the Henry Mountains and Navajo Mountain. Laccoliths form when molten rock pushes up beneath and through sedimentary layers, bulging the rock into a dome-shaped mountain but not breaking through to form a volcano.

Usually smooth and rounded, laccolithic mountains become more ragged looking as erosion wears away the sedimentary layers, exposing jagged fins of basaltic rock. Occasionally, the entire intrusive neck comes into view. In the Henry Mountains, the intrusive rock is exposed in many places, forming rugged looking topography, while on Navajo Mountain, the basaltic rock has yet to be exposed. Some of this rock is called granite. You can see granite cobblestones which have originated from the Henry Mountains in the drainages of Trachyte, Twomile, Fourmile and Smith Fork Canyons.

Geologic formations are not stagnant; their forms are constantly changing as erosion continuously wears away at the stone. Even large plateaus slowly turn into mesas, mesas evolve into buttes, buttes become spires, and spires crumble. The eventual fate of all formations, regardless of shape or size, is collapse and/or erosion.

GEOLOGY CROSS SECTION--LAKE POWELL

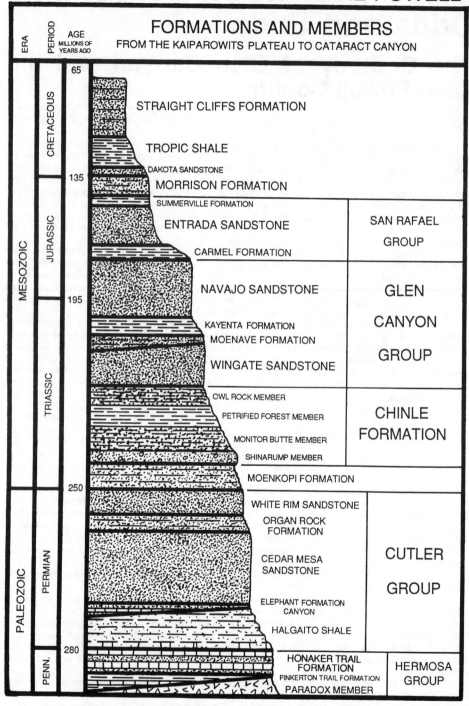

FORMATIONS AND MEMBERS
FROM THE KAIPAROWITS PLATEAU TO CATARACT CANYON

ERA	PERIOD	AGE MILLIONS OF YEARS AGO	FORMATIONS AND MEMBERS	Group
MESOZOIC	CRETACEOUS	65	STRAIGHT CLIFFS FORMATION	
			TROPIC SHALE	
		135	DAKOTA SANDSTONE	
			MORRISON FORMATION	
	JURASSIC		SUMMERVILLE FORMATION	SAN RAFAEL GROUP
			ENTRADA SANDSTONE	
			CARMEL FORMATION	
		195	NAVAJO SANDSTONE	GLEN CANYON GROUP
			KAYENTA FORMATION	
			MOENAVE FORMATION	
	TRIASSIC		WINGATE SANDSTONE	
			OWL ROCK MEMBER	CHINLE FORMATION
			PETRIFIED FOREST MEMBER	
			MONITOR BUTTE MEMBER	
			SHINARUMP MEMBER	
		250	MOENKOPI FORMATION	
PALEOZOIC	PERMIAN		WHITE RIM SANDSTONE	CUTLER GROUP
			ORGAN ROCK FORMATION	
			CEDAR MESA SANDSTONE	
			ELEPHANT CANYON FORMATION	
			HALGAITO SHALE	
	PENN.	280	HONAKER TRAIL FORMATION	HERMOSA GROUP
			PINKERTON TRAIL FORMATION	
			PARADOX MEMBER	

Geologic Formations and Where They're Exposed

Below is a list of all the formations found within just a few short kms of the shores of Lake Powell. The youngest rocks are the Straight Cliffs Formation, found at the top of Fiftymile Mountain(Kaiparowits Plateau), just to the north of the Dangling Rope Marina. The oldest rocks, the Paradox Formation, are found in the far upper or northern end of the lake in Cataract Canyon.

Straight Cliffs Formation Type Locality: The long straight cliffs on the northeast side of the Kaiparowits Plateau, usually known as Fiftymile Mountain, Kane County, Utah. This formation is a cliff maker and is seen as the upper most layer of rocks on top of the Kaiparowits. This a light colored brown or yellow sandstone, sometimes mixed with shale and mudstone. In the southern parts where this formation is exposed, it's divided into four members: Drip Tank, John Henry, Smoky Hollow and Tibbet Canyon Members. 333 meters thick.

Tropic Shale Type Locality: In Bryce Valley around the small town of Tropic, Garfield County, Utah. This is a dark gray marine shale, with thin layers of sandstone near the top, and thin fossiliferous limestone in the lower part. This formation makes a bench and is the first layer below the Straight Cliffs Formation on the Kaiparowits Plateau above Grand Bench. However it is buried by talus and landslide slopes, and almost never exposed at that location. It's also seen above the lake in Wahweap and Warm Creek Canyons. 185 to 195 meters thick.

Dakota Sandstone Type Locality: Near Dakota City, Dakota County, Nebraska. This is generally a pale brown, course-grained sandstone, with some beds of mudstone and some coal seams. It's sometimes seen on the outskirts of the first broad bench below the top-most cliffs of the Kaiparowits Plateau, and to the west and southwest just above the flat-topped benches which were created by the Morrison Formation below. It's the bed where the Spencer Mines are found in Crosby Canyon, a tributary to Warm Creek. It's a cliff making formation, but it hardly forms a cliff in this region, because it's so thin. 10 to 30 meters thick.

Morrison Formation Type Locality: Near Morrison, Jefferson County, Colorado. Made up mostly of continental beds of sandstone, but with conglomeratic sandstone and mudstones. This formation is definitely a cliff former, and seen just up lake, or east of Wahweap, and in the cliffs on both sides of the lake. It forms the upper half of the cliffs in Warm Creek, Padre, Last Chance, Rock Creek, and Dangling Rope Bays, and others to the east and south of the lake. 0 to 155 meters thick.

Summerville Formation Type Locality: Summerville Point, north end of the San Rafael Swell, Emery County, Utah. Reddish to pale brown sandstone, mixed with shaley siltstone. In many locations, this narrow band is in the middle of the big cliffs formed by the Morrison and the Entrada Formations. It's hard to pick out in the middle of the cliffs above Warm Creek, Padre, Last Chance, Rock Creek and Dangling Rope Bays, or in the cliffs above Wetherill, West and Face Canyons. 5 to 25 meters thick.

Entrada Sandstone Type Locality: Entrada Point, north end of the San Rafael Swell, Emery County, Utah. In the Lake Powell area, it is mostly the reddish brown massive, or solid sandstone you see in the walls of the big cliffs between Wahweap and the Dangling Rope Marinas, on both the north and south sides of the lake. Generally, this forms the lower half of the cliffs, with the Morrison making up the top half. 185 to 230 meters thick.

Carmel Formation Type Locality: Mount Carmel, Kane County, Utah. These are thin beds of dusky red limy siltstone, and reddish brown sandstone, with occasional pink limestone beds. It is seen to form the benches where camping is so fine in Gunsight Canyon, Warm Creek, Labyrinth and Face Canyon Bays, and at the upper end of the three bays forming Rock Creek. It's also the bench where employee housing sits at the Dangling Rope Marina. It's always a bench former and always on top of the ever present Navajo Sandstone. 60 to 120 meters thick.

Navajo Sandstone Type Locality: Navajo Canyon, Coconino County, Arizona. This thick layer of solid or massive sandstone is usually a pale brown, or buff colored. It's a cliff maker, and one which makes up many of the very narrow slots canyons on the Colorado Plateau. It's seen in Navajo Canyon, all the canyons of the Escalante River Arm, in the area of the Great Bend of the San Juan Arm, and on top of the big walls, forming the bluffs to the west of Hite Marina. Rainbow Bridge is perhaps the best example of the Navajo Sandstone. It's also the most prominent formation making the walls of Zion Park and in the Paria River Canyon to the west of Lake Powell. 290 to 425 meters thick.

EXPLANATION: In recent years, and with better transportation into the Lake Powell county, more studies have been made of the Carmel Formation and the Navajo Sandstone. It's been found in the area from Dangling Rope Marina, Page, Arizona, and the middle part of the Paria River in Utah, there are divisions in the lower Carmel and the top part of the Navajo. Geologists have come up with a new cross section. On top is the **Carmel Formation,** which in some areas to the west has about three members. Next, is what used to be the top of the Navajo, but now is called the **Page Sandstone,** which includes the **Thousand Pockets Tongue.** From all the author can gather, both of these mentioned members are one in the same formation. Under the Page Sandstone is the **Judd Hollow Tongue of the Carmel Formation.** Then immediately under this thin layer is the main body of the **Navajo Sandstone.** Up to date, only a few of the very latest maps have any mention of this new classification. These date from the early to mid-1980's. All other geology maps retain the older and still used names of just the Carmel and Navajo Formations. Since newer maps with the new names still don't cover all areas, the author has left them as they are.

Kayenta Formation Type Locality: Just north of the town of Kayenta, Navajo County, Arizona. This is the reddish brown fluvial made sandstone, siltstone and shale layer which is always sandwiched in between the Navajo above, and the Wingate or the Moenave below. This one is a bench former, and often has several minor terraces itself. It can be seen in the Escalante River Canyon, in the area of the mouth of Bowns and Long Canyons, and between Good Hope Bay and Hite. 75 to 120 meters thick.

Moenave Formation Type Locality: Near Moenave and Tuba City, Coconino County, Arizona. Mostly a reddish brown sandstone, with thin layers of siltstone and mudstone. This formation is exposed in the big cliffs you see to the south of the San Juan Arm of the lake. It's near the top of the massive Wingate Sandstone walls on Piute Mesa. It thins out completely by The Rincon, and is non-existent in areas to the north. It replaces the Wingate Sandstone to the west, in the area of Zion Park, and south into Arizona. The cliffs to the east of Lee's Ferry are mostly Moenave, with just a little Wingate. 0 to 125 meters thick.

Wingate Sandstone Type Locality: Cliffs north of Fort Wingate, McKinley County, New Mexico. Reddish brown and light brown, fine grained, and massive crossbedded sandstone. This one makes the big cliffs or walls surrounding The Rincon, and is the lower part of the wall in the area of the mouth of Bowns and Long Canyons. It makes most of the big wall you see on the north and east side of Piute Mesa, and where the Williams Trail zig zags up the steepest part. 70 to 105 meters thick.

Chinle Formation Type Locality: Chinle Valley, Apache County, Arizona. There is great variation between the four main members of the Chinle, but mostly it's famous for many clay beds. The *Owl Rock Member* is a reddish brown silt mudstone. The *Petrified Forest Member* has lots of petrified wood in it. It was in these clay beds that Charles H. Spencer tried to dig out gold at Lee's Ferry and later at Pahreah, Utah. A reddish brown mudstone is the third member from the top and is called the *Monitor Butte Member.* The lowest member is the *Shinarump Conglomerate.* It's a white colored, course sandstone and conglomerate, again with lots of petrified wood. In some localities, it was known as the Black Ledge, because it's often covered with black desert varnish. This one is famous also as one of the primary formations on the Colorado Plateau which contains uranium. It's an area-wide formation, and uranium was mined in it from the San Rafael Swell to Arizona. Many of the old mine exploration tracks you see in the San Juan Arm and in the area of Hite and The Rincon, led miners to explore this member of the Chinle. 15 to 380 meters thick.

Moenkopi Formation Type Locality: Moenkopi Wash, Coconino County, Arizona. In some places there are some thin beds of limestone in this formation, but mostly it's a dark reddish chocolate brown, ripple marked sandstone, with thin lenses of shale and mudstone. The Moenkopi is seen in the ledges across the channel from Hite, and in the area of Piute Canyon, Zahn Bay and Nokai Dome. Most of the dark reddish-brown soil you see as you drive along White Canyon to the east of Hite, is from the Moenkopi. 90 to 120 meters thick.

White Rim Sandstone Type Locality: White Rim escarpment between the Green and Colorado Rivers, San Juan County, Utah. A white to yellow, thin, fine grained, crossbedded, massive sandstone in the White Canyon and Dirty Devil River Canyon areas. Some geologists believe this to be the same as the Coconino Sandstone, which is to the north and southwest. The Coconino is a common formation in the top layers of the rim of the Grand Canyon. Around Lake Powell it is seen in the lower part of the Dirty Devil River and around White Canyon, and also surrounding Zahn Bay and on the slopes of Nokai Dome, in the San Juan Arm. 0 to 120 meters thick.

Organ Rock Shale Type Locality: Organ Rock, Monument Valley, San Juan County, Utah. This is a reddish brown siltstone with sandy shales. It forms a slope and ledge on the cliffs across the channel from Hite Marina, and on both sides of Zahn Bay in the San Juan Arm of the lake. Some of these rocks appear similar to the rocks seen in Goblin Valley, next to Utah's San Rafael Swell. 90 to 150 meters thick.

Cedar Mesa Sandstone Type Locality: Cedar Mesa, west and northwest of Mexican Hat, San

Juan County, Utah. This covers the top of the mesa to the south and southwest of the Abajo Mountains. It's mostly white to pale light yellow, crossbedded, massive sandstone. It makes some of the finest narrows hikes around, especially in the lower White Canyon. This is the same formation where all or most of the Anasazi ruins are found in the areas south of the Abajos, and especially in Grand Gulch. You can see this as the massive sandstone walls in Narrow Canyon, and as you get further up and into Cataract Canyon, this is the top-most layer on those high walls. It's also the top layer as you hike into all the tributary canyons of Cataract. It's always a big cliff maker. 365 to 400 meters thick.

Elephant Canyon Formation Type Locality: Elephant Canyon, near the Confluence of the Green and Colorado Rivers, Canyonlands National Park, San Juan County, Utah. It's made of cherty limestones and some dolomites, interbedded with pale reddish sandstones. This one forms a cliff, but with some slopes and terraces as well. You can only see this one in the far upper end of the lake in Cataract Canyon. 125 to 450 meters thick.

Halgaito Shale Type Locality: Halgaito Springs, southwest of Mexican Hat, San Juan County, Utah. The Halgaito is made up of reddish brown sandstones, red siltstones, and conglomerates with thin limestone beds. It forms a slope or bench at the bottom of the Cedar Mesa Sandstone in the upper part of Narrow Canyon, and throughout Cataract Canyon. 125 to 210 meters thick.

Honaker Trail Formation Type Locality: Honaker Trail, in the San Juan River Canyon west of Mexican Hat, San Juan County, Utah. This formation is composed of dark colored thick limestone, interbedded with gray cherty limestone, and red and gray shales and sandstones. This is a cliff maker. It forms the lower part of the walls from Freddies Cistern and Dark Canyon up to the Palmer and Gypsum Canyon area of Cataract Canyon. These beds form the cliffs or falls you have to get around in the lower end of Calf, Cove, Palmer and Imperial Canyons. 300 to 500 meters thick.

Pinkerton Trail Formation Type Locality: Pinkerton Trail, along the San Juan River Gorge west of Mexican Hat, San Juan County, Utah. This formation is a pickish gray series of limestones beds, with intertongues of siltstone. It also contains gypsum beds. This one is only seen in the lowest end of the San Juan River Canyon above Clay Hills Crossing. 45 to 60 meters thick.

Paradox Formation Type Locality: Paradox Valley, Montrose County, Colorado. You likely won't see this one, as it's difficult to differentiate with others, and much of it is covered with talus slopes. This is a slope and cliff maker, and you may see it only in the upper end of Cataract Canyon, near the mouths of Palmer and Gypsum Canyons. It's basically black shales and limestone, interbedded with salt anhydrite and gypsum. The author believes this is the blackish rock which has made Gypsum Falls in Gypsum Canyon. The Paradox Formation is a result of a large anticline in western Colorado and eastern Utah. In the middle parts of the anticline, the beds are made of salts, a result of evaporation of a large shallow inland sea(perhaps similar to the Caspian Sea). But along the outer fringes, one sees mostly limestone beds. This would be the result of marine shell fish sedimentation during younger stages of the same salty sea. Since we see mostly limestone beds in Cataract Canyon, it's assumed this region was along the outer most edges of that ancient sea. 150 to 1500 meters thick.

Maps of Lake Powell County

One thing to keep in mind when using this book as your guide to Lake Powell, you must also have one of the larger maps available which shows the lake in it's entirety. The only maps in this book which show the entire lake are the ones showing some of the United States Geological Survey(USGS) maps, and the Reference Map of Hikes.

There are several full sized maps of the lake, one of which must be used along with to this book. The most popular one is **Stan Jones' Boating and Exploring Map of Lake Powell.** It is double sided with lots of information about boating rules and regulations, wildlife, fishing regulations, etc. By itself, it's surely the best map of the lake and the one this author recommends. It's also the best selling lake map available. Stan Jones updates the map and its information about every year or two.

Another good one is called **Lake Powell Map Guide.** It too is double sided, with lots of tidbits of information, including weather and water temperatures, fishing and boating tips, and a little about the marinas. This one is published by the American Adventures Association.

Still another commercial map of the lake is entitled **Lake Powell, Finding Your Way.** This one is published by someone in Chico California, and uses the 1:62,500 scale USGS maps of the region as it's base. It shows the lake in 4 sections, and it may be the most accurate of all the lake maps available when it comes to showing the inlets and bays. Perhaps the best thing about this one is that it specializes in showing all the buoys on the lake. Beyond that, it has no other information.

The three maps above are all commercial ventures and in 1988, all cost $3.00. They can be purchased in the Del Webb marina stores around the lake and in other businesses in the vicinity. In addition to these, there are some free maps put out by the National Park Service. One is called **Glen Canyon: Official Map and Guide.** It has a little information about all aspects of the lake and is a good one. Another one put out by the NPS is titled **Glen Canyon Dam and National Recreation Area.** It's very similar to the one above, but appears to be an older version. It's an adequate map as well. Both of these maps can be found at National Park Service Visitor Centers around the lake, and in some cases at visitor centers at the other national parks in the region. Sometimes BLM offices will carry them as well.

There are two more maps showing all of Lake Powell. The Utah Travel Council has a series of maps covering the state, and in the old series **Map # 1, Southeastern Utah,** covers the lake very well, especially the access roads leading to the GCNRA. This a good map, but it shows nothing of the lake on the Arizona side of the line. In the new map series, look for the one titled, **Southeastern Utah.** Both the old and the new cover about the same area.

One more map put out by the USGS, the Bureau of Reclamation, and the NPS, is called **Glen Canyon National Recreation Area.** It is based on the 1:250,000 scale USGS maps of the region, and is the very best one to show the northern end of the lake in Cataract Canyon(up to the confluence of the Green and Colorado Rivers). It too is a very good map of the lake and region.

Shown on this index map are the new **USGS 1:100,000 scale Metric** topographic maps of southeastern Utah. It takes five of these to cover the lake, and are undoubtedly the best maps available. The ones you'll need are: Hanksville, Hite Crossing, Navajo Mountain, Smoky Mountain and Glen Canyon Dam. In addition to these USGS maps, the Bureau of Land Management(BLM) also puts out maps which are identical except theirs come in different colors which depict land ownership. For example, public lands are shown in yellow, private lands are in white, and Forest Service lands are in green, etc. If you buy any of the BLM maps, be sure to order those in the series called *Surface Management Status.* These are easier to read than maps having to do with mineral leases.

Some of the good things about these new USGS metric maps dating from the 1980's are that all show the lake at the high water mark(HWM), they show all of the newer roads leading to the lake and the marinas, and they show lots more detail than any of the maps above, which show the entire lake. This makes them good for both boating and hiking.

In addition to these new metric maps, there are the older USGS maps of the area at **1:62,500 scale.** These are good maps and show detail better than any maps available; but they are old, most dating from the 1950's or earlier. This means they were made when Lake Powell was just a dream, so they don't have the newer access roads, marinas, or the lake's shore line. The serious hiker could still get by with these, but it would be guess work to decide where the shore line of the lake is located. The best map for hiking is listed under each of the area maps in this book. That short list includes both the 1:100,000 and 1:62,500 scale maps available.

INDEX TO 1:100,000 SCALE TOPOGRAPHIC MAPS OF LAKE POWELL

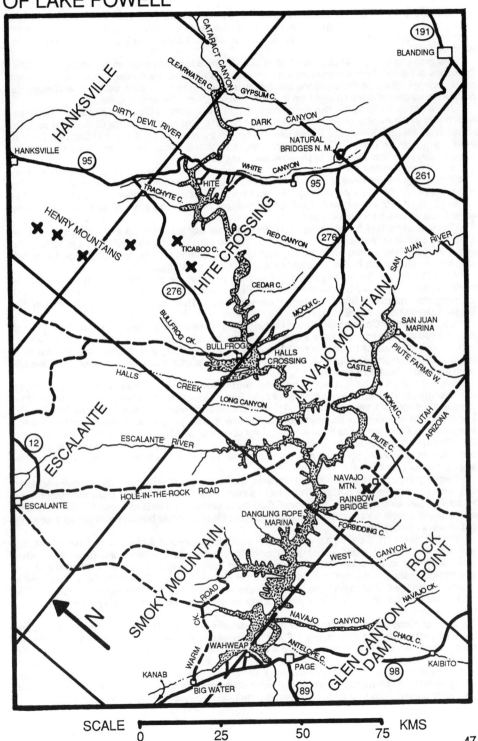

SCALE

0   25   50   75   KMS

47

Odds and Ends of Information

One of the first things you'll have to do before you get onto the lake, and before you even begin to plan a trip, is to get a **large map covering the entire lake.** You can't use this book effectively, unless you have one. See the section on *Maps of Lake Powell Country,* for a list of the maps available.

The map you buy should show on it, all or many of the **buoys** one sees while boating on the lake. The buoys in the middle of the channel, which tell boaters where deeper water is, also have numbers and sometimes letters on them. Those with letters don't seem to mean a lot, but those with numbers, indicate the number of miles up lake from the Glen Canyon Dam. The dam is at mile 0.

There are no buoys in the San Juan Arm of the lake to indicate mileage or kilomage. Neither are there buoys at the mouths of any of the side canyons. The numbers the author uses in that part, are the old river mileage before Lake Powell came to be. In the north end of the lake in Cataract Canyon, there are no buoys either. On the canyon maps in those parts, the author has extended the mileage(kilomage) from the dam, to show relative distances.

In this book, and on the various maps of the canyons, there will be numbers and letters such as **M24(K38).** This means there is a buoy in that area that is marked with a number indicating the miles from the dam. In this case 24 miles up lake from the dam. The second letter and number are not on the buoys, but it is the conversion of miles to kilometers(kms). In this case 24 miles equals 38 kms, the distance up lake from Glen Canyon Dam.

The reason each of the buoys marked in this book are labeled with miles and kms, is because the rest of this book is in **metrics.** It's not meant to confuse people, but surely will do that to some. The reason it's used here is that when the day comes for the USA to change over to metrics, the author won't have to change his books. The author feels that day is fast approaching.

In 1975, the US Congress passed a resolution to begin the process of changing over to the metric system. They did this because the USA, Burma, and Brunei were the only countries on earth still using the antiquated British System of measurement. This progressive move ended with the Reagan Administration in 1981.

Use the **Metric Conversion Table** for help in the conversion process. It's easy to learn and use once you get started. Just keep a few things in mind: 1 mile is just over 1.5 kms, 2 miles is about 3 kms, and 6 miles is about 10 kms. Also, 100 meters is just over 100 yards, 2000 meters is about 6600 feet, and 3000 meters is about 10,000 feet. A liter and a quart are roughly the same, and one US gallon jug holds about 3.75 liters.

When it comes to the subject of **boating regulations,** this is something you'll have to get more of some place else. The regulations for Lake Powell appear to be virtually the same as for other waters in the states of Utah and Arizona. There's no difference when you cross the state line. Briefly, all boats with motors must be licenced with the numbers showing on the boat. Boats must have a fire extinguisher, a life jacket for each passenger, a set of oars or paddles, and a whistle or horn of some kind. Other highly recommended items would be: an anchor or anchor line, maps, simple tool kit and good boat shoes. Also, plenty of gasoline(more than you think you'll need), food, water, and the camping gear of your choice.

Before going to Lake Powell for the first time, it's best to check your own state's requirements for equipment and other safety devices. Also, have a map of the lake which gives more information than this book. Stan Jones' Map of Lake Powell Country is perhaps the best all-around. This map and other sources should be consulted concerning the markings on other buoys, travel at night, boater's right-of-ways, fishing, etc,.

For the most part, there is little or no danger in striking a piece of **driftwood** on Lake Powell, but there are a couple of areas where you'll have to be observant. The worst place the author encountered was in the upper end of Navajo Canyon Inlet. It's very thick near the south end, but some floaters make it to the half way mark. The other place is Cataract Canyon in the northern end of the lake, where the Colorado River enters. The water is always muddy in that region, but there isn't as much floating wood as you might expect. Sand or silt bars can be bigger problems up there than driftwood.

If you're hiking into any of the slot or narrow canyons around the lake, remember to get out and stay out if **bad weather** is threatening. Flash floods of the magnitude which can wash people out of narrow canyons don't come very often, but when they do, you'd better not be in their way. Most of the big gully washing floods come in the late summer and early fall. They come about during cloud-burst type storms. The all-day type rainstorms which pass over the area in winter, usually put some running water in these narrow canyons, but ankle-deep water is not a problem. A few years ago, 5 hikers were carried away in a big flood in Zion Narrows, so be aware of this potential danger.

REFERENCE MAP OF CANYONS & HIKES

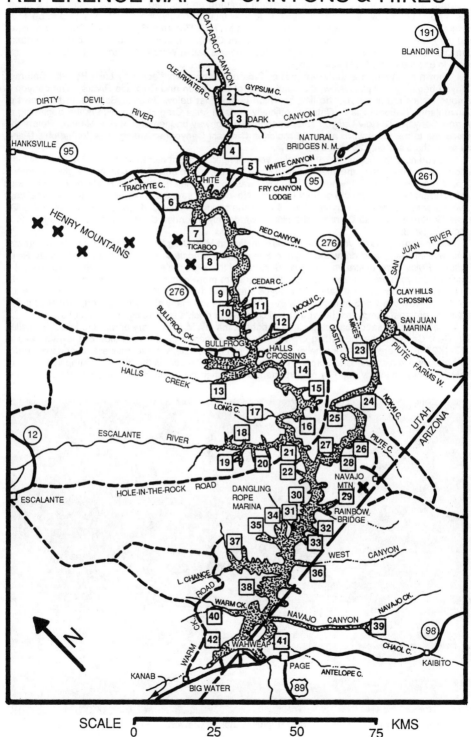

Cataract, Imperial, and Calf Canyons

Location and Campsites The three canyons featured on this map are located right at the upper most end of Lake Powell. When the lake is at maximum capacity, the elevation is said to be 1128 meters, and reaches into Cataract Canyon to about M172(K276) from Glen Canyon Dam. This upper end also reaches to what rafters call the Ten Cent Campsite, just north of the mouth of Imperial Canyon. On some maps, the Calf Canyon shown here is called Waterhole Canyon; but boaters maps seem to use the name Calf most often.

Shown on the map is the lower part of Cataract Canyon unaffected by Lake Powell. Cataract Canyon begins at, or just below, the confluence of the Green and Colorado Rivers. The canyon is famous for it's many rapids, the first of which begins just below Spanish Bottoms in the heart of Canyonlands National Park. Cataract officially ends at Mille Crag Bend, which is the beginning of Narrow Canyon. Narrow Canyon ends at about the highway bridge north of Hite Marina. Before the lake came to be, there were about 62 rapids in Cataract Canyon(according to Dellenbaugh's Diary), but today there are only 25 above the HWM.

As you near the upper end of the lake, you will notice a slight current. Its speed will vary with the amount of water entering the lake and how close you are to the end of the lake at any given moment. Upon the author's July visit, when the lake level was about 2 meters below the HWM, he could detect a slight current below the mouth of Dark Canyon. Needless to say, the upper end of the lake will always have water that is less than crystal clear. During the spring runoff, cloudy water is seen past Hite. On a late September visit to Cataract, the cloudy water only extended down canyon to the beginning of Mille Crag Bend.

As you boat up lake, you will see a warning sign at Mille Crag Bend which states: *Swift currents, shallow sand bars, and driftwood beyond this point. Campsites above here are needed by River Rafters. Please limit upstream camping.* Because of this sign, the author saw no other lake boaters in Cataract Canyon; only the rafters. Actually, there are more campsites than this sign might indicate, but everyone wants the nice sandy beach-type sites, and these are definitely limited. However, when the water levels are 4 or 5 meters below the HWM, there are many silt bars exposed. Not all of these make the greatest campsites, but you can pitch a tent or dock a boat up against most of them.

The very best sandy camping place is right at the HWM at the very end of the lake. It's called Ten Cent Campsite by the rafting crowd. It's a large beach on the east side of the river-lake at M171(K274). There's another smaller sandy site just across the water to the west. Just down around the bend and across the lake from the mouth of Imperial Canyon, is the Imperial Campsite. Both of these sites are regularly used by river runners during their six month rafting season. If you camp at

Large rafts running through the Big Drop Rapids, Cataract Canyon.

MAP 1, CATARACT, IMPERIAL & CALF CANYONS

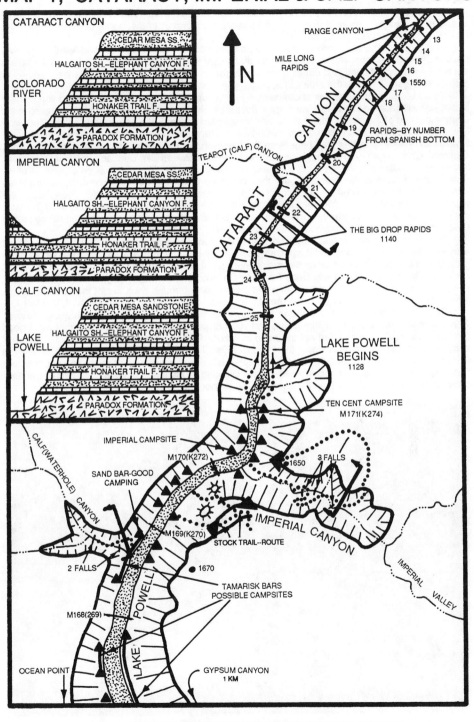

CATARACT CANYON
CEDAR MESA SS.
HALGAITO SH.–ELEPHANT CANYON F.
COLORADO RIVER
HONAKER TRAIL F.
PARADOX FORMATION

IMPERIAL CANYON
CEDAR MESA SS.
HALGAITO SH.–ELEPHANT CANYON F.
HONAKER TRAIL F.
PARADOX FORMATION

CALF CANYON
CEDAR MESA SANDSTONE
LAKE POWELL
HALGAITO SH.–ELEPHANT CANYON F.
HONAKER TRAIL F.
PARADOX FORMATION

N

RANGE CANYON
MILE LONG RAPIDS
13
14
15
16
• 1550
17
18
19
RAPIDS–BY NUMBER FROM SPANISH BOTTOM
20
TEAPOT (CALF) CANYON
CATARACT CANYON
21
22
THE BIG DROP RAPIDS 1140
23
24
25
LAKE POWELL BEGINS 1128
TEN CENT CAMPSITE M171(K274)
IMPERIAL CAMPSITE
M170(K272)
1650
3 FALLS
SAND BAR–GOOD CAMPING
CALF (WATERHOLE) CANYON
M169(K270)
STOCK TRAIL--ROUTE
IMPERIAL CANYON
IMPERIAL VALLEY
2 FALLS
• 1670
TAMARISK BARS POSSIBLE CAMPSITES
M168(269)
LAKE POWELL
OCEAN POINT
GYPSUM CANYON 1 KM

SCALE
0   1   2   3   4   KMS

51

either of these sites, do so at one end or the other, so when the rafters come in during the afternoons, you will all have plenty of room.

Down canyon a bit further, there are numerous campsites with tamarisks, all of which are of questionable quality. There is one very good little site just north of the mouth of Calf Canyon. It's labeled *sand bar-good camping,* on the map.

In this part of the lake or river, the available campsites will depend on the lake level. Generally speaking, the lower the water level, the better these sites are. These sites exposed when the lake is low will be mostly silt bars, and not as desirable as the sandy beaches. In the future there should be more and bigger silt bars in the area just down canyon from this mapped area.

Some of the negative things about camping in this upper end of the lake are, when you want to bathe, you will often be standing in mud ankle deep, sometimes deeper. The best place to bathe in the upper-most end of the lake is where there's a current which doesn't allow the mud to settle. The water is always a little muddy too. These factors limit water sports such as water skiing and swimming.

Routes or Trails The first hike here is up the lower end of the present-day river part of **Cataract Canyon.** Chances are you will begin walking somewhere between Ten Cent and Imperial Campsites. There are no trails up along the river, but the walking is fairly easy. You can walk on either side of the river. Staying close to the river is usually the best place to walk. There are however, some places with lots of driftwood and others with large boulders. Some parts are even sandy. Even though the hike is almost a flat track, you'll feel it in your legs if you're not is good shape, because of all the rock-hopping involved. If you have the inclination, you could walk all the way through the remaining part of Cataract Canyon to the confluence of the Green and the Colorado Rivers.

One destination on this hike would be Teapot Canyon, about 3 kms above the HWM. You could also go to as far as the mouth of Range Canyon on a day-hike, but perhaps the best plan would be to go to the first really big rapids along the river. There are three rapids(the author counted 4) in a short stretch of the river called, the **Big Drop Rapids.** On river runners maps, they are numbered 21, 22, and 23. Most of the time, the rafters stop just before going through each to plot their course. If you arrive around mid-day, you may meet some of these people taking the plunge through white water.

Begin the walk up **Imperial Canyon** from anywhere along the wide open mouth along the river. After about one km, the canyon constricts, and you'll reach some narrows and a big dry fall. A good climber could scale this one, but not the ordinary hiker. At that point, regress 50 meters or so, and head due north; first on a talus slope, then up two cliffs. This part is almost vertical, but there are lots of hand holds, and it isn't as difficult as it first appears. For some groups, it might be best to take a short rope to help those not accustomed to rock climbing. This is the most difficult part of the hike, and descending is more risky than the ascent. The author had no trouble doing it alone.

Looking north from the rim of Cataract Canyon. Imperial Canyon coming in from the right, or east.

Once through these ledges, you'll be on a bench or terrace. Walk east into the narrows again, where you'll be above one dry fall, but below still another. Instead of trying to climb the fall, continue west on the same level, and to the south side, directly across from where you scaled the first cliffs. From there, head up-slope to the south route-finding your way up through about three easy-to-climb ledges. Once on the next terrace, bench-walk to the east again and into the upper basin.

About 300 meters above the second dry fall, route-find left and onto still another easy-to-reach terrace to avoid a third fall. After you pass this last fall, gradually veer to the left or north, and walk up the steep but easy talus slope to the canyon rim. To reach the overlook of Cataract Canyon at 1650 meters altitude, first walk due north before turning west, to avoid a minor drainage. You'll come out at a point where you can look straight down on Imperial Camp. About mid-day or just after noon would be the best time to take fotos.

About half way between the mouths of Imperial and Calf Canyons, on the east side of the lake(river), is another easy and interesting way to the rim of Cataract Canyon. This route(in places it's sort of a trail) is up to the rim of the canyon overlooking the mouth of Imperial Canyon.

To get onto this route or trail, boat north from the mouth of Calf Canyon about 1 or 1 1/2 kms. As you do, observe a couple of big slide areas coming down from the rim to your right, or east. Probably the one easiest to climb is the second, or the one furtherest north. Dock at the bottom and walk up a steep but easy talus slope. As you do, you will first be walking east, then will veer to the northeast. At the top of this first slope will be a small butte on your left, and a low ridge to your right, or southeast. Walk to the southeast and over an easy-to-climb little ridge. At the top look to the east, and to still another rim about 300 meters away. Walk toward it but veer to the left just a bit. On the lower part of this slope you'll find some stone cairns and what looks like a very old and faded trail. Near the top, veer to the left and skirt to the north of this rim. Once on the north side, this faded trail zig zags up to the south. Once on top of this slope or rim, again walk south and look for an easy way up one last minor bench or terrace.

As you near the top, you'll have some fine views to the north and into both Imperial and Cataract Canyons. Due north and along side the river, will be the Imperial Campsite. It you want, you can return via another steep gully about 300-400 meters to the south of the route just described.

The last hike is a short climb into the middle basin of **Calf Canyon.** About 200 meters back from the lake is a high dry fall of perhaps 70 meters. This part of the canyon is likely the Paradox Formation of the Hermosa Group. You can't climb it there, so look to the north side of the now filled-in bay, and you'll see a slide area . Walk up this steep, but easy-to-climb talus slope. At a convenient location, and at about the same elevation as the top of the first fall, veer to the left or west, and bench-walk to a point just above the fall. From there you will climb over a little rise and down into the

Looking down on the Ten Cent Campsite from the overlook above the mouth of Imperial Canyon.

middle basin.

After another 400 meters or so, you'll come to yet another big dry fall, perhaps 80 to 90 meters in height. This one is in an alcove that is dark in the afternoons. This wall must be the Honaker Trail Formation. There will likely be several large potholes in the middle basin and especially at the bottom of the dry fall. From this middle part it appears there is no way to the upper basin of Calf Canyon.

Hike Length and Time Needed In Cataract Canyon, from the Ten Cent Campsite to the mouth of Teapot is about 3 1/2 kms. Since it's slow and go for part of the way, plan to take an hour and a half each way, or about 3 hours round-trip. If you hike to Range Canyon, it will likely be an all day trip.

To make the climb up Imperial Canyon to the rim and back, will take most people 5 or 6 hours. The author did this one in 4 hours. The distance is only 3 to 4 kms, one way, but it can't be done quickly. The Calf Canyon hike is only about one km in length, and can be completed in an hour or two. Going up to the east rim between Calf and Imperial Canyons will take a couple of hours, one way.

Boots or Shoes For all hikes a pair of rugged boots are best, but running shoes would work fine for the walk up Cataract Canyon.

Water There are no springs in this area, so take your own water.

Main Attractions A hike up one of the most spectacular canyons in the world and a chance to see rafters run some of the best rapids around. Also, some interesting climbing to the rim of the plateau for some excellent views of Cataract Canyon.

Hiking Maps USGS or BLM map Hanksville(1:100,000), or Orange Cliffs(1:62,500), or Canyonlands National Park(1:62,500).

Rafters floating down stream without a raft, in the upper end of the lake near the mouth of Imperial Canyon.

From the eastern rim, looking down into Cataract and Calf Canyons(background).

Sandy campsite just north of the mouth of Calf Canyon.

Looking northeast from about half way between Calf and Imperial Canyons. Shown are two routes to the eastern rim of Cataract Canyon; one on the far left, another gully on the right.

Looking down into Cataract from above the lower falls in Calf Canyon.

The mouth of Gypsum Canyon as seen from Ocean Point.

Looking north into Cataract Canyon from Ocean Point.

Gypsum, Palmer, Easter Pasture, Clearwater & Bowdie Canyons and the Ocean Point Hike

Location and Campsites There are five canyons on this map; Gypsum, Palmer, Easter Pasture, Clearwater, and Bowdie. Combined with Easter Pasture Canyon is a hike to the rim of Cataract Canyon at a place called Ocean Point. There is an old stock trail up to the east rim of Cataract just north of the mouth of Gypsum, and another route out of Gypsum to the east rim. This group of canyons and hikes is found not far below the upper end of the lake in Cataract. The mouth of Gypsum Canyon is near M166(K266), while Bowdie Canyon empties into the lake at about M161(K258).

There are many campsite symbols on this map, almost all of which are silt bars with lots of tamarisks(on the higher parts). It's in this section the lake waters are moving more slowly, therefore silt is deposited, especially next to shore and at the mouths of the many tiny coves or inlets. When the lake is three or four meters below the HWM, you will see many little ponds of water behind the silt bars. During times of low water, there's one straight main channel with dike-like bars and backwater ponds behind, all along this section of the lake.

The highest parts of these silt bars are so thickly covered with tamarisks, that it may be difficult to find an open place for a tent. Consider taking an ax, along with a shovel, when the lake waters are high. With so much silt being deposited along the shore line, it's sometimes a little unpleasant for camping. Just under water will be thick mud; and just above, the tamarisks. When everything is covered with mud, it's difficult to enjoy a bath.

When the lake level is low, with much larger silt bars exposed, it means lots more campsites. But you'll have to look for places where the water is deep right next to the silt bar, otherwise it's hard to get out of your boat--without stepping into a quagmire. Other than this minor problem, it's a nice quiet area to visit.

About the only camping place regularly used by rafters on this map is in the area of Clearwater Canyon. One site is inside the shallow bay; the other just across from the bay on the east side. During times of low water levels, you won't be able to get into Clearwater Bay, as it's completely filled in by sand and silt. There are other generally good sites at the mouth of Gypsum and Bowdie Canyons, depending on lake levels.

It's in this region that the oldest rocks seen along the shores of Lake Powell are exposed. These belong to the Paradox Member of the Hermosa Formation. They are exposed in just a few places between Spanish Bottom(upper end of Cataract Canyon) and Palmer Canyon. It's difficult to see differences in the rocks of the Paradox(some are gypsum) from others above.

Gypsum Falls in Gypsum Canyon. First whiteman to see this was John W. Powell in 1869.

MAP 2, GYPSUM, PALMER, EASTER PASTURE, CLEARWATER, BOWDIE CANYONS & OCEAN POINT HIKE

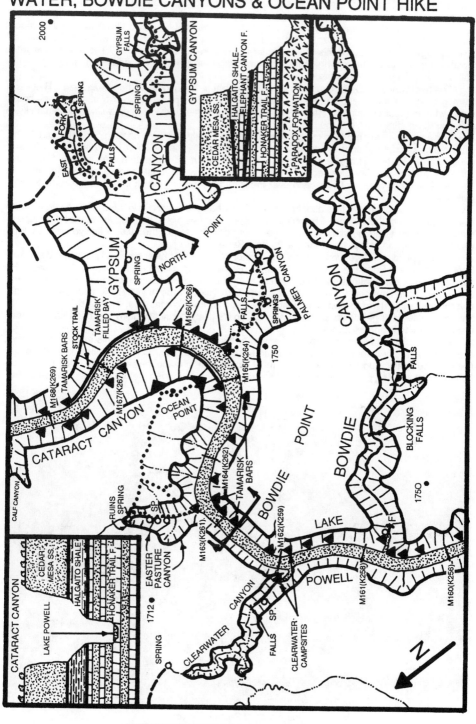

SCALE

0 1 2 3 4 5 KMS

Routes or Trails After the author was in this area twice in warm weather, he had a chance to discuss an old trail down into Gypsum Canyon with John Scorup of the BLM in Monticello. John is a grandson of Jim Scorup, of the old Scorup Brothers cattle outfit. He stated that a **stock trail,** which had been built long ago, came down from the rim about 1 1/2 kms up Cataract from the mouth of Gypsum Canyon on the east side. This he guesses, was built by David Goudelock of the Dugout Ranch some time about the turn of the century or just after. John Scorup was probably the last cowboy to take horses down this trail to winter in the lower end of Gypsum. The author has yet to locate this one, but he thought he could see something from the rim at Ocean Point. Looking for this trail will be exciting for an avid hiker.

The best way to walk up **Gypsum Canyon** is right in the middle of the stream bed. There is a running stream all the way, but in a long dry spell, it could dry up in a place or two. The creek bed is rather wide in most places and the walking very easy, as there are no trees, willows or tamarisks to slow you down after you leave the bay area.

The canyon is very broad in the lower end, then gradually becomes narrower. After about 8 kms, you'll reach a couple of tight bends as the canyon constricts, then you'll come to blocking cliffs and the **Gypsum Falls.** The author estimates it to be about 40-45 meters high and is completely enclosed, making a rather dark secluded place. This is surely the most spectacular waterfall on Lake Powell. The water appears to cascade over the Paradox Member, which in this case seems to be a dark limestone.

If you regress from the falls about a km, to where the upper spring is located, you can find a route to the upper part of the canyon. The only way to the upper basin is to head up the steep talus slope to the west and to a bench which will take you around to the top of the falls. After you get past the waterfall, you will be able to go all the way to Beef Basin above.

In the middle of Gypsum Canyon, the author met another hiker who had just come down from Beef Basin. It was Brian Blackstock of Colorado. He had taken a leisurely trip down in 2 1/2 days. He stated that one can make it into Beef Basin OK, but there are a number of small waterfalls to get around--which is time consuming, but not so difficult. Take a rope anyway. He also told the author that the vast majority of the water pouring over Gypsum Falls comes from springs below other falls, and that cattle can't get down to it from above. So it's likely(but not certain) you can drink Gypsum Creek water and live to tell about it.

John W. Powell hiked up Gypsum Canyon to the falls during the first of his epic river journeys, then later found a way out of the canyon in an eastern side canyon. On the author's second trip into Cataract, he finally found the route Powell must have taken to reach the canyon rim. As you walk up from the bottom of Gypsum, you will pass two side canyons on the left before reaching the waterfall.

From Ocean Point, looking south at the mouth of Palmer Canyon.

60

It's the second one you'll be interested in, called East Fork.

Right where the dry creek bed of East Fork meets Gypsum Creek, turn left, or east. First, walk up onto a low bench on the north side of the dry creek. From there you'll see a big dry fall at the mouth of East Fork. Your goal then is to walk up a steep talus slope on the left and to the top of a high bench or terrace north of the fall. This allows you to enter the upper basin above a couple of blocking falls. Once inside the upper basin, you'll have a choice of two routes out to the rim. For this description, the author's circular route will be described.

As you enter the upper basin, continue on the same horizontal bench until you're in the bottom of the dry creek bed about half way into the upper basin. At that point you'll see several cottonwood trees and willows indicating a seasonal seep. Continue up canyon to the southeast, along the easiest route. Higher up, you'll come to another green spot and cottonwoods, where is located a very good year-round spring. There are no cattle or beaver in this area, so this water will be good to drink.

From this spring, head up and to the south side of the little drainage coming down into the canyon from the east. Then walk east to within about 50 meters of the highest dry fall, which forms the upper most rim. There on the south side, you'll come to a 10 meter high crack in the yellow sandstone. This crack is steep, but it has lots of good hand and foot holds and is easy to climb. You can return this same way, but there's another way in or out about 600 meters to the northwest.

From the rim above the spring and first exit, walk northwest to find a shallow drainage dropping off the rim. Right where that dry creek falls over the rim, look for an easy way down with two minor dropoffs. From there, walk down to the west a ways, then when you reach the first terrace, veer to the right, or northwest, and bench-walk another 700-800 meters. When you reach a landslide area, walk down to the terrace you were on when you entered the upper basin at the beginning of the hike. It was in this area the author ran onto a single young big horn ram.

J.W. Powell's Report In Powell's book on his explorations of the Colorado, he describes his party's exploration of Gypsum Canyon. On July 26, 1869, he writes, *About ten o'clock, Powell, Bradley, Howland, Hall, and I start up a side canyon to the east. We soon come to pools of water; then to a brook, which is lost in the sands below; and passing up the brook, we see that the canyon narrows, the walls close in and are often overhanging, and at last we find ourselves in a vast amphitheater, with a pool of deep, clear, cold water on the bottom.* This was what is now known as Gypsum Falls. They tried to get out of the canyon there, but failed. The party then retreated and each member set out to find a route to the rim by himself.

Powell went up a side canyon on the northeast, and after some work, found a route up. Near the top he states, *I came to a place where the wall is again broken down, so I can climb up still farther; and in an hour I reach the summit. I hang up my barometer to give it a few minutes time to settle, and*

Looking southeast into Cataract from the rim of Easter Pasture Canyon.

occupy myself in collecting resin from the pinyon pines, which are found in great abundance. One of the principal objects in making this climb was to get this resin for the purpose of smearing our boats; At the end of that days entry he states, *Great quantities of gypsum are found at the bottom of the gorge; so we name it Gypsum Canyon.*

In reading Powell's account of his river expeditions, keep in mind he had but one arm; he lost the other in the Civil War. In **Dellenbaugh's Diary,** *Canyon Voyage,* he makes a statement concerning Powell's handicap. The scene was somewhere in middle Cataract Canyon and on September 20, 1871(Powell's second trip). He states, *The Major having no right arm, he sometimes got in a difficult situation when climbing, if his right side came against a smooth surface where there was nothing opposite. We had learned to go down by the same route followed up, because otherwise one is never sure of arriving at the bottom, as a ledge half-way down might compel a return to the summit. We remembered that at one point there was no way for him to hold on, the cliff being smooth on the right, while on the left was empty air, with a sheer drop of several hundred feet. The footing too was narrow. I climbed down first, and, bracing myself below with my back to the abyss, I was able to plant my right foot securely in such a manner that my right knee formed a solid step for him at the critical moment. On this improvised step he placed his left foot, and in a twinkling had made the passage in safety.*

The first canyon down stream from Gypsum is **Palmer Canyon.** If you stay in the creek bed, you can only walk into it less than a km, then you come to some high blocking falls. But there's a way around these dry falls and into the upper basin.

You can dock your boat just around the corner of Palmer to the west and walk up-slope from there until you're on to the terrace at the same elevation as the falls. Then bench-walk at the same level around the falls and into the upper basin. Or you can begin at the bottom of the canyon about 300 meters below the falls. At that point, look up and to the southwest and locate an easy route up the steep talus slope to the level or terrace just above the level of the falls. Walk up the slope to that bench and head south into the canyon.

As you walk into the upper basin, you'll first be in a dry creek bed, but after a ways, you'll come to the first spring and some running water. Not far beyond that point you'll come to the place where a short side canyon comes in from the west. It has some running water, and you'll have to skirt around a fall and pourover pool to the left. Above this, there are several minor falls you'll have to get around. Finally, you'll reach a point at about the bottom of the Cedar Mesa Sandstone, where there's a trickle of running water and unclimbable falls. It appears this is the end of the line for hikers, and that there is no way out of Palmer Canyon to the rim.

However, in the 1940's, a team of archaeologists from the Carnegie Museum of Pittsburgh, explored the upper parts of this canyon(what they called John Palmer Canyon) from the rim, and found three different Anasazi ruins. One site was said to be in a crack in the Navajo Sandstone(it could only

One of several small Anasazi ruins in the upper end of Easter Pasture Canyon.

be the Cedar Mesa Sandstone!). The other two sites were only 150 meters above the elevation of the river, and about 1 1/2 kms from the Colorado River. This would put them in the area about where the side canyon from the west enters the main drainage(where the pourover pool is).

These three sites were called the Andrew Delaney, Henrys, and Sandy Camp sites. There were Mesa Verde style potsherds found at all three ruins, one of which was dated between 1026 AD to 1127 AD; another dated from between 1070 AD to 1164 AD. At the time of the author's visit, he was unaware of the existence of these sites, so he didn't see them, nor did he see any way out of the canyon to the rim. It appears the only way out would be up the west side canyon. If anyone finds either the ruins or a route out of Palmer, the author would be interested to hear about it.

There is no trail up **Easter Pasture Canyon**, but you can easily climb up it to the rim. For some strange reason, the big falls or cliffs which block passage in other nearby canyons, have been filled in with debris in this one. This makes it one of the few side canyons in Cataract which you can exit. Just walk up this steep and mostly dry creek bed. After 600-700 meters, you'll come to one tree; below it's branches is a small seep. Not far above that are three cottonwood trees and another trickle of water(on the author's September trip to this canyon, these two sites were nearly dry).

Further up you'll come to some minor cliffs, which you pass on the left, or north side. After a couple of these cliffs, you'll have to walk to the right, or south, across a very small stream, then climb up a talus slope, to avoid one little waterfall. Above this is a dry section of the canyon, but just ahead is a big dry fall and right beneath it are several places where the water seeps out from under the lowest part of the Cedar Mesa Sandstone. About 30 meters to the left of the main spring are four small Anasazi structures; one was a living quarters, the other three were for storage. They're all in pretty bad condition today.

From the upper spring, veer to the east and route-find up through the minor ledges. To reach the top of the rim, which is the top of the Cedar Mesa Sandstone, you'll have to zig zag your way up through half a dozen terraces. There are easy ways up through each, but you have to look for them. At one point, the author thought he detected the remains of an old constructed trail, but it may have been a naturally-made rock terrace.

Once on top, you can route-find to the southwest, where you can see down into lower Easter Pasture and Cataract. But to reach the best canyon overlook on Lake Powell, which is **Ocean Point,** go southeast from the spring and ruins. By first starting out going east, you avoid the heads of two minor drainages. When you reach the rim of Cataract, veer south to the Point. From various locations in that area, you can see up and down Cataract, and into Gypsum and Palmer Canyons. The altitude of the lake at the HWM is 1128 meters; while Ocean Point is about 1800. This is nearly 700 vertical meters(2300 ft) above the water, and one of the best hikes around.

In **Clearwater Canyon,** you simply walk up along side the small stream. However, you can't

On the rim of Easter Pasture Canyon looking southwest at the deepest part of Cataract Canyon.

go far, as you'll come to blocking falls less than 2 kms up from the mouth of the canyon. Along the way you'll see some cottonwood trees, a result of the small, clear, year-round flowing stream in the lower portion of the canyon. The author saw a rattlesnake there, the only one he saw while doing the footwork for this book.

J. W. Powell's Report From Powell's diary, which centered mostly on his 1869 trip down the Colorado, he mentions the area around Clearwater Canyon. On July 27 he states, *We have more rapids and falls until noon; then we come to a narrow place in the canyon, with vertical walls for several hundred feet, above which are steep steps and sloping rocks back to the summits. The river is very narrow, and we make our way with great care and much anxiety, hugging the wall on the left and carefully examining the way before us. Late in the afternoon we.....discover a flock of mountain sheep on the rocks more than a hundred feet[30 meters] above us. We land quickly in a cove out of sight, and away go all the hunters with their guns, for the sheep have not discovered us. Soon we hear firing, and those of us who have remained in the boats climb up to see what success the hunters have had.*

They end up with two young sheep, which they apparently needed very badly as he later writes. *We lash our prizes to the deck of one of the boats and go on for a short distance; but fresh meat is too tempting for us, and we stop early to have a feast......We care not for bread or beans or dried apples to-night; coffee and mutton are all we ask.* Apparently there were no stops at either Easter Pasture, Clearwater or Bowdie Canyons, all of which are in this very deep and narrow area.

There are no trails in **Bowdie Canyon,** in fact you can't hike up very far. Right at the HWM you'll be in a limestone bed of the Honaker Trail Formation. Nearby is a small spring and normally some running water, which flows over some smooth water-worn cliffs. The first pothole you see can be skirted(very carefully) on the right, but then you've got another pothole always full of water just above that. You'll have to wade or swim this one. One hiker, who went without camera, maps, watch or wallet, said he went about 1 1/2 km up canyon before being stopped by a high falls. Carl Mahon of Monticello, told the author there must be a route down the canyon some way, because he has seen big horn sheep go down. However, this author will guarantee it won't be easy to find that sheep route!

On one trip down into the canyon from the top end, the author came to within about 3 kms of the lake, only to be stopped be a big waterfall. It's possible this is the same fall mentioned by the second hiker, but it's also likely there is a series of falls in the lower end of Bowdie. This leaves room for someone who enjoys exploring, to look for a way up and out of Bowdie. Be prepared to do some deep wading and possibly some pothole swimming in this canyon.

There is one discouraging thing about Bowdie Canyon. On the author's late September trip to the area, with the lake water about four meters below the HWM, there was a silt bar across the mouth of Bowdie Bay, with deep water behind. At that lake level, it would have meant swimming a couple of hundred meters into the bay to begin the hike. However, expect things to change in the next few

The mouth of Clearwater Canyon is just a narrow slit in the wall of Cataract Canyon.

years, perhaps a filling in of the bay(on the author's first trip he boated into the inlet).

Hike Length and Time Needed It's about 8 or 9 kms from the lake to the falls in Gypsum Canyon. The author did the round-trip hike in about 4 1/2 hours. Some hikers may want 5 or 6 hours, so consider taking a lunch. On the author's second trip, which took him to the rim, it took about 5 hours, round-trip.

It's about 2 1/2 kms from the lake to the ruins and spring in Easter Pasture Canyon, and about 7 kms from the lake to Ocean Point. The author hiked for about 7 hours, but he did some back tracking and re-fotographing because of a brief rainstorm earlier that morning. Most people will want all or most of one day to do this hike, so take water from the spring and a lunch.

You can only go up Clearwater Canyon about 2 kms or less, so it will take only about an hour for this hike. To get more than a 100 meters or so above the HWM in Bowdie Canyon, you'll have to leave behind your camera and anything that can be damaged by water. If you plan accordingly, you can get up this canyon about 1 1/2 kms which shouldn't take long. Because of the possibility of swimming, do this one in warm weather only.

Boots or Shoes Use rugged hiking boots in Gypsum, Palmer and Easter Pasture Canyons, but any shoe will be OK in Clearwater. In Bowdie, use wading type shoes.

Water There is normally water running the length of Gypsum Canyon below the falls, but it almost dries up in a place or two. This water looked a little muddy on the author's first visit, but later is was clear. It comes from spring mostly below Beef Basin, so it couldn't be too bad if you have to drink it as is. However, it's best to stock up on water from the two springs seen on the map. The first spring bubbles out of the creek bed about 2 kms from the lake. It should be good to drink, as it's cold when coming out of the ground. Immediately above this spring there is very little running water, but more appears the further you walk up canyon. About one bend below the falls, several cold water seeps come out of the rock on the left at creek level.

There are several little springs and some running water in the upper basin of Palmer Canyon, which will always be safe to drink. In Easter Pasture Canyon, there is water at several locations, but the best is at the spring source near the Anasazi ruins. In Clearwater Canyon, there is a spring about 300 meters above the HWM. It should be good water any where along this stream's short course. There is a small seep in Bowdie Canyon, just at the HWM. Above this there will likely be some water coming down from the upper canyon.

Main Attractions One of the best waterfalls near Lake Powell, a walk to Anasazi ruins and to the best overlook in Cataract Canyon. You will see the deepest and steepest part of Cataract which is between Easter Pasture and Bowdie Canyons, and a chance to see big horn sheep on the cliffs and crags of Bowdie Point.

Hiking Maps USGS or BLM maps Hanksville and Hite Crossing(1:100,000), or Orange Cliffs and Mouth of Dark Canyon(1:62,500), or Canyonlands National Park(1:62,500).

The source of the little stream in Clearwater Canyon.

Cove, Rockfall and Dark Canyons

Location and Campsites Cove, Rockfall and Dark Canyons, are all located in the lower end of Cataract Canyon. The mouth of Cove is very near M156(K249), Rockfall is at about M154(K246), and the mouth of Dark Canyon is M153(K245) distance from Glen Canyon Dam. Rockfall Canyon gets it's name from a big rockfall or land slide about 300-400 meters up canyon from the HWM. You can see where it has fallen off the high wall as you boat down canyon from the north.

Dark Canyon has its beginnings on the western slopes of the Abajo Mountains and in the area to the north and east of Natural Bridges National Monument. Most of this canyon has been set aside as an official wilderness area and is a popular hiking region.

Most people who hike into Dark enter at Peavine or Woodenshoe Canyons on the southwest slopes of the Abajo's, or via the Sundance Trail. The Sundance is reached by Road 208A, which begins about half a km above the Hite turnoff on Highway 95(near mile post 49). After 14 kms, you must turn left onto Road 209A, then drive 4 kms to the Car-park as shown on the map. The trail on the mesa top is marked with cairns and is used often. The last part of the Sundance Trail is down the steep side of lower Dark Canyon. Only the lower quarter or so of the drainage is shown on this map, as that's the area of interest to boaters.

At or near the mouth of Cove Canyon, there are few if any campsites exposed during times of high lake levels, but when the water drops, there are many silt bars all along this part of the lake. The normally very good campsite at the mouth of Rockfall Canyon is a regular stop for river runners heading down Cataract, but in times of low water, you may be blocked from entry by a silt bar across the mouth of the bay.

River runners often make Dark Canyon one of their campsites, but the author was there once in early July, with water extending up to very near the HWM. At that time and at that water level, there were no possibilities for finding a campsite in the inlet or along the main channel. But during a late September trip, with lower lake levels, no water extended into Dark Canyon Inlet; it just ended right at the mouth of the canyon. At that time the sand was very wet just above the lake level. If the lake had been a meter or two lower, some good dry sandy campsites would likely have been available. It appears this is a low water level and/or a late season campsite only.

COVE CANYON

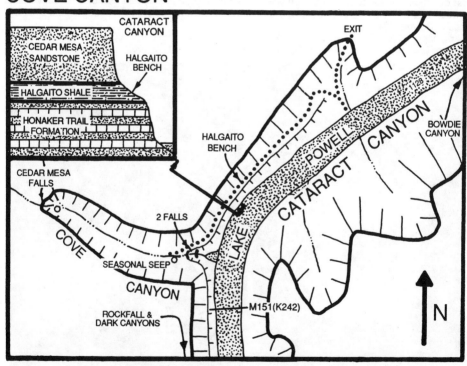

MAP 3, ROCKFALL AND DARK CANYONS

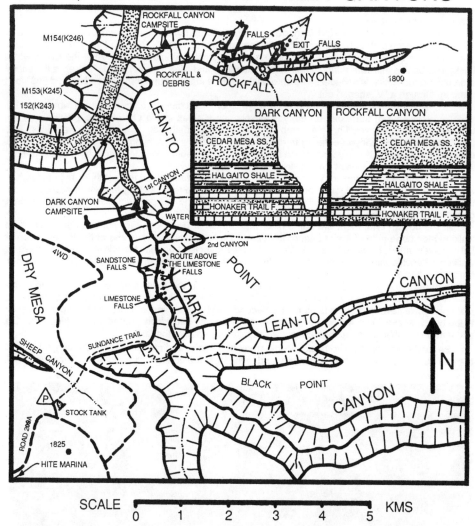

SCALE

0   1   2   3   4   5   KMS

Routes or Trails The first drainage to be covered here is **Cove Canyon.** When you first look at the bottom of this canyon from the lake, it appears to be un-hikable. But there's a way into an upper basin. From the mouth of the little bay, boat up-lake to the northeast about 2 kms, and dock on the left side where you see a landslide debris slope coming down from above. Walk straight up this steep slope until you're at or just above the Halgaito terrace which is about half way up to the rim(at that point it appears you can continue to walk north and reach the canyon rim, as shown by the word *exit,* on the map). Once on this intermediate level, walk to the southwest along the Halgaito bench toward Cove Canyon.

Once you reach the lower end of Cove, you'll have to drop down a ways to reach the dry creek bed. At that point, you'll be above two big falls, which appear to be in the upper part of the Honaker Trail Formation. Just above the second fall, you may see a minor seep, a pool or two, and some cottonwood trees.

From that point, you can walk up canyon about a km or a little more, before coming to blocking falls in the Cedar Mesa Sandstone. Along most of the way there will be cottonwood trees, but likely no running water, unless you arrive at the end of a wet spell. The walking is easy and fast. At the upper end you'll find some big boulders just below the falls and a minor seep just below. It's likely some water will be there at any time.

There is no trail up **Rockfall Canyon**; you just walk up the mostly dry creek bed. A little ways up canyon, a large slab of Cedar Mesa Sandstone has broken off near the top of the wall on the south side and fallen to the canyon floor. This has created a jumbled jungle of rocks. After the crash, water backed up behind this dam during times of flash flooding, and filled it in with sand. There's a flat sandy area behind the rocks, which looks like an old lake bed. Finally it burst through its dam and you now climb up through a "V" shaped cut.

Above the dam it's easy walking for a ways, then you come to a limestone fall which can be passed easily. From that point on up, you'll likely see a small trickle of water most of the way up canyon. After a ways, you'll have to climb up to the right, or south side, to avoid three waterfalls. Not far beyond, is a side canyon entering from the north. On this side canyon's east side, you can climb out onto the plateau, the only such place in the canyon. It would take some time, but you could rim-walk to the west and to a point overlooking Cataract Canyon.

If you continue up canyon, you'll have to pass another waterfall on the south, or right side, then after a walk through a small forest of cottonwoods, you'll come to a blocking fall, which appears to be the bottom part of the Cedar Mesa Sandstone. All the way up to this point you'll see numerous springs on the south side of the canyon wall.

In the bottom end, there are some hiker-made trails in **Dark Canyon,** but often times you'll be walking along one side of the stream or the other. Dark Canyon Creek is one of the largest to enter Lake Powell and it flows year-round. When the lake level is at or near the HWM, you'll first have to walk on a bench beside the water on one side of the bay or the other, then further along get down into the stream bed.

Just after you pass the second canyon on the left, you will enter a narrow section. First, you pass a sandstone waterfall; then you'll be stopped by a series of limestone falls in a short narrows. At that point you'll have to regress to nearly the second canyon, then find and follow a trail up a little gully to the bench above. This will put you on top of the limestone bed which created the blocking falls. On that terrace you'll be on a much-used trail which takes you above the falls.

Beyond the falls, you'll be back into the creek bed again, and not far beyond, the canyon begins to open up. To the left is Lean-to Canyon; and to the right will be the lower end of the Sundance Trail,

This is what the upper end of the lake looks like when the water level is low. Dikes form along the sides of the lake as sediment is dropped in the slow moving water. Near the mouth of Cove Canyon.

the popular entry/exit route into the lower end of the canyon. You can walk into Lean-to Canyon on its east side, as there's a hiker-made trail going that way from near the bottom of the Sundance. Big game guide Carl Mahon told the author there's an old stock trail in the upper end, where you can exit to the Dark Canyon Plateau.

Hike Length and Time Needed To hike to the end of Cove Canyon will take about half a day. The author hurried up and back just before dark, and did it round-trip in less than three hours. You can only walk 4 or 5 kms up Rockfall Canyon, but it's slow going, so you'll need at least half a day just to reach the blocking fall and return. Much more time would be needed to reach the rim of Cataract and return.

It's only 4 or 5 kms from the HWM in Dark, to the bottom end of the Sundance Trail. But you'll likely have to do some backtracking and route-finding to get above the falls, so count on at least half a day for a round-trip hike to the Sundance. The author got to very near that trail, and returned in less than three hours. On another trip he walked part way up Lean-to, then returned in 4 hours.

Boots or Shoes Hiking boots are best in Cove and Rockfall Canyons, but it might pay to have waders in Dark Canyon. However, the author used leather hiking boots going into Lean-to, and never did get them wet.

Water You likely will find some water in upper Cove Canyon, but it's best to take your own. There are several springs with good water in Rockfall, originating at the contact point between the Cedar Mesa S.S. above, and the Halgaito Shale below. The creek in Dark Canyon begins to flow about half way down its long course, so the water couldn't be too bad as there are no cattle in the lower end. But it's best to drink from the little side drainage the author calls second canyon(this may dry up at times).

Main Attractions A chance to exit Cataract near Cove Canyon. In Rockfall Canyon, good water, waterfalls, and a chance to exit to the rim. In Dark, a very deep and rugged canyon, perhaps the most spectacular one to enter the upper end of Lake Powell.

Hiking Maps USGS or BLM map Hite Crossing(1:100,000), or Mouth of Dark Canyon(1:62,500), or Canyonlands National Park(1:62,500).

J.W. Powell's Report On July 28, 1869, Powell must have been very near Rockfall and Dark Canyons when he wrote. *During the afternoon we run a chute more than half a mile[700 meters] in length, narrow and rapid. This chute has a floor of marble; the rocks dip in the direction in which we are going, and the fall of the stream conforms to the inclination of the beds; so we float on water that is gliding down an inclined plane....After this the walls suddenly close in, so that the canyon is narrower than we have ever known it. The water fills it from wall to wall, giving us no landing place at the foot of the cliff; the river is very swift and the canyon very torturous, so that we can see but a few hundreds*

Half way up Rockfall Canyon are two impressive waterfalls(dry part of the time).

yards ahead; the walls tower over us, often overhanging so as almost to shut out the light. I stand on deck, watching with intense anxiety, lest this may lead us into some danger; but we glide along, with no obstruction, no falls, no rocks, and in a mile and a half[2 1/2 kms] emerge from the narrow gorge into a more open and broken portion of the canyon. Now that it is past, it seems a very simple thing indeed to run through such a place, but the fear of what might be ahead made a deep impression on us.

In the middle part of Rockfall Canyon is this unusual bridge and dry fall.

The lower end of Dark Canyon.

The mouth of Dark Canyon in the background and rafters with outboards heading for Hite Marina.

Large rafts with outboard motors. They begin near Moab, finish at Hite.

Freddies Cistern, Sheep, Narrow & Rock Canyons

Location and Campsites The mouth of Sheep Canyon is located at the point separating the lower Cataract and the upper part of Narrow Canyon, and right at M147(K235). This canyon drains into part of the Colorado River Canyon known as Mille Crag Bend, which is very noticeable on the map.

There are several good campsites in the area. The best is what the rafters call Sheep Canyon Campsite, which they use often. Please don't squat right in the middle of it. If you need to use it, camp at one end or the other. It's a large site and can accommodate many.

Another small sandy site is right at the head of Sheep Canyon Bay. Also, just above and below Sheep, are several small ledges just above the HWM which could be used, but they are not the best of campsites. Just around the bend to the west of Sheep Canyon are more ledges, including one good site the rafters call Ledges Campsite. In 1988, this site was next to the floating sign which warned lake boaters of the problems in finding good campsites in the lake above. It reads, *Swift currents, shallow sand bars, and driftwood beyond this point. Campsites above here are needed by River Rafters. Please limit upstream camping.* The truth is, during times of low water, there are many silt bars exposed, making many campsites. Read about this situation under Maps 1, 2, and 3, which cover Cataract Canyon.

Routes or Trails About the only place you can hike in this area is into **Sheep Canyon.** There are no trails up this drainage; you just route-find up along the dry creek bed. The north side looked best to the author. It's slow and go all the way because you weave in and out of large boulders. After about 3 kms, you'll be able to climb up the slope to the left, or north, and get out onto the rim easily. There's one good viewpoint there, or you could rim-walk to the west for a better view of the lake and Mille Crag Bend.

Hike Length and Time Needed The first place you come to where you can exit is about 3 kms. In less than half a day, you can hike the canyon and get up on the rim for some fine views. The author spent 2 hrs. 40 minutes on his round-trip hike.

Boots or Shoes Hiking boots are best, but running type shoes will do.

Water There are no springs or streams in the area. Take your own.

Main Attractions From above, good views of Mille Crag Bend and the lake.

Hiking Maps USGS or BLM map Hite Crossing(1:100,000), or Browns Rim(1:62,500).

J.W. Powell's Report On July 28, 1869, the Powell Party passed this way, and here is an excerpt from Powell's diary. *At three o'clock we arrive at the foot of Cataract Canyon. Here a long canyon valley comes down from the east, and the river turns sharply to the west in a continuation of the line of the lateral valley[Sheep Canyon]. In the bend on the right vast numbers of crags and pinnacles and tower-shaped rocks are seen. We call it Mille Crag Bend.*

Late season driftwood slick at the upper end of Mille Crag Bend.

MAP 4, FREDDIES CISTERN AND SHEEP, NARROW AND ROCK CANYONS

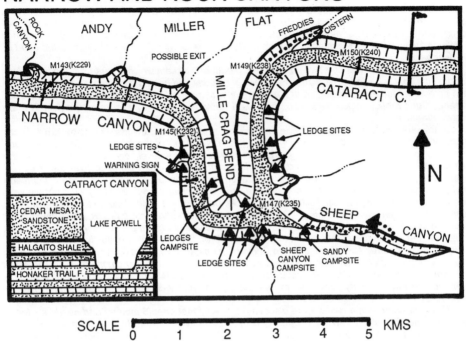

SCALE |0———1———2———3———4———5| KMS

From the head of Sheep Canyon, one looks down on Mille Crag Bend. Henry Mountains in the background.

And now we wheel into another canyon on swift water unobstructed by rocks. This new canyon is very narrow and very straight, with walls vertical below and terraced above. Where we enter it the brink of the cliff is 1,300 feet[400 meters] above the water, but the rocks dip to the west, and as the course of the canyon is in that direction the walls are seen slowly to decrease in altitude. Floating down this narrow channel and looking out through the canyon crevice away in the distance, the river is seen to turn again to the left, and beyond this point, away many miles, a great mountain is seen. Still floating down, we see other mountains, now on the right, now on the left, until a great mountain range is unfolded to view[Henry Mountains]. We name this Narrow Canyon, and it terminates at the bend of the river below.

As we go down to this point we discover the mouth of a stream which enters from the right. Into this our little boat is turned. The water is exceedingly muddy and has an unpleasant odor. One of the men in the boat following, seeing what we have done, shouts to Dunn and asks whether it is a trout stream. Dunn replies, much disgusted, that it is a "dirty devil," and by this name the river is to be known hereafter.

In this area of lower Cataract, Mille Crag Bend, and Narrow Canyons, **Dellenbaugh's Diary** states on September 29, 1871. Morning brought a continuation of the rain, which fell in a deluge, driving us to the shelter of a projecting ledge, from which comparatively dry retreat we watched the rain cascades that soon began their display. Everywhere they came plunging over the walls, all sizes, and varying their volume with every variation in the downpour. Some dropped a thousand feet[300 meters] to vanish in spray; others were broken into many falls. By half-past eight we were able to proceed, running the rapid without any trouble, but a wave drenched me so that all my efforts to keep out of the rain went for nothing. By ten o'clock we had run four more rapids, and arrived at the place the Major had named Millecrag Bend, from the multitude of rugged pinnacles into which the cliffs broke. On the left we camped to permit the Major and Prof. to make their prospective climb to the top. A large canyon entered from the left[Sheep Canyon], terminating Cataract Canyon, which we credited with forty-one miles[66 kms], and in which I counted sixty-two rapids and cataracts,..... The Major and Prof. reached the summit at an altitude of fifteen hundred feet[450 meters]. They had a wide view over the unknown country, and saw mountains to the west with snow on their summits[Henry Mountains].

Near our camp some caves were discovered, twenty feet deep[6 meters] and nearly six feet[2 meters] in height, which had once been occupied by natives. Walls had been laid across the entrances, and inside were corncobs and other evidences usual in this region, now so well known. Pottery fragments were also abundant[these caves are now under water].

Other Canyons On this map is another short canyon which is not really hikable. This is **Freddies**

Warning sign for lake boaters at Mille Crag Bend.

Cistern. It's a long drainage, but you see only the last part as it falls over the Cedar Mesa Sandstone walls. The author hasn't tried hiking there, but if you dock about 300 meters to the west of the mouth, you can get upon the highest bench of the Halgaito Shale, then walk northeast and into the lower end of Freddies. From the lake, it appears there is no exit, but if there is, one would have a fine view of lower Cataract Canyon from the rim. There are few, if any campsites in that area.

Still another canyon, part of which is on this map, is **Narrow Canyon.** This short section of the former Colorado River lies between Mille Crag Bend(the end of Cataract Canyon), and the mouth of the Dirty Devil River, which is the beginning of Glen Canyon. There was never any mining, nor any other activities in this section of the Colorado.

Another interesting drainage, but with no hiking possibilities, is **Rock Canyon.** It's to the west of Mille Crag Bend in about the middle of Narrow Canyon. It's a long drainage, but you can see the very bottom end below a high dry fall. There is but one small possible campsite in the back of the tiny inlet where it enters the lake. On ledges just above the HWM, are several flat spots which could be used by people with tents that don't use stakes(it's mostly on slickrock). There are even places which are sandy, but they are right where water comes down during flash floods. This is a very cool and shaded campsite.

A cool shaded alcove at the bottom end of Rock Canyon drainage.

Dirty Devil River, North Wash and Farley & White Canyons

Location and Campsites Of all the drainages discussed in this section, White Canyon is the only one with hiking possibilities. White Canyon Inlet is located 7 or 8 kms south of the Hite Marina. Out in the main channel you will likely find a buoy with M135(K216) or M135 A on it. From the main channel you can enter either Farley or White Canyons. As shown on the map, you can drive from Highway 95 down into White or Farley Canyons and camp or launch a boat. There are many campsites at the head of the each inlet. Just as you boat into White Canyon Inlet, you'll find several good sites for putting up a tent from a boat.

Routes or Trails This lower end of **White Canyon** is one of the most challenging and exciting hiking canyons on the entire Colorado Plateau. Non-boaters normally visit the most interesting part of the canyon, called the Black Hole. They enter the canyon just north of mile post 57, and exit at m.p. 55, as shown on the map. But boaters can also walk up the canyon from the lake.

Walking from the lake, the drainage at first is shallow, but gets deeper with every bend. If there has been a recent rainstorm, expect to wade through potholes, beginning near the highway bridge. It's moderately narrow and deep until after about 10 or 11 kms, then it really tightens up, and you'll have to start wading. After a ways, you'll have to swim to get through the narrowest part. There is one section of the Black Hole where you have to walk under a large pile of tree trunks and other debris. This pile of debris is about 10 meters above you and about 15 meters in length. Just above this tunnel is the part where you'll have to swim. It could be difficult to get through, if the potholes are low on water. Don't hike into this canyon during periods of bad weather.

If you have no camera, watch, or wallet, you can make it very easy; but if you have anything that can be damaged by water, you'll have to take some kind of float device(inner tube, child's play pool, etc.) to keep them dry. Another tip, keep your clothes dry in plastic bags, so you can warm up quickly at the end of the swimming part. Because it's so dry, the water evaporates quickly, leaving behind refrigerator-cold water that never sees the sun. Hypothermia is a real danger. Do this hike only in warm or hot weather--from June 1 to mid-September.

Also, take along a rope at least 10 meters long. The exit at m.p. 55 can be difficult for some. The exit at m.p. 57 is easy. Also, if you're taking younger people through, you might equip them with life preservers; and everyone should be hanging onto something that floats. The cold water really effects the body! Go prepared, and this can be the best hike on Lake Powell. This is for experienced hikers only.

Hike Length and Time Needed It's about 16 kms from the HWM through the canyon to the exit at m.p. 57; then another 8 or 9 kms by road back to the HWM. A very long all-day hike. You might consider seeing the lower end from your boat, and the Black Hole part from your car.

Lower White Canyon, with the highway bridge in the upper background.

MAP 5, FARLEY & LOWER WHITE CANYONS

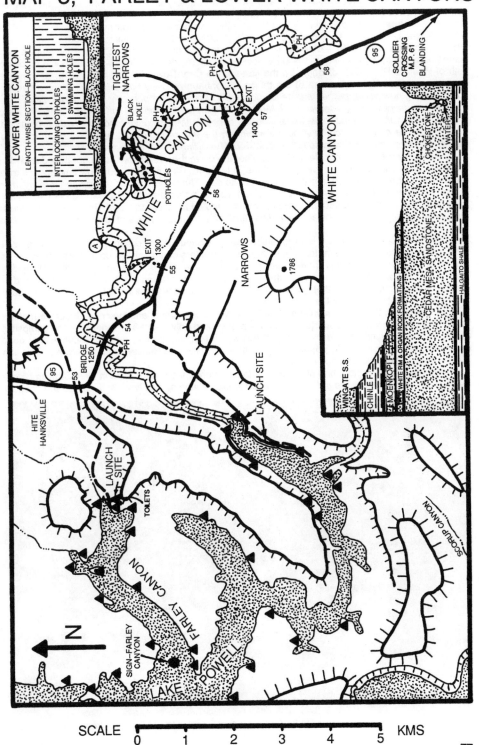

SCALE

0 1 2 3 4 5 KMS

Boots or Shoes Wading type shoes.
Water Some pothole water could be drank, but best to take your own.   There could be lots of traffic down through this canyon in the next few years.
Main Attractions The most exciting and challenging narrows hike found anywhere.
Hiking Maps USGS or BLM map Hite Crossing(1:100,000), or Browns Rim(1:100,000).
Other Canyons and J.W. Powell's & Dellenbaugh's Diaries Just north of Hite Marina and the mouth of North Wash is where the Dirty Devil River enters the lake. This was a stopping place for both of Powell's River Expeditions. On the first trip the Dirty Devil was given its name. During the second expedition here are some of the things Dellenbaugh's Diary had to say on September 30, 1871. *Having now accomplished a distance down this turbulent river of nearly six hundred miles[1000 kms], with a descent toward sea-level of 2607 feet[800 meters], without a serious accident, We were all in a happy frame of mind, notwithstanding the exceedingly diminutive food supply that remained. We felt that we could overcome almost anything in the line of rapids the world might afford, and Steward declared our party was so efficient he would be willing to "run the Gates of Hell".....*

Apparently they were considering still another trip down the river in the future, for they decided to leave one of their three boats at the mouth of the Dirty Devil. Their supplies were low anyway and they had no need for three boats. Dellenbaugh went on to say, *The Canonita was chosen and the day after our arrival, Sunday, October 1st, we ran her down a short distance on the right, and there carried her back about two hundred feet[60 meters] to a low cliff and up thirty or forty feet[10 to 12 meters] above the prevailing stage of water, where we hid her under an enormous mass of rock which had so fallen from the top......*

The **Dirty Devil River** is a long drainage with a sinuous lower canyon, but in the summer of 1988 with the lake level at 2 meters below the HWM, boaters could only go up a short distance. As the name implies, this is a very muddy river much of the time, and is filling up with sediment rapidly. Because of the north-south situation of the canyon and the prevailing south winds, the driftwood is constantly pushed into the northern part of the inlet. This, along with the sand bars, makes it virtually impossible to get to the end of the lake waters.

The canyon walls along the inlet are the Cedar Mesa Sandstone and they rise abruptly out of the water. There are no hiking opportunities in this region and only about 3 or 4 not-so-good campsites above the highway bridge.   However, just below the highway bridge, there are many very good campsites right along Highway 95, the main link between Hite, and Hanksville and Blanding. This is a popular camping and boat launching area.

According to Crampton, one of the men who researched the historic sites in Glen Canyon before Lake Powell times, *during the gold mining period in Glen Canyon, the Dirty Devil marked the practical*

At the bottom of the Black Hole in White Canyon is this tunnel made of logs and tree limbs.

upper limits of prospecting. It does not appear from any records or from physical evidence that any extensive placering took place above it. Robert B. Stanton in 1897, in anticipation of mining operations for the Hoskaninni Company, actually surveyed two dam sites in the narrow lower canyon of the Dirty Devil. He planned to use the dammed waters of the river downstream along the Colorado for mining purposes, and for the generation of electric power.

Going back in time now to the second Powell Expedition of 1871. From the Dirty Devil River and their camp, part of the men went down stream a ways to the mouth of **North Wash** where they found an Indian trail. This is where *Prof. and Cap.* climbed out, after following the trail up the gulch six miles[10 kms], and they saw that it went toward the Unknown Mountains[Henry Mountains], which now lay very near us on the west. Steward....with his glass was able to study their formation and determined that lava from below had spread out between the sedimentary strata, forming what he called "blisters." He could see where one side of a blister had been eroded, showing the surrounding stratification. These blisters were later called laccoliths by G. K. Gilbert in his study of the Henry Mountains in the mid-1870's.

As the 1871 party left the mouth of North Wash, they were traveling in two boats, the Dean and the Nell. Dellenbaugh went on to state, *Each man had charge of a cabin and this was Cap.'s special pride. He daily packed it so methodically that it became a standing joke with us, and we often asked him whether he always placed that thermometer back of the fifth rib or in front of the third, or some such nonsensical question, which of course Cap. took in good part and only arranged his cabin still more carefully.*

Just across the lake from the present-day Hite Marina, is the mouth of North Wash. If you are driving south from Hanksville heading for Hite, this is the canyon the present day highway runs through. In the old days before Lake Powell, the road across southeastern Utah went down North Wash, then along the Colorado River to Hite and to Dandy Crossing where the ferry was located. Originally, and in the days of Cass Hite and the Glen Canyon Gold Rush(about 1884 to 1900), the trail to this region was down Trachyte Creek, then up White Canyon to Bluff.

In 1889, Robert B. Stanton, who was originally a railroad engineer, brought boats down to the Colorado River via North Wash and went down the river. He worked for a group of investors who were considering running a railroad down the Colorado River to California. Read more on his story under Map 12, Stanton Canyon and in this book's introduction.

The original name for North Wash was Crescent Creek, but sometime during the later gold rush days it's name was changed. The upper part of this drainage on the east side of Mt. Ellen, is still called Crescent Creek. There was much placer mining activity along the mouth of North Wash prior to about 1900, then during the 1950's uranium boom, there was still more activity in the lower end of the

You have to swim and wade nearly 200 meters to get through the Black Hole in White Canyon.

canyon where the Chinle clay beds are exposed.

Farley Canyon shares the same common mouth with White. Farley is one of the places you can drive to from the highway(about 3 kms) and launch a boat. There are many good campsites(with a couple of toilets) at the end of the improved road, as well as along the inlet leading to the main channel. If you're driving to this launch site, turn west off Highway 95 at mile post 53, about 7 kms south of the turnoff to Hite Marina.

The first Powell Expedition stopped at the very mouth of White and Farley Canyon on July 29, 1869. For that day Powell states, *We enter a canyon to-day, with low, red walls. A short distance below it's head we discover the ruins of an old building on the left wall. There is a narrow plain between the river and the wall just here, and on the brink of a rock 200 feet[60 meters] high stands this old house. Its walls are of stone, laid in mortar with much regularity. It was probably built three stories high; the lower story is yet almost intact; the second is much broken down, and scarcely anything is left of the third. Great quantities of flint chips are found on the rocks near by, and many arrowheads, some perfect, others broken; and fragments of pottery are strewn about in great profusion. On the face of the cliff, under the building and along down the river for 200 or 300 yards[180 to 270 meters], there are many etchings.*

In the days of the gold rush when Hite was having it's hey day, this structure was given the name **Fort Moqui.** It seems that everyone who passed that way stopped and had a look around. Crampton, who visited the canyon just before Lake Powell covered this site, made a list of the names which were inscribed on the walls of Fort Moqui. The oldest readable date was from 1884. Read more on Hite and the ferry under Map 6, Trachyte and Swett Canyons.

It was on October 2, 1871 and during the second Powell Expedition, that Dellenbaugh describes the state of the river below the mouth of White Canyon and Hite. *The river, some three hundred and fifty feet[110 meters] wide, was low, causing many shoals, which formed the small rapids. We often had to walk alongside to lighten the boats, but otherwise these places were easy. A trifle more water would have done away with them, or at least would have enabled us to ignore them completely.*

An interesting event happened in the middle part of White Canyon in 1884. The story actually began on July 7, near the Utah-Colorado state line, in a tributary canyon in the lower end of Montezuma Creek. There was an argument between a group of Piutes and several cowboys over the rightful ownership of a horse. The whites were quick to claim the horse, and ended up wounding one Indian by the name of Brooks. Then there was a big shootout with two cowboys being wounded as they tried to leave the scene.

The cowboys escaped and some headed for Colorado where they rounded up a group of whites including soldiers, and began hot pursuit The Piutes, which included a whole band of men, women and

Hite Ferry in operation in July, 1963(Crampton foto).

children, went north and northwest around the southern part of the Abajo Mountains. All the time they stayed just out of rifle range, and just ahead of the their pursuers. From the area of the Woodenshoe Buttes, just north of Natural Bridges National Monument, they heading southwest into White Canyon.

In the middle part White Canyon between Short and Fortknocker Canyons, the Indians headed south over what has been known ever since as Piute Pass(near mile post 61 on Highway 95). To reach the top of Piute Pass, it was necessary to go up a narrow trail under some cliffs. The Indians waited on top, while two white men advanced into a trap. There was another gun battle, and the two whites were shot and left to lie in the hot sun. That day was July 14, 1884. The Piutes pinned down the rest of the soldiers, not allowing them to come to the aid their two wounded companions. In the night the Piutes took all the valuables from the two men, who were by then dead. One of the men was a soldier named Worthington, the other a cowboy named Wilson.

From Piute Pass, the Indians headed south into Red Canyon and to the Colorado River. From there a trail went south along the river to what is now Good Hope Bay. They got to the canyon rim along an old trail on the southwest side of the bay(this was later developed into a stock trail). From the rim(according to Melvin Dalton of Monticello) they must have dropped down into a north fork of Cedar Canyon, then moved up the main fork, over a divide, and down into the upper end of Moqui Canyon(cowboys always knew this as North Gulch). They left upper Moqui by way of a big sand slide north of Burnt Spring, and finally headed southwest to Lake Pagahrit.

The Piutes camped at Lake Pagahrit for one week. They vented some of their frustration toward the whites by shooting all the cattle they could. They feasted on some of the beef, while other cows were shot with arrows and left to run around looking like pin cushions. When they left, it's believed they headed southwest over Wilson and Grey Mesas, down Wilson Canyon and to the San Juan. The soldiers and cowboys in pursuit, lost the trail not far from Pagahrit, and never knew for sure which way they went.

Perhaps the first man to write about this story was Albert R. Lyman. In his book, *The Outlaw of Navaho Mountain,* he called much of this route, at least that part from White Canyon to the San Juan, the **Old Trail.** It was quite obviously a trail well known by the various Indian groups, but not the whites. It appears Lyman had gotten at least part of his information from some of the Piute Indians who were in that group.

The author has never stopped to see, but there is some kind of marker or monument along Highway 95 just below Piute Pass, at what locals call **Soldier Crossing.** Look for something very near mile post 61. Apparently the dead cowboy and soldier were buried there, and the graves are now in a small enclosure.

Looking west from Narrow Canyon toward the Highway 95 bridge and the Henry Mountains.

81

Trachyte and Swett Creek Canyons

Location and Campsites The bay of Trachyte Creek Canyon is located about 8 kms southwest of the Hite Marina. The buoy in the channel reads M134(K214). The bay is about 5 kms long and seems to be a fairly popular place to camp, although there aren't that many good campsites. There will always be some kind of camping place at the very mouth of Trachyte or Swett Creeks, and several more further down, but they are on the less desirable clay beds of the Chinle Formation.

Routes or Trails Trachyte Creek is a wide canyon with a year-round flowing stream. It's used during the winter for cattle grazing. As a result you'll find some trails, but normally you just walk in or beside the creek. This canyon has no obstructions and it was the original route to Hite or Dandy Crossing before the road was built down North Wash, which was the better route for wagons. Three kms up Trachyte Creek(from the HWM) is a side drainage coming in from the left, or west. This is **Woodruff Canyon.** You can walk up Woodruff quite easily; first past one large chokestone which has made a pool of water on the lee-side(maybe some wading), then up and over one waterfall(on the right side), and finally up along a small stream to Highway 276 near mile post 12.

About 7 kms past Woodruff Canyon is **Trail Canyon.** This drainage is featureless, but it's an easy and quick way to enter or exit the Trachyte Valley. Another canyon and small stream enters Trachyte Creek from the west about one km above Trail. This is **Maidenwater Canyon,** and it's the most interesting side drainage to Trachyte Creek. It has a live beaver population and some small pools. At one point, you'll encounter a large chokestone which has made a pool of water behind it, which you may have to wade(neck deep sometimes!). There are some pretty good narrows, then finally another chokestone which rises two meters above a large pool. Most people will have to stop there. You could come down this part from the highway, but it would be difficult to get back up.

Now for **Swett Creek.** You'll first come to a short falls and a little running water, then the canyon narrows and deepens. After about 7 kms you'll come to the Wingate Narrows. Above this, the canyon really narrows where it winds through the Navajo Sandstone. You can walk all the way to Highway 276, between mile posts 13 and 14. In the **South Fork** of Swett Creek, you will find a moderately narrow canyon with several seeps and places where large boulders have fallen down to the creek bed. The author went about half way up and it appears that one could use this canyon to reach the summit of Mt. Holmes.

Hike Length and Time Needed All of the hikes to the various side canyons discussed here are day hikes, with none being too long. The walk to the upper pool in Maidenwater(about 13 kms) is an all day affair, as is the hike to the highway through Swett Creek. To go half way up the South Fork of Swett Creek and back, is half a day or less.

Large pothole behind a chokestone in Maidenwater Canyon.

MAP 6, TRACHYTE & SWETT CK. CANYONS

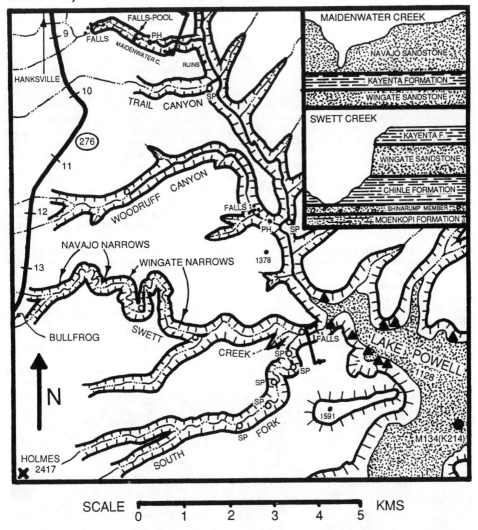

Boots or Shoes Take wading shoes into the Trachyte drainage and dry weather boots or shoes into Swett Creek.
Water Better not drink the water in the Trachyte Canyons; cattle graze somewhere in that drainage much of the year. However, there is at least one spring near the creek just above the confluence with Woodruff Canyon. There's also a minor seep in lower Trail Canyon which should be good.
   The author recalls at least three minor seeps along Swett Creek. Take water where it comes out of the ground and it should be good as there are no cattle around. South Fork seeps have good water; at least the author didn't get sick after tanking up at four different waterholes.
Main Attractions Good narrows, wading in some deep pools, a live beaver population, and someone mentioned a small Anasazi shelter exists between Trail and Maidenwater Canyons.
Hiking Maps USGS or BLM map Hite Crossing(1:100,000), or Browns Rim and Mt. Hillers(1:62,500).
History of Hite and Dandy Crossing Much of the following information comes from the work of

C. Gregory Crampton, who studied Glen Canyon in the late 1950's and early 1960's. His research has been written up in the *Anthropological Papers* published by the University of Utah.

According to Crampton, who interviewed Art Chaffin in 1960, the first white occupant in the Hite area was Joshua Swett, a squaw man, who allegedly stole horses on one side of the river and sold them on the other. He had arrived in 1872 and built a cabin at the mouth of Swett Creek, the south fork of Trachyte, about 6 or 7 kms from the Colorado. When Hite arrived in 1883, Swett left. Then Hite moved the Swett Cabin to the river, where it stayed until Lake Powell covered it.

The town of **Hite** was founded upon the arrival of Cass Hite to Glen Canyon on September 19, 1883. He had fled Arizona under threats of being scalped by Navajos, and had entered the area via White Canyon on the east. Chief Hoskaninni of the Navajos had told him of gold in the canyon. The location where Cass Hite first settled and what was later known as Hite City, is about 8 kms south, or downstream from present day Hite Marina, and at the mouth of White and Trachyte Canyons.

When Hite first reached the Colorado from the east through White Canyon, he found a good place to cross, which he called **Dandy Crossing.** As it turned out, it was the best crossing of the Colorado in all of Glen Canyon. The normal way through southeastern Utah in the days after Hite's arrival, was to pass through Hanksville and go down Trachyte Creek(later, the normal route went down North Wash), cross at Dandy Crossing, then go on up White Canyon and on to Blanding or Bluff.

Soon after Hite arrived, he discovered gold in the sand bars of the Colorado. This led to two minor gold rushes; one lasting from about 1884 until around 1890, the other from about 1893 until 1900. Crampton believes there were probably no more than a thousand men in the canyon at any one time, so the Glen Canyon Gold Rush wasn't of the same magnitude as the California or Yukon Gold Rushes.

As it turned out the gold was very hard to get out of the sand. It was in the form of fine gold dust, which tended to float away in the panning process. Another problem miners encountered was the lack of water. It proved difficult to get river water up to the higher bars, where most of the gold was located. There were a few side canyon streams, but they flooded periodically, washing everything away. Water wheels were used in a place or two, but with little success, and pumping the muddy water out of the river quickly wore out the pumps. The best way to get the gold was simply with a shovel, some form of sluice, and a pan.

After Hite moved the Swett Cabin down to the river, he was followed by his two brothers. The family ran the post office, which opened in 1889, and a store for many years. The Hite brothers stayed in the canyon until Cass Hite died at his ranch on Ticaboo Creek in 1914.

Cass Hite may have put his name on the town and ferry crossing, but he never did build or operate a real ferry himself. For years those who wanted to cross just swam their animals over, or

Lower Maidenwater Canyon has a year-round stream.

floated their wagons across on drift logs found along the river. There was never really a ferry, and it was never a ford, because animals always had to swim. Actually, Hite did have a small row boat, which some people either borrowed or rented. The Scorups used it several times in the 1890's to help get some of their stubborn cattle across the river.

In 1907 or 1908, a man named **Harshberger** built and operated the first real **ferry** at Hite, but it was about 5 kms upstream or north of Hite, and the later Hite Ferry. The boat itself measured about 4 x 9 meters. At the time, the price of copper was high, and Harshberger had found some deposits in upper White Canyon and established a mine. With the use of the ferry, he was able to take the copper to the railway at Green River, via North Wash and Hanksville. Apparently the ferry service stopped, when the price of copper dropped after only a year or two.

There is no record of regular ferry service at Hite again until 1946. Arthur L. Chaffin moved to Hite in 1932, and ran a farm. It was he and other local people who, over the years, opened a real road from Hanksville to Hite. Finally the state got involved, and built a road from Hanksville to Blanding. It was Chaffin who supplied the last link. He opened the first auto ferry service at Hite on September 17, 1946. This ferry, along with a small store, ran continuously until June 5, 1964, when the rising waters of Lake Powell forced the closure.

Because of the opening of the road and ferry, more mineral exploration began in the area. Uranium was found in upper White Canyon, and in 1949, the Vanadium Corp. of America and the Atomic Energy Commisson opened an experimental mill just across the river from Hite at the mouth of White Canyon. Shortly after, a one-room school opened with 30 pupils. A post office opened as well. The school closed about the time the mill shut down in 1954, but the post office stayed open until 1964.

The lower end of the Dirty Devil River Canyon as it enters upper Glen Canyon.

Twomile, Fourmile, Scorup, Blue Notch & Red Canyons

Location and Campsites The two hikable canyons here, Twomile and Fourmile, are only 2 to 3 kms apart, and together they are 12 to 14 kms southwest, or down lake from Hite Marina. The buoy nearest Twomile Canyon Bay is marked M132(K211); while near Fourmile C. Bay one is labeled M130B(K208).

This is an area with limited campsites; the shore lines are either rough and rocky, or in some cases the Chinle clay beds extend down to the shore. In other places the Shinarump Member of the Chinle is exposed at the shore line, and it creates a flat-top bench and a short cliff. Not many places to pitch a tent! In Twomile, there is one sandy place right where the creek bed enters the lake near the HWM. In Fourmile, there are many more sites available, at least when the lake is high.

Routes or Trails In **Twomile Canyon**, you'll begin at about where the Shinarump Member of the Chinle Formation is exposed. First you'll pass a falls, then a series of potholes as the usually dry stream bed drops down through a sandstone layer(Shinarump). A km past the potholes is a steep place in the canyon, where boulders have come down near a spring. In hot weather, you'll enjoy drinking this spring water; it's seems very cold on a hot day and tastes good too. Drink it where it flows from beneath a large boulder right in the creek bed.

On the author's visit he went around the south side of these big boulders located at what he is calling Coldwater Spring. However, in talking about the canyon with Riter Ekker, old time cowboy of Hanksville, he was told there is a trail of some kind around the north side of these boulders, on the slope with all the cottonwood trees and other greenery. Years ago, a man named Tom Humphrey ran cattle in Twomile Canyon, and he built this trail around the boulders which allowed his stock to graze the upper and lower ends of the drainage. If it's there and clearly visible, would someone please contact the author about it.

Beyond the Coldwater Spring, it's fairly easy walking, with about three more minor seeps with good water. In the upper end, you can route-find up to the right, or north, and exit the canyon. It's possible to climb Mt. Holmes via this canyon.

Right at the HWM in Fourmile Bay, there is a good little seep and running water, which the author drank on two different trips. **Fourmile Canyon** is similar to Twomile, with the same geologic formations. There are several seeps and water which flows for short distances. Then further along, you'll come to some narrows and potholes. This is where the stream bed cuts down and drops through the Wingate Sandstone. Further up is the Fourmile Spring, once used by stockmen.

From near Fourmile Spring, you could walk north and climb the rugged Mt. Holmes. You could also continue straight up the canyon to the west, go over a pass, and end up on Highway 276 at mile post 20. From near that pass, you could climb south and reach the summit of Mt. Ellsworth, but it's a lot easier to climb from the highway and m.p. 20.

Mt. Ellsworth dominates the western skyline from the mouth of Twomile Canyon.

MAP 7, TWOMILE & FOURMILE CANYONS

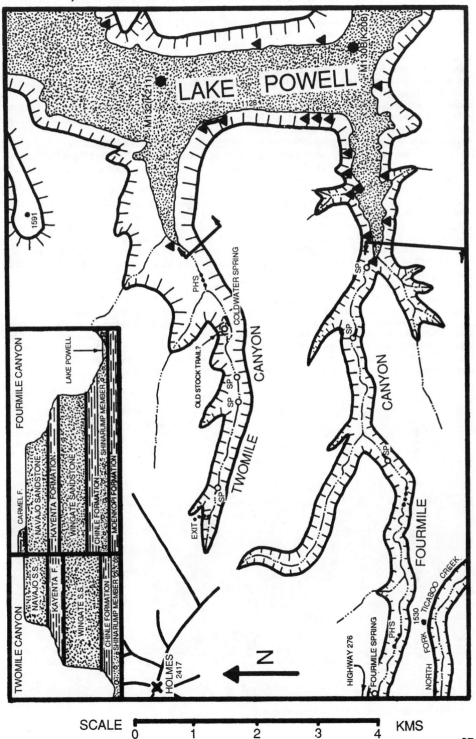

SCALE

0   1   2   3   4   KMS

You could also walk south from the upper end of Fourmile, and drop down into the upper end of the North Fork of Ticaboo Creek. If you had two boats and drivers, hikers could walk up Fourmile and down North Fork of Ticaboo.

Hike Length and Time Needed It's about 6 kms from the HWM to the exit in upper Twomile Canyon. The author's trip lasted 3 1/2 hours, so you'll need at least half a day round-trip, maybe more. The author once walked from the highway to the lake in Fourmile Canyon in 8 1/2 hours, round-trip. A long hike.

Boots or Shoes Any kind of walking boots or shoes are OK.

Water There are several seeps and springs in both canyons which the author drank from. Hopefully, most of these seeps will be there on a year-round basis.

Main Attractions Solitude in seldom visited canyons, and for hardy climbers a chance to climb either of the two peaks making up the Little Rockies part of the Henry Mountains. The Little Rockies are Mts. Ellsworth(2510 m) and Holmes(2417 m).

Hiking Maps USGS or BLM map Hite Crossing(1:100,000), or Browns Rim(1:62,500).

Other Canyons and History Just a few kms south or down lake from Two and Fourmile Canyons, are three more canyons, two of which share a common mouth. These are Scorup, Red and Blue Notch Canyons.

About 5 or 6 kms down lake[near buoy M169R(K206)] around the big horseshoe bend called The Horn, and on the east side of the lake, is a small drainage called **Scorup Canyon.** If you were to walk up this short drainage, you'd end up in the lower end of White Canyon, just over a low divide. It got its name from the Scorup Brothers cattle outfit, who ran stock in this area from 1891 until 1959. Read all about the Scorups in the introduction under *History of the Cattle Industry.*

Just inside the broad mouth of Red Canyon, which is located at about M125(K198) and buoy O and N, and just after you pass around Castle Butte on your left, you can enter the short inlet of **Blue Notch Canyon.** This is a short tributary of the much larger Red Canyon. At the end of the inlet, you will see a road. This 4WD track leaves Highway 95 between mile posts 59 and 60, and runs southwest over Blue Notch Pass and down to the lake. Before Lake Powell, this road was used for access to copper and uranium mines in the area. There are a number of good campsites in this inlet.

If you continue southeast from the mouth of Blue Notch, you'll be in the larger **Red Canyon Bay.** This is another bay with shallow waters along the shore line. Some of the shore line rocks are part of the Moenkopi Formation, while just above these reddish siltstones are the clay beds of the Chinle Formation. There are many uranium mines, prospects and old mining exploration roads in this canyon above the lake. Mining was most active in Red Canyon in the 1950's.

A scene from the upper end of Twomile Canyon.

The roads you see heading southeast from the head of the inlet, reach pavement on Highway 276, which links Highway 95 and Halls Crossing Marina. The canyon has running water in some places and at certain times, but coming out of the clay beds, it probably won't taste good. There are many good sandy and gravely type campsites.

In the pre-Lake Powell days, there was an interesting old miners log cabin located at the mouth of Red Canyon. It measured 3 x 5 meters, was built with squared logs, and had a stone fireplace. No one seems to know for sure who built it or when it was built, but it must have been in the gold rush days, sometime between 1884 and 1900. In 1909, a miner named Albert "Bert" Loper moved in, and lived there for five years. Loper called it his **Hermitage.** He apparently left in 1914, the same year Cass Hite died at his ranch on Ticaboo Creek.

Loper it was said, dammed Red Creek in order to have water to run his placer mining operation on the nearby river bar, and to irrigate a small farm of about one hectare(two acres). Loper brought several pieces of farm equipment to the canyon. In later years(1952) it was reported by a river runner that a family was living in the cabin and doing a little farming themselves.

Years later, Bert Loper became a river guide and took many people down the Colorado. He did this until he was 80 years of age. In July of 1949, he was drowned in the Colorado River somewhere in the Grand Canyon.

The Bert Loper Cabin. It was located near the mouth of Red Canyon.

Ticaboo Creek and South Fork

Location and Campsites The mouth of Ticaboo Creek is about 27 lake kms southwest of Hite Marina and near to what should be M122(K195). Near this bay is a buoy marked "I".

There are not too many campsites in this region, either in Ticaboo Bay or the main channel. However, there's a good one at the head of the bay and at the HWM. Not far away, there are some really great sandy beaches to the south of Ticaboo and on the southeastern shore of Good Hope Bay.

Routes or Trails Right at the HWM at the upper end of the Ticaboo Bay, you'll find running water and a nice spring coming out of a crack in the wall on the left. The author has called this Wall Spring. This will be one of the best places around to stock up on water. About 150 meters above this spring is the beginning of the stream which used to flow past the now submerged Ticaboo Ranch belonging to Cass Hite, and on to the Colorado River(read more on Cass Hite below).

Just up canyon a short distance from the beginning of the running water, is a fork in the drainage. The one on the right, or north, is Ticaboo Creek. The one on the left, or south, is the South Fork of Ticaboo.

South Fork is the most interesting canyon in the immediate area. After 5 or 6 kms, you'll see a short side drainage to the left, or south. Up this a ways on the east side is a large cave once used by Indians, probably the Fremonts. After another 3 or 4 kms, and just before the canyon begins to really narrow, look to your left on the south side wall, to locate an old stock trail.

One person told the author this trail had been built during the Depression by the CCC workers. However, Riter Ekker of Hanksville, told the author that a Keith Taylor of Teasdale, Utah(located just east of Capitol Reef National Park), who used to have a permit to run cattle in the canyon, did most of the work on this trail during the 1940's and 1950's. The author guesses the trail has been there a long time, going back to Anasazi and Fremont Indian times, but that Taylor was probably the last to use and maintain the **South Fork Trail.**

At the top of this trail is a metal water tank called the Ticaboo Tank. It holds water from a small spring on the ledges above. Beside it is a watering trough, both of which should have water year-round. This was installed by the BLM in recent years to provide water and water storage for the cattle of the grazing permit holders. Continuing up the South Fork. The canyon gradually narrows to almost nothing, then it's blocked by a falls in the Navajo Sandstone. There are several little side cracks in the upper end which are worth looking at.

Now back to the main **Ticaboo Canyon.** Less than one km above where the South Fork enters, and on the left wall, is another good spring. It flows over a ledge, making a small waterfall. As you walk up canyon the walls gradually fade away and it becomes less deep. Four or 5 kms above the little waterfall, you'll come to cottonwood trees and willows, and a stream flowing for about 200 meters.

Wall Spring, at the lower end of Ticaboo Creek Canyon.

MAP 8, TICABOO CREEK & SOUTH FORK

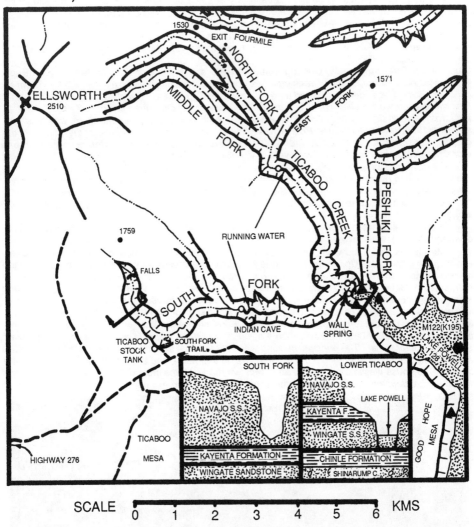

SCALE
0 1 2 3 4 5 6 KMS

Not far above this wooded area is the **Middle Fork;** and just a short distance beyond that the **North Fork** enters on the left. The author only knows the North Fork. In it you'll pass through some moderately narrow sections of the Navajo Sandstone, then about 3 kms into North Fork, you'll come to the emerging Kayenta Formation which makes some shallow narrows. At that point you can walk up the slope to the right, or east, and exit the canyon. From there you'll have a fine view of Ellsworth and Holmes.

Back to the lake and **Peshliki Fork.** You'll have to do some scrambling to get into this one; or when the lake is low, you may not get above the Wingate falls at the mouth. If you can get into Peshliki, it could prove interesting.

Hike Length and Time Needed It's about 11 kms from the HWM to the exit in North Fork. The author did this one in less than 4 1/2 hours, round-trip. You would need most of a day for the same trip which is pretty easy walking all the way. On another trip, the author drove from Highway 276 to the Ticaboo Tank, and walked to the lake and back in about half a day.

Boots or Shoes Any boots or shoes are OK.

Water There doesn't seem to be any cattle in any of these canyons today, so all water should be good for drinking, especially at the source of each spring or seep. Also at Ticaboo Tank.

Main Attractions An Indian cave, the narrows and the old stock trail of upper South Fork, great views of the mountains, and several narrow side canyons.

Hiking Maps USGS or BLM map Hite Crossing(1:100,000), or Browns Rim and Mt. Ellsworth(1:62.500).

Cass Hite's Ticaboo Ranch Quoting from Crampton's University of Utah Anthropological Paper #72. *At the point where Ticaboo Creek emerges from a narrow canyon about a mile[1 1/2 kms] from the Colorado River, Cass Hite established a home--usually called Ticaboo Ranch--where he lived much of the time that he was in Glen Canyon after 1883. There in an open area of about 3 acres[about 1.2 hectares] alongside Ticaboo Creek is where he built a cabin, the chimney of which is still standing[1959, and before Lake Powell reached the area]. The foundations of the cabin on the outside measured about 18 by 30 feet[6 by 10 meters]and may have consisted of more than one room.* Crampton goes on to say there were many objects of various kinds lying about.

The cabin was near the canyon wall just to the west, and the area was fenced. There was a corral in one place. and nearby a fenced-off vineyard. *A few of the vines, though they had not been irrigated in years, still clung to life. When Julius Stone visited Cass Hite at Ticaboo Ranch October 23, 1909, his host treated him to grapes and melons fresh off the vine, and was given a sackful of raisins to take along.*

Crampton also noted, right next to the corral and vineyard was a large boulder which had rolled down the slope. It was covered with petroglyphs.

Hite always had good water at the cabin, but just down stream, Ticaboo Creek sank into the sands of the gravel bar. Up stream about one km was a fine stream where it flowed over bedrock and a low waterfall. *In 1914 Cass Hite died at his ranch at Ticaboo and is buried there. The grave is marked by a rectangular enclosure composed of boards nailed to four posts. Another grave along side that of Hite, and with a similar enclosure, is reported to be the resting place of one Frank Dehlin.* The water of Lake Powell covered these ruins and historic site sometime in the mid-1960's.

J.W. Powell's Report Powell mentions finding ruins near what later would be Hite, then in the afternoon of July 29, 1869, he says, *then we run down fifteen miles[24 kms] farther, and discover another group[of ruins]. The principal building was situated on a summit of the hill. A part of the walls are standing, to the height of eight or ten feet[2 1/2 to 3 meters], and the mortar yet remains in some places. The house was in the shape of an L, with five rooms on the ground floor,--one in the angle and two in each extension. In the space in the angle there is a deep excavation. From what we know of*

The South Fork Trail, in the middle part of the South Fork of Ticaboo Creek.

the people in the Province of Tusayan[Hopi Land], who are, doubtless, of the same race as the former inhabitants of these ruins, we conclude that this was a kiva, or underground chamber in which their religious ceremonies were performed. These ruins must have been not far above the mouth of Ticaboo Creek.

A narrow side drainage of the South Fork of Ticaboo Creek.

The remains of the cabin built by Cass Hite at Ticaboo Ranch(Crampton foto, 1959).

93

Sevenmile & Cedar Canyons and Good Hope Bay

Location and Campsites The two canyons featured here are Sevenmile and Cedar. The buoy nearest the mouth of Sevenmile is M113(K181); while near the mouth of Cedar Canyon Inlet is buoy M110(K176). The name *Sevenmile* came about because the mouth of this canyon was 7 miles(11 kms) down Glen Canyon from Cass Hite's Ticaboo Ranch on Ticaboo Creek. Before Lake Powell, there was a road and trail running along the west side of the river, extending all the way from Hite and Dandy Crossing to Sevenmile Creek.

There are several campsites in each canyon, some much better than others. At the upper end of each inlet, you'll find at least one small campsite which is sandy. If you like a lot of sand, then consider heading for **Good Hope Bay**. On the southeast and eastern sides of this bay are many sandy beaches, as well as some very good springs. The best spring puts out a lot of water that's good tasting and cold--at least in hot weather. The author counted 8 or 9 springs on the hillsides below the Wingate Sandstone walls.

Routes or Trails From the HWM in the upper end of the inlet to **Sevenmile Canyon,** you'll first encounter a small stream lined with cottonwood trees and other water loving plants. There are enough people hiking up this canyon to have created some hiker-made trails. These trails extend all the way up canyon to the big boulders and narrows, which is the end of hiking for all except perhaps a few rugged rock climbers. If it's possible to get above this blockage, then surely more good narrows lie beyond. The main Sevenmile Canyon is as deep and narrow as any canyon on Lake Powell. The Navajo Sandstone walls are very high and impressive.

Paralleling the main fork to the east is what the author is calling the **East Fork.** It has a short inlet with a couple of campsites. After walking about 200-300 meters above the HWM, you'll come to a dry fall, below which is a minor spring(which may dry up during long dry spells). You can skirt this obstacle on the left, or west. Then you walk right up the dry creek bed and into some pretty good narrows with very high Navajo walls. About a km above the dry fall you'll come to a place with large boulders jammed into the gorge. Most hikers will be stopped at that point, but energetic folk can likely get around this to surely find more good narrows beyond.

Just to the south of the mouth of East Fork you may be able to find an old **miners trail** heading up to the east and southeast to the top of the Kayenta bench. This trail, according to Crampton, was apparently used by miners during the Glen Canyon Gold Rush days from about 1884 until 1900. It started at Hite and went south along the west bank of the river. It was a wagon road at first, then gradually narrowed to a horse trail. It's shown on old river maps to run south to Sevenmile, then heads up over the rim and southwest to the head of Hansen Creek, where a wagon road ran down to the river in the dry creek bed. Going north from Hansen Creek was the standard route to Hanksville.

The upper end of the deeply entrenched Sevenmile Canyon Inlet.

MAP 9, SEVENMILE & CEDAR CANYONS AND GOOD HOPE BAY

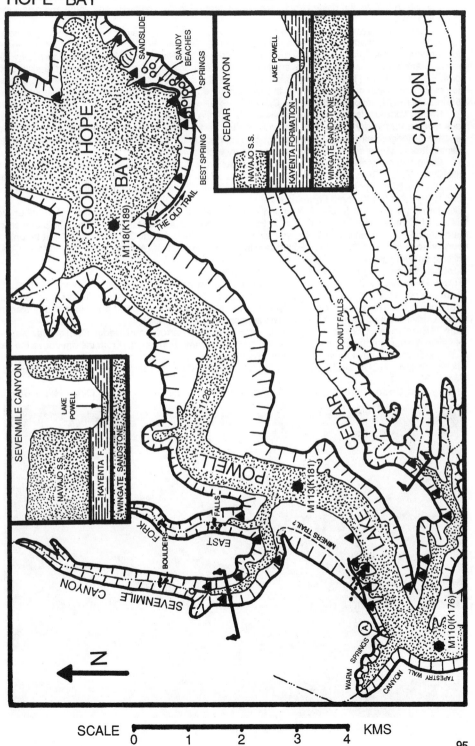

SCALE

0   1   2   3   4   KMS

95

This is what the author found. He boated into the main inlet about a km past the mouth of East Fork and docked where the Kayenta bench is seen coming out of the water. At that point there is a faint trail, which follows the rising bench as it curves around to the southeast and south and below the big Navajo walls.

On top of the Kayenta bench, there are about half a dozen stone cairns to mark a route around to the southwest and nearly to the mouth of Warm Springs Canyon. When the cairns end, someone on foot can easily walk up one of several routes to the top of the Navajo rim. While this is an easy walk for the infantry, the cavalry could never make it. The author never saw any cairns on the slickrock, nor any steps cut out. It seems that if this was indeed a real trail, it was not used by horses, but by foot traffic only. You could also get to this old trail by docking along the main channel about 2 kms northeast of the mouth of Warm Springs Canyon.

Cedar Canyon is not so impressive as Sevenmile. Its walls aren't too high and they're set back away from the dry creek bed. As you walk up Cedar Canyon, you'll be walking along Kayenta benches or ledges, all or most of the way. You can go up for two or three days, but maps seem to indicate it doesn't get any more interesting, scenery wise.

As you go up canyon, you'll have to pass by several small falls, before reaching what the author calls Donut Falls. There, the flood waters have created a small donut-shaped bridge across the top of a usually dry fall. There are also several places with potholes and special erosional features in the various layers of the Kayenta Formation.

Hike Length and Time Needed You can only walk about one km up Sevenmile. The author did this round-trip hike in less than an hour. In East Fork, the time and distance are about the same as in the main fork. It's about 5 kms from the HWM to Donut Falls in Cedar Canyon. This might be only 3 hours or so round-trip. The author did this one in an even two hours. Walking along the old miners trail will take only an hour or so.

Boots or Shoes Any kind of boots or shoes are OK.

Water There seems to be a year-round stream in the lower 100-200 meters of Sevenmile Canyon. There are no cattle or deer there, so it should be good drinking unless you see fresh sign of beaver. East Fork is dry except for a minor seep under the falls. The author found a number of potholes in Cedar Canyon, but otherwise it's dry with no springs(up to Donut Falls).

Main Attractions Sevenmile Canyon is very deep and narrow, and Cedar Canyon has some fotogenic erosional potholes and other features in the Kayenta Formation. From the rim above the old miners trail, you will have some good views in all directions.

Hiking Maps USGS or BLM map Hite Crossing(1:100,000), or Mt. Ellsworth and Mancos Mesa(1:62,500)).

History and Good Hope Bay In the upper right hand corner of this map is **Good Hope Bay.** It

Erosional features in the Kayenta Sandstone in Cedar Canyon.

provides the best campsites around, plus there's a couple of interesting short hikes. On the southwest side of the bay is an old **stock trail** used during the time before Lake Powell, to take cattle and other livestock down to the river.

To find this trail, first locate the most westerly talus slope which can be climbed to the rim in the southwest corner of the bay. The author placed a large cairn near the bottom and just above the HWM. From the lake the trail heads up and to the west, part of which is next to a recent slip scarp, created by slippage of the talus slope. This slope is on top of the Chinle clay beds which the rising lake water has lubricated, thus the slip scarp. Once you get on the trail, it's very easy to follow. It runs diagonally up about 400 meters to the rim, then seems to disappear.

At the rim, where you'll have fine views to the west and the Henry Mountains, is a rock wall which kept the livestock either in, or out of the canyon. This stock trail appears to be part of the **Old Trail**, discussed by Albert R. Lyman in his book, *The Outlaw of Navajo Mountain*. This was an old Indian trail which began somewhere near the Woodenshoe Buttes, then ran down White Canyon and south along the Colorado River, and finally over the mesa tops to the San Juan River. In 1884, a band of Piutes had an altercation with some cowboys and there was a shoot-out near the Utah-Colorado state line. Later, when cowboys and soldiers followed the Piutes, there was still another gun battle on the rim of White Canyon. Two white men were killed in an ambush, and the Piutes escaped to Navajo Mountain along this trail. See all the details under Map 5 and White Canyon.

A second little hike you could take is up the big prominent **sand slide** on the east side of Good Hope Bay. The author had thought there might be a trail up this slope, but if there ever was one there, it's now lost in time. Cattle could likely be taken up the sand slide, but then they'd have to bench-walk for several kms before they could find flat ground. One nice thing about taking the time for this hike is, from the top you'll have perhaps the best view anywhere of the Henry Mountains to the west.

Under the lake waters and on the west side of the bay, is what was called **Good Hope Bar.** This was one of the better placer gold mining gravel bars in Glen Canyon during the gold rush which lasted from about 1884 until 1900. Gold was discovered in February of 1887, and a company founded by Cass Hite and J. S. Burgess. At some point in time, and before 1897, Burgess and Hite built a 12 meter high water wheel on the rivers edge. When Stanton visited the place in 1897, he called this the *Egyptian Wheel,* which must have resembled water wheels on the Nile River.

This wheel was connected to a 225 meter long, 12 meters high flume, which took water to a reservoir a distance away, where it was used in the placer mining operation. In later years, when uranium prospecting was in full swing, there was a landing strip built along the bar on the west side of the river. When Crampton visited the bar in 1964, they found such things as shovels, a post-hole digger, drills, cogwheels, scrapers and screens. Now that era has vanished under the lake waters.

A telefoto lens view of the eastern side of Mt. Ellsworth, with the mouth of Ticaboo Bay in the foreground.

This foto was taken from the canyon rim half way between Sevenmile and Warm Creek Canyons. Navajo Mountain is in the far background.

This is part of the Old Trail, leading up and out of Good Hope Bay.

From the top of the sandslide on the east side of Good Hope Bay, you have good views of the Henry Mountains to the northwest.

The Ryan Cabin, was located along the Colorado, opposite the mouth of Sevenmile Canyon. In 1897, Robert B. Stanton called it *O'Keefe's Lone Star Rock House*. It was built during the Glen Canyon Gold Rush by miners Mike Ryan or Timothy O'Keefe before 1897(foto by Crampton, 1961).

Tapestry Wall Hike, Smith Fork, & Warm Springs Canyon

Location and Campsites The mouth of Smith Fork Canyon is about 20 kms northeast or up-lake from the mouth of Bullfrog Bay. The buoy closest to Smith Fork is marked M106(K170); the one in front of Tapestry Wall, is M110(K176).

There are very few campsites in this region. The reason is, the Navajo Sandstone walls come right down to the waters edge. There are a couple of sites at or near the beginning of the Tapestry Wall Hike, and there should be two good sandy sites at the head of Smith Fork Inlet, right where the creek flows into the lake. There could also be a couple of slickrock sites in Smith Fork Inlet. Warm Springs Canyon has nothing but sheer walls everywhere.

Routes or Trails Smith Fork is one of the premier narrow or slot canyon hikes in this book. As you walk up canyon, you will find some cottonwood trees growing along side the small stream which begins to flows maybe 200 meters above the HWM. In this same area there is also a short side canyon coming in from the right, or northeast. It's narrow and dark for a ways and ends in a cool grotto.

Going up the main canyon, you'll find some of the best narrows on Lake Powell beginning about half a km above the HWM. For a short distance, this slot is as impressive as the Buckskin Gulch of the Paria River. Above the best narrows, the canyon isn't so deep, but it's narrow all the way up. You'll find several little side canyons, which could prove interesting, and there is one chokestone you'll have to climb over. In the upper end you'll come to a large rockfall, which will stop all but the hardiest of climbers. In the upper sections, note all the granite cobblestones which have come down from Mt. Ellsworth.

Now for the **Tapestry Wall Hike.** Park and/or camp just across the channel from the mouth of Knowles Canyon. There are several campsites right at the corner of a small inlet, with lots of driftwood lying about. From the water, head up a shallow drainage in the slickrock to the west. In places it can be steep, but there are several different ways up to choose from. It's easy hiking for the whole family.

As you walk up to the west, you'll also be looking down on another shallow drainage to the north. This one has many potholes, which are often filled with water. After a ways, begin to veer to the north, then just below the Carmel Rim, cross the upper part of this little drainage to the east side. Finally, you'll climb onto the Carmel Rim, then it's an easy stroll to the top of the wall, where is found a little pyramid of limestone, a part of the Carmel Formation. This little pyramid is the highest point around. On top is a USGS bench mark reading *Mancos*. From there you'll have excellent views of the Henry Mountains to the northwest, and of the lake, 226 meters below.

Hike Length and Time Needed In Smith Fork, you can walk up canyon about 6 kms. The author made this hike round-trip in about 2 hours, but you may want 3 or 4 hours. Stay out of this drainage in times of bad weather. From the lake to the top of Tapestry Wall is about 3 or 3 1/2 kms, and will take

Tapestry Wall, with Mt. Ellsworth in the far right background.

MAP 10, TAPESTRY WALL HIKE & SMITH FORK & WARM SPRINGS CANYONS

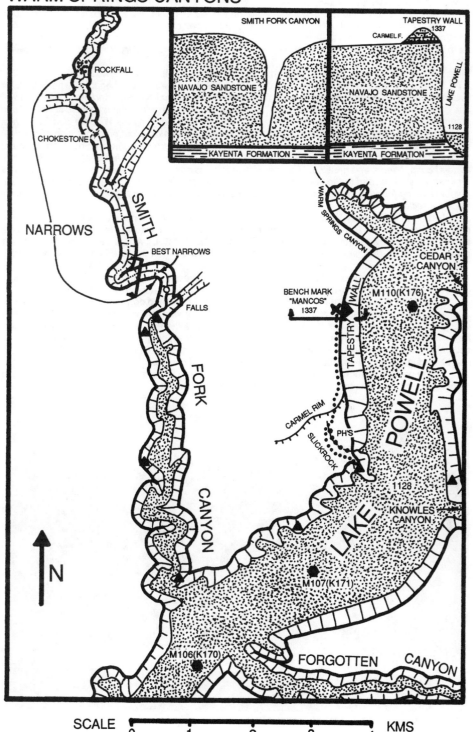

SMITH FORK CANYON

TAPESTRY WALL

CARMEL F.

1337

NAVAJO SANDSTONE

NAVAJO SANDSTONE

LAKE POWELL

1128

KAYENTA FORMATION

KAYENTA FORMATION

ROCKFALL

CHOKESTONE

NARROWS

SMITH

BEST NARROWS

FALLS

FORK

CANYON

N

WARM SPRINGS CANYON

CEDAR CANYON

BENCH MARK "MANCOS" 1337

M110(K176)

TAPESTRY WALL

CARMEL RIM

PH'S

SLICKROCK

LAKE POWELL

1128

KNOWLES CANYON

M107(K171)

M106(K170)

FORGOTTEN CANYON

SCALE 0 1 2 3 4 KMS

most people 2 hours round-trip. The author did the round-trip in 1 hr. 15 min.

Boots or Shoes Any dry weather boots or shoes will do on Tapestry Wall, as half the hike is on slickrock. After rains, take wading shoes into Smith Fork; otherwise it's a dry hike.

Water After rains you'll find lots of pothole water on the Tapestry Wall Hike. Also, a small year-round seep exists in the lower end of Smith Fork. There are no cattle or beaver there, so it should be good drinking.

Main Attractions Some of the best narrows anywhere, and great views from the top of Tapestry Wall.

Hiking Maps USGS or BLM map Hite Crossing(1:100,000), or Mt. Ellsworth(1:62,500).

J.W. Powell's Report and History On July 29, 1869, the Powell Party began at what was later Hite, and ended up in the area of Tapestry Wall. Here's part of what he said. *And now I climb the wall and go out into the back country for a walk. The sandstone through which the canyon is cut is red and homogeneous, being the same as that through which Labyrinth Canyon runs[Wingate Sandstone now below the lake]. The smooth, naked rock[Navajo Sandstone] stretches out on either side of the river for many miles, but curiously carved mounds and cones are scattered everywhere and deep holes are worn out. Many of these pockets are filled with water. In one of these holes or wells, 20 feet[6 meters] deep, I find a tree growing. The excavation is so narrow that I can step from it's brink to a limb on the tree and descend to the bottom of the well down a growing ladder. Many of these pockets are potholes, being found in the courses of little rills or brooks that run during the rains which occasionally fall in the region.*

Just north of Tapestry Wall, just across the main channel from the mouth of Cedar Canyon, and near buoy marked M110(K176), is a short narrow bay with high vertical Navajo Sandstone walls throughout its entire length. This is **Warm Springs Creek Inlet.** At the very end of the inlet it dead-ends in high falls, and there's not one campsite—at least when the lake is at or near the HWM. The name Warm Springs was given to it by early-day prospectors, although there were never any warm springs in the canyon. There was however, a small year-round stream flowing out the bottom end before the coming of Lake Powell, and was a regular waterhole stop for river runners.

Just across the river from the mouth of Warm Springs Creek and down the Colorado River about 2 kms, was another historic site called **Olympia Bar.** It was an important placer mining site dating back to as early as the 1890's. When Crampton was there in the early 1960's, studying the historic sites of Glen Canyon, he noticed extensive placer mining operations had occurred. At several locations there was a terrace about 60 meters above the level of the river, where gravel beds had been dug out and taken down to river levels by means of chutes.

At one point, a water wheel had been placed in the river to lift water to a flume, which carried it to a nearby gravel bar. The geologist Charles B. Hunt was there in 1953, and reported this wheel was the

Looking southeast from the top of Tapestry Wall.

102

one originally located at Good Hope Bar, further up stream. It was moved to Olympia Bar in 1910, and was called the Bennett Wheel, according to Frank Bennett(this Frank Bennett is the same fellow who in 1920-21, drilled for oil at Oil Seep Bar, down river across from The Rincon). At various places on the bar were found ore cars, old wooden tracks, scrapers, screens, wooden wheel barrows, and remains of the old camp.

From the top of Tapestry Wall one has fine views of the lake 226 meters below.

The mouth of Cedar Canyon seen from the top of Tapestry Wall.

103

Side canyon of Smith Fork.

The narrows of Smith Fork, one of the best slot canyons around.

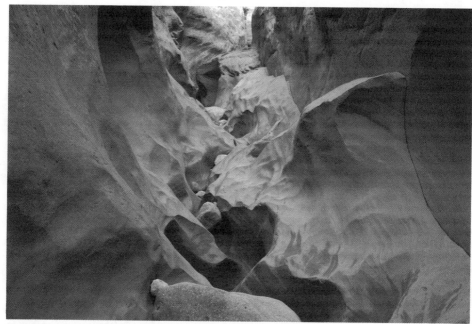

Typical scene in the upper end of Smith Fork Canyon.

Fresh sign of beaver population in the North Fork of Forgotten Canyon.

Knowles, Forgotten, Hansen & Crystal Springs Canyons

Location and Campsites The mouths of Forgotten and Knowles Canyons are located about 20 kms northeast, or up-lake, from the mouth of Bullfrog Bay. Near the mouth of Forgotten Inlet, is a buoy marked M106(K170), while near Knowles another buoy reads M107A(K171).

Each inlet is long and narrow, with small campsites in the upper ends of each. That's where the Kayenta Formation is exposed forming ledges just below the Navajo Sandstone walls. Right where the small streams of each canyon enters the lake, will be at least one sandy campsite. Hansen Creek Inlet has many good campsites, while there's but one very good site in Crystal Springs Canyon Inlet.

Routes or Trails There are hiker-made trails running up **Forgotten Canyon,** but half way up these tend to disappear and the upper part is more pristine. There is a year-round stream which is lined with willows, cottonwoods and gamble oak. At the end of the canyon you'll find a high dry fall or dropoff. Under it is a spring and sometimes a pool of water. The benches you'll be walking on are made of the Kayenta Formation, while the walls above are all Navajo Sandstone.

The North Fork of Forgotten is similar to the main canyon, with a stream from end to end, and big falls at the head of the canyon. The author found fresh sign of beaver in both forks, and a small beaver dam in the North Fork.

Both forks of Forgotten are box canyons with no exits. In the upper part of the inlet in the main fork, look to the left or north side, and into south-facing alcoves. Located there are two sets of Anasazi ruins. The first you'll see are called Crumbling Kiva Ruins, the next is known as Defiance House. This one gets it's name from a pictograph on the wall, which shows three warriors with shields and clubs of some kind. The Defiance House Ruins have been restored by the NPS. They are discussed below.

Knowles Canyon is very similar to Forgotten, but has a slightly wider inlet. The canyon has running water throughout most of it's lower course, and water in a few places higher up; therefore it has trees and some brush. The hike isn't considered a bushwhack however.

In the lower parts you'll find some hiker-made trails, but higher up are cattle trails. This canyon has at least one entry trail at the top end, so there are cattle around from October to June each year, and deer year-round. As you near the upper end of the canyon, you'll have a couple of falls and pourover pools to pass. Look to the right, or south side of each, for cattle trails by-passing the obstructions. These two pourovers are less than a km apart.

As you pass the upper falls on the south side, continue veering to the right, until you're heading back in a southwest direction. Look for stone cairns and obvious routes up through the last series of ledges. As you near the top, evidence of a constructed cattle trail will be seen in places. This trail

Floating sign at the mouth of Forgotten Canyon.

MAP 11, KNOWLES, FORGOTTEN AND CRYSTAL SPRINGS CANYONS

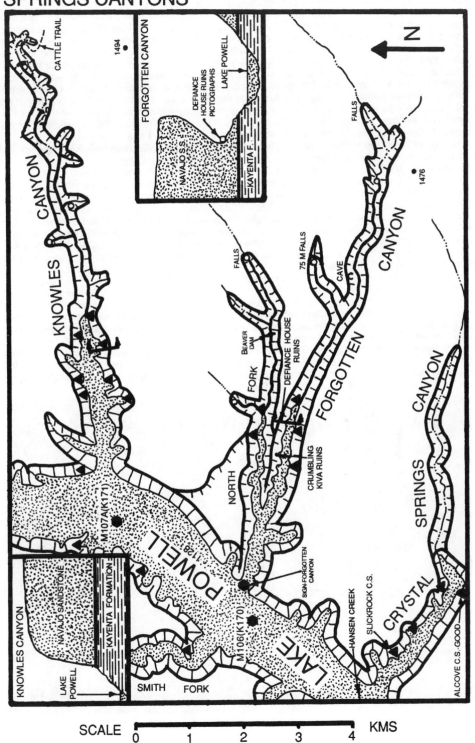

SCALE 0 1 2 3 4 KMS

was surely built by a pair of brothers named Knowles. It's not certain when they were in this part of the country, but according to John Redd of Monticello it was in the 1890's.

Hike Length and Time Needed From the HWM to the head of the main fork of Forgotten is 7 or 8 kms, and will take at least half a day for a round-trip hike. The North Fork of Forgotten is shorter, around 5 kms to the headwall. The author did this one in 2 hrs. 40 min., while his hike in the main fork lasted about 3 hours. It's about 7 kms to the cattle trail in Knowles Canyon, and this one took the author just over 3 hours to complete. Most people would want 4 or 5 hours for this round-trip hike.

Boots or Shoes There is running water in both canyons, so it's best to use a wading type shoe.

Water The small streams in both forks of Forgotten Canyon are clear and should be good to drink much of the time, but there's likely to be beaver in the lower ends of each. Best to drink water at the spring source if possible. In Knowles the water is more suspect, because of the cattle. Normally, cattle are permitted in these canyons from October 1 until mid-June--then they're removed for the summer. Only drink directly from, or very near, unpolluted springs in Knowles Canyon.

Main Attractions Moderately narrow canyons, high falls, one historic cattle trail, many springs and small streams(good tasting water), and the Anasazi ruins in Forgotten Canyon.

Hiking Maps USGS or BLM map Hite Crossing(1:100,000), or Mt. Ellsworth(1:62,500).

Anasazi Ruins and History Studies made in the Glen Canyon area in the late 1950's and early 1960's by the University of Utah and University of Northern Arizona Archaeology Departments, included the ruins in Forgotten Canyon. Their studies indicate both of these habitation sites were occupied for short periods of time. They surmise this because the trash heaps were very small. This would indicated they were camps associated with seasonal agriculture, or possibly were short-lived attempts to settle and establish year-round homes. The length of habitation at Crumbling Kiva site was estimated to be from about 1225 to 1250 AD; while the Defiance House structures were occupied from 1250 to 1285 AD, or thereabouts.

Pottery remains from Crumbing Kiva, which was closer to the Colorado River, indicated it was used mostly by people who came up the river and are considered to be attached to the Kayenta Anasazi group. The Defiance House homes, it is theorized, were built by a group of people believed to have come from the east, and from over the high mesa country around the Abajo Mountains. These peoples have been classed as the Mesa Verde Anasazi(but keep in mind, this is a box canyon and all who entered it must have come via the river?!).

Crumbling Kiva has not been restored and is in poor condition. Please don't help the aging process. The Defiance House site has been stablized and there's a short trail from the water to the occupied ledge. This may be the most visited archaeology site on the lake. It's been restored to what the NPS believes is close to the original condition.

These are pictographs for which Defiance House Ruins are named.

Just off the map to the west, and across the channel from the mouth of Crystal Springs Canyon is **Hansen Creek Inlet.** Near each of these two canyons is a buoy marked M104(K166). Hansen Creek today is an inlet with low canyon walls or no walls at all. For the most part the rocks exposed at the shore line are from the Carmel Formation; that's the reason for the low bench around the HWM, or in some cases no bench at all. On the northeast shore line, the Carmel Formation is often exposed, while some of the bluffs on the southwest shore line are made of the Entrada Sandstone. Because of all the sands in the area, there are numerous beaches and good campsites, many of which offer good views of the Henry Mountains to the north.

Hansen Creek was an important canyon to the miners during the Glen Canyon Gold Rush, which lasted from about 1884 until 1900. This canyon offered an easy route to the Colorado from the Henry Mountains. A wagon road was opened as early as 1888. Hansen Creek was the only easy and usable route into Glen Canyon between Hite and Halls Crossing on the west side of the river. It served three important mining locations along the river; California, Smith and Moqui Bars.

Across the river and upstream about 2 kms from the mouth of Hansen Creek, was the **California Bar**(just below the mouth of Forgotten Canyon), another important placer mining site in Glen Canyon. It was first mined in 1888 by miners Hawthorn, Brown, Keeler and Haskell. Sometime later, Bert Loper and Louis Chaffin worked it over. Supplies for the mining operation were brought down Hansen Creek, then usually ferried across to the bar. Chaffin, who was interviewed by Crampton, stated that on one occasion when the river was low, he was able to drive a team of horses and a wagon across. Robert B. Stanton, who was staking claims there in 1899, stated that $30,000 had been taken from the bar up to that point. This bar saw intermittent activity until the mid-1940's.

Most of the gold bearing gravels at California Bar were on a low terrace. The gravel was loaded into ore cars, taken to the edge of the terrace and dumped down a chute. About 300 meters upstream from this area was a large steam boiler and a second placer mining site. In the early 1960's, there were scattered remains of the old mining days which included ore cars, tracks, a chute, an old cook stove, and the walls of a two room rock house. Also on the bar, a grave was found marked; *A. B. Tuner[Turner], died April 23, 1923, age 69.*

Just above, and just below the mouth of Hansen Creek, was a large sandy embankment. In the days before Lake Powell, it was known as **Smith Bar.** It's believed it was first prospected by a pair of Smith brothers, but the first dated claim was located by N. and Theodore Hansen and others in 1888. In 1961, researchers reported all that was left of the mining era were the remains of a small water reservoir, the ruins of three stone cabins, plus other miscellaneous camp litter. Right at the end of the road coming down Hansen Creek, was an abandoned steam boiler.

At the upper end of Forgotten Canyon is this big dry fall. A spring seeps out at the bottom.

Across the channel from Hansen Creek is **Crystal Springs Canyon Inlet.** Today this is a moderately short inlet, with vertical Navajo Sandstone walls rising from the waters edge. There are several alcoves, one of which has a small but very nice sandy campsite. Off at one end is *toilet paper alley.* Why not take along and use a shovel to bury it in such places? The end of the inlet is nearby, and one would have to swim up a very narrow channel to have any chance of getting into the canyon's

Part of Defiance House Ruins, one of the most visited Anasazi Sites on Lake Powell.

The stock trail built by Knowles brothers sometime near the end of the 19th century.

upper basin. The author believes this is a dim possibility.

Just down stream from the mouths of Crystal Springs Canyon and Hansen Creek is another mining site called **Moqui Bar.** Access to this gravel and sand bar was via both Hansen Creek Canyon, and an old trail which came off the low benches to the west.

Another scene in upper Forgotten Canyon. This is where one of the springs begins to flow.

One of the nicest campsites anywhere is this one at the head of Crystal Springs Canyon Inlet.

North Gulch, Moqui & Stanton Canyons, and Bullfrog Bay

Location and Campsites The opening of the inlet to Moqui Canyon and it's north fork called North Gulch, is just around the corner from Bullfrog Bay and Halls Crossing Marina. Buoy number M99(K158) sits near the mouth of the bay.

Moqui Canyon Inlet is long, narrow and rather entrenched. It's one of the more popular canyons around; partly because it's close to two marinas, and partly because of its beauty, its Anasazi ruins, and its good sandy campsites in the upper end of the inlet. The best campsite in the canyon is in the area of the sandslide right across the inlet from the first ruins you pass. There are several small campsites in North Gulch as well.

Routes or Trails Most of the time, the upper end of **Moqui Canyon** Inlet will not extend past the first ruins and sandslide. So one fun hike is to walk to the top of the sandslide right near the better campsites, then use a hiker-made **ledge trail** to reach the canyon rim. It's an easy hike with good views from the top. This trail could be hiker-made, but it also could have had it's beginnings with Indians or the early-day cattlemen who roamed the area before the turn of the century.

To get up stream, walk on the north side of the stream to the Kayenta ledges, and locate a hikers trail heading east, up canyon. The lower end of the canyon is well traveled, as there are some good ruins about a km east of the sandslide on the north side of the creek. This is as far as most hikers go, with few going further up canyon.

Moqui has a year-round stream throughout the canyon, so it has lots of trees and willows. In some places you have to route-find up through the vegetation; but it's easy going if you walk right in the middle of the sandy stream bed, which is normally less than 5 cms deep.

About 3 kms above the main ruins, you'll be in an area with several springs issuing from the south side of the canyon wall, and one small Anasazi site on a ledge just above the stream(north side). The author saw no more ruins above that. Another 3 kms above the third ruin, a second sandslide appears on the south wall(it's the weathering of the Navajo Sandstone and the prevailing south winds which have created at least four sandslides which make entry/exits points to the canyon). You can easily walk up this slide to the rim. The author did just that, then made his way to Camp Canyon to the east, where he descended a third sandslide, and found running water and two easily passable waterfalls in the Wingate Sandstone. Moqui Canyon goes on for many kms, but scenery seems less interesting to the east. In the early days of San Juan County, this main canyon was known to cowboys as *North Gulch*.

North Gulch is another seemingly endless canyon with a year-round flowing stream. The author didn't hike far up this creek, but he did find fresh sign of beaver, a beaver pond, some bushwhacking, and several good springs. Big game guide Carl Mahon of Monticello, Utah, stated that

A granary and part of the ruins found in Moqui Canyon.

MAP 12, MOQUI CANYON & NORTH GULCH

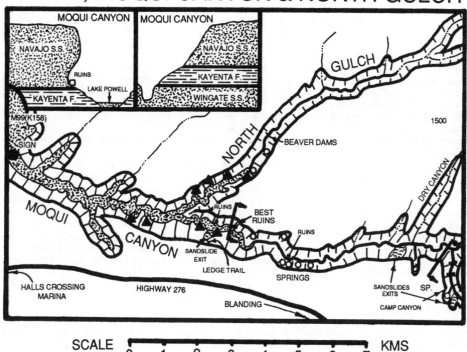

MOQUI CANYON

NAVAJO S.S.

RUINS

LAKE POWELL

KAYENTA F.

MOQUI CANYON

NAVAJO S.S.

KAYENTA F.

WINGATE S.S.

M99(K158)

SIGN

MOQUI

CANYON

NORTH

GULCH

BEAVER DAMS

1500

DRY CANYON

RUINS

BEST RUINS

RUINS

SANDSLIDE EXIT

LEDGE TRAIL

SPRINGS

SANDSLIDES EXITS

SP.

CAMP CANYON

HALLS CROSSING MARINA

HIGHWAY 276

BLANDING

SCALE   0 1 2 3 4 5 6 7   KMS

Looking north at the upper inlet and the first sandslide in Moqui Canyon.

you can walk out of the upper end of North Gulch, which used to be a regular cattle route in the early days of the cattle industry of San Juan County.

Hike Length and Time Needed When the lake level is at or near the HWM you can visit the best ruins in a few minutes. You can climb the first sandslide and reach the canyon rim in less than half an hour. To hike up to Camp Canyon and back, similar to what the author did, will take you all day,so it's best to take a lunch. The author did it in 5 hrs. 11 min., round-trip. Maps indicate one can walk for many kms up North Gulch. This leaves room for exploration.

Boots or Shoes Both canyons have streams so use wading type shoes.

Water There are cattle in the main Moqui Canyon, so don't touch the stream water. There seems to be no cattle in North Gulch, but many sign of beaver are evident. Drinking directly from un-muddied springs should be safe in either canyon.

Main Attractions A deep and narrow inlet, a well watered and green desert valley, a couple of good campsites, and Anasazi ruins.

Hiking Maps USGS or BLM map Navajo Mtn.(1:100,000), or Lake Canyon and Mt. Ellsworth(1:62,500).

Anasazi Ruins, Bullfrog Bay and Stanton Canyon During the pre-Lake Powell archaeological studies in Moqui Canyon, 100 sites were found. Many are now below the lake, and those up canyon are less visible than the commonly seen cliff dwellings.

Seven to eight hundred years ago, there were many inhabitants in Moqui Canyon. That's because of a sizable and year-round flowing stream, a broad alluvial-filled canyon bottom, many overhanging alcoves, and a number of natural entry/exits to the canyon(three sandslides in this local area, and a fourth higher up canyon).This place must have looked pretty good to an agricultural people.

Studies on cliff dwellings now under water, indicated Moqui Canyon was inhabited from about 1125 to 1275 AD. In examining the potsherds in those sites, it was found that about half of the cultural affiliation came from the Kayenta Anasazi; about half from the Mesa Verde. Those sites in the upper canyon indicated a strong tendency to have been influenced by the Mesa Verde people to the east and the Abajo Mountains, as opposed to Kayenta people who likely migrated up the Colorado River Gorge.

As you hike up canyon, notice the soil or alluvial benches just back from the stream, but below the Navajo walls or the Kayenta benches. This erosion or down cutting of the soil deposits, has taken place all over the Colorado Plateau, and the primary reason for it is believed to be overgrazing by the whiteman's cattle herds. Lake Canyon is another good example of this recent down cutting, and the reason for it is obviously overgrazing. The author believes a similar pattern of down cutting may have occurred with a dense population of Anasazi, thus the eventual evacuation. If indeed that occurred,

Another sandslide in the upper part of Moqui Canyon. This is called Camp Canyon.

then these canyons refilled themselves with sand and soil up to the time of the cattle boom just before and after the turn of the 20th century.   Since then it's been in another cycle of down cutting, but it seems to be abating now, perhaps even beginning to restore itself.

Not far to the west of the mouth of Moqui Canyon is **Bullfrog Bay**, which is the location of Bullfrog Marina, the number one launching site for northern Utah boaters. Bullfrog Bay is one of the largest open bodies of water on Lake Powell. The southern part of the bay is merely a transit corridor for boats going up or down lake, and to Halls Crossing Marina just to the south of Bullfrog and on the east side of the lake.

The northern or upper part of the bay is very popular for people who enjoy water skiing and other water sports.   It also has many sandy beaches and excellent campsites with both boater and automobile access. See Map 13, of Halls Creek and the Waterpocket Fold Canyons, for a better look at campsites in Bullfrog Bay.

Before Lake Powell, there was a small or minor set of rapids at the mouth of Bullfrog Creek, one of the few in the entire length of Glen Canyon. The river dropped only about one meter in a km, so it was mostly just a ripple.   The Bullfrog drainage begins on the south slope of Mt. Hillers, and was originally called Pine Alcove Creek by the 1873 Wheeler Survey. The name Bullfrog probably came about during the gold rush days just before the turn of the century.

As far as history of Glen Canyon is concerned, not a lot happened in the area of Bullfrog Bay. However, there were several sand bars in the vicinity of the mouth of the creek which were fairly important in the gold rush days. There was the **Wilson Bar**, right at the mouth of Stanton Canyon. It served as a camp for the Hoskaninni Company, when they were operating their dredge(see below).

Another of the more important sites in the area, was **New Years Bar**. It was found directly across the river from the mouth of Stanton Canyon, and extending upstream.   Records show it was placer mined from 1888, and mining equipment littered the area in 1959. At the upper end of the bar was one of the few sites where agriculture was undertaken in Glen Canyon. Crampton reported that a Dan E. Miller had planted melons, peanuts, and other crops sometime before August, 1958. By the next year, it had been abandoned.   Left there was an old trailer house, a one-room log cabin, a chicken coop and corrals.

Perhaps the most important site in Glen Canyon, as far as mining history is concerned, was the **Hoskaninni Company** operations at **Camp Stone** and **Stanton Canyon.**   This area was up stream a couple of kms from the mouth of Bullfrog Creek and had to do with the Stanton Dredge.

Robert Brewster Stanton was an engineer, educated at the University of Miami, in Ohio. One of his first jobs was in Colorado, working on a railway line to Leadville. Surveying potential railroad grades became his specialty. He once met a Frank M. Brown, who in 1889 founded the Colorado

A typical alcove and spring found in North Gulch of Moqui Canyon.

115

Canyon and Pacific Railroad Company, for the purpose of constructing a watergrade railroad from Grand Junction, Colorado, to the seaboard, through the canyons of the Colorado River, connecting the coal fields of the Rocky Mountains with southern California.

Brown hired Stanton to help assess the potential route. During 1889-90, they went down Glen Canyon surveying a route for the railway. However, while boating the Colorado just below Lee's Ferry, Brown and two others were drowned in the upper part of Marble Canyon. That pretty well ended the big plans for a railway through the Grand Canyon. But Stanton remembered the gold mining in Glen Canyon.

After a few years, Stanton and several interested business men, went back to Hite and Glen Canyon, and made some tests of the gold diggings. They thought they had something, so on March 28, 1898, the Hoskaninni Company was founded, with Julius F. Stone as president, and Mills, Brooks, Morton and Ramsey as co-owners and investors. Robert B. Stanton was brought into the firm as a vice president, engineer and as superintendent.

In the year 1898, a crew made the trip from North Wash to Lee's Ferry, and re-staked all old claims. In all, the company had 145 continuous claims from about 3 kms above Hite to Lee's Ferry, a distance of 265 kms.

Early in 1900, a contract was let out to the Bucyrus-Erie Company of Milwaukee, to build a gold dredge. Later in the spring it was shipped by rail to Green River, Utah. Moving the dredge the 160 kms to the river required the building of a road from the areas between Granite and Trachyte Ranches, just east of the Henry Mountains, up Benson Creek to South or Stanton Pass between Mt. Hillers and Pennell, and down Hansen Creek, passing Stanton's Coal Mine on the way. From the lower part of Hansen Creek, the route went south over the low divide and down Stanton Canyon to the river. It took about 25 men and several wagons, with 4 to 8 horses each, and 75 to 100 horses total, to haul the dredge from Green River. It took 8 days.

For some reason, Stanton ordered the dredge to be assembled not at the mouth of Stanton Canyon, where a dugway was built out of solid rock, but at a site about 1 1/2 kms up-river. This site was called Camp Stone, and was a couple of kms downstream from the mouth of Moqui Canyon. The dredge was built on a barge measuring about 12 x 25 meters. The construction started in June of 1900, and took about 7 months to complete(January, 1901). The dredge worked for about 6 months and quit; a total failure. It failed because the equipment was unable to separate the fine gold dust from the sand and gravel. Estimates on the total cost to the company ranged between $100,000 and $350,000.

Sometime later, the dredge was moved down stream to the mouth of Stanton Canyon, where it gradually sank in the river. For many years it was a regular stopping place for river runners on the

Evidence of an active beaver population in North Gulch of Moqui Canyon.

Colorado. It now sits below about 100 meters of water.

Crampton reports in his Anthropological Paper, #61, that in 1902 or 1903, one A. L. Chaffin operated a trading post at the site of the gold dredge, and directly across from New Year Bar. At that time it was a frequent stop for Navajos.

Wagons taking parts of the Stanton Dredge down into Stanton Canyon(Stanton foto, 1900).

The completed Stanton Dredge(Stanton foto, 1900).

Halls Creek & Waterpocket Fold Hikes and Lost Eden Canyon & Halls Creek Bay

Location and Campsites Halls Creek is the very long intermittent stream running along side the Waterpocket Fold. It begins in the north in Capitol Reef National Park and flows south to Halls Creek Bay. This large bay is immediately next to, and southwest of Bullfrog Bay. It's a quick ride to the mouth of Halls Creek, or the face of the Waterpocket Fold, from the marinas at Bullfrog or Halls Crossing.

Halls Creek Bay is one of the best places on the lake for camping and water skiing. There are many sandy beaches and good campsites, some of which are on small islands made of the Entrada Sandstone. Most campsites are on the south or southwest side of the bay, where it makes contact with the Waterpocket Fold.

Routes or Trails The walk up **Halls Creek** to the narrows and Hall Divide is one of the longer hikes in this book. But it's also one of the best, because it has one of the most spectacular narrow canyons on the Colorado Plateau.

To begin, start walking northward on the southwest side of Halls Creek. It probably isn't visible, but there is an old road running north along the western side of the creek. This is the original road built and used by Charles T. Hall during his years at the ferry crossing on the Colorado River. More on Hall below.

This old road is all but invisible until you get further up stream and near Hall Divide, then it's easy to find and follow. The road follows the creek, until the stream takes a strange twisting course to the west. The road itself crosses over a kind of natural divide, avoiding about 4 kms of canyon narrows. A few million years ago, the stream was already entrenched, when the final uplift came to this part of the Waterpocket Fold. That's the reason the stream runs off to the west as it does, rather than cutting across the natural low point of the divide.

Once you reach this area, it's likely best to walk the road to the north side of the narrows first, then walk down stream through the slot. This will also give you a chance to walk to the rim of the narrows and see down into a most impressive gorge. The road you see there now was probably last used about the time the lake began to fill in the early 1960's.

Going down the narrows, you'll find at one point a dry fall about 100 meters high, coming off the wall to the right, or west--one of the highest the author has seen. There's also one place where the water was waist deep for the author, but the depth of that hole will vary with the season, and the length of time since the last flood. There are also several springs in this part, which seep out at the contact point between the Navajo and Kayenta Formations.

Telefoto lens view of the face of Waterpocket Fold. The rock exposed is the Navajo Sandstone.

MAP13, HALLS CK. & WATERPOCKET FOLD HIKES AND HALLS CK.& BULLFROG BAYS, & LOST EDEN CANYON

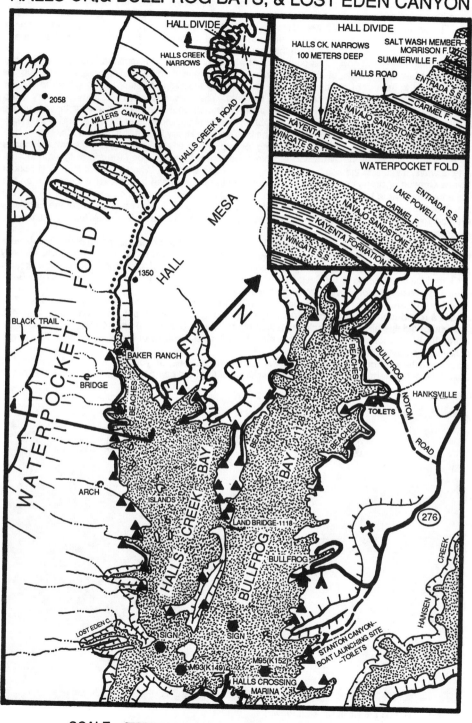

As you walk along Halls Creek, the **Waterpocket Fold** is best seen on the west, but you're actually in the center of the fold(see the geology cross section). To the west are seen many short and narrow canyons coming off this monocline. The top most rock exposed is the Navajo Sandstone, and when it's subjected to erosion, it creates many potholes or waterpockets; thus the name of the fold.

The largest canyon is **Millers Creek.** It's very deep and narrow at the mouth, and it has a year-round flowing stream with small minnows. Up and to the west, it opens up and Kayenta and Wingate rocks are exposed underneath the Navajo.

Heading southeast now. Just southwest of where the old Baker Ranch was situated, and at the head of the bay during times of high lake levels, is a canyon with an interesting bridge. To get up this one, it's best to get out of the canyon itself, and walk up the slickrock face. This would be true for hiking any of the short little slot canyons on the Fold. The reason is, each slot canyon is very steep and narrow with one big pothole, pourover pool, or dry fall after another. It's easier to walk up the slickrock face in most places. Just pick a spot anywhere along the face of the Fold, and start hiking. From on top, you'll have some fine views of the lake and the Henry Mountains to the north.

Another thing to look for is the beginning, or end, of the **Black Trail.** This old stock trail heads up the slickrock face of the Waterpocket Fold, then runs southeast along the top of this monocline. After a ways, it veers to the south, and to the west of Long Canyon. When it reaches the East Fork of Bowns Canyon, it drops down in and runs nearly to the mouth, then heads over a low divide on the Kayenta Bench, and follows this same bench southeast in Glen Canyon, then west, and north into the mouth of the Escalante River Arm. Part of it is submerged today. It then ran west out of the Escalante Canyon just north of the mouth of Clear Creek, and connected to the Hole-in-the-Rock Road, then to the town of Escalante.

The reason it got the name Black Trail, is that in a small alcove near the mouth of the Escalante is written in charcoal, "J W Black, Feb. 2, 1896". It probably was put there by a John Black, an early pioneer of the town of Boulder. Along the way other trails headed off to the east, such as the Schock Trail, and the one running to Oil Seep Bar, just north of The Rincon. If there is any sign of it near Baker Ranch, it'll be some stone cairns up along the slickrock.

Hike Length and Time Needed From the HWM to the top of Hall Divide is about 14-15 kms. This means a round-trip hike will be over 30 kms!; a rather long all day walk, but the going is easy and fast. The author did this hike, which included a side trip up Millers Creek, in 9 hrs. 10 min. A hike up to the top of the Waterpocket Fold directly from the lake, will take a couple of hours, round-trip. Any length of hike can be taken on the Fold.

Boots or Shoes For the Halls Creek hike, take wading shoes, as you'll likely be wading almost all the 4 kms of the narrows. Walking up the slickrock of the Fold can be done with any kind of boots or

Looking down into the Halls Creek narrows.

shoes.

Water Halls Creek has running water much of the time, but does dry up in June, the driest month of the year in Utah. But don't drink the water. After rains, there will be hundreds of potholes full of good water on the Fold. At the same time, there will be little seeps and some sweet running water coming out the bottom of each slot canyon for a few days, or a week or two, after a good rainstorm.

Main Attractions Great slickrock hiking, and one of the deepest, narrowest and most impressive gorges on the Colorado Plateau. Also, interesting geology in the Waterpocket Fold.

Hiking Maps USGS or BLM map Hite Crossing(1:100,000), or Hall Mesa(1:62,500).

Halls Crossing, Baker Ranch, and other History The history of Halls Crossing begins further down stream at Hole-in-the-Rock. A man by the name of Charles T. Hall was a carpenter living in Escalante, Utah, when the San Juan Party made its epic journey from southwestern Utah, through the Hole-in-the-Rock in 1879-80. They made their way to, and settled Bluff, Utah, located on the San Juan River.

Hall was called upon by Mormon Church authorities to assist the party by building a boat to ferry wagons across the Colorado. He then stayed on the Colorado operating the ferry through 1880, but the route to the river was so incredibly difficult, almost no one gave him business. Later, Hall got word of a better route further upstream. He scouted the region, and moved the ferry up river to what would be known as **Halls Crossing** and **Halls Ferry.**

The approaches to Halls Crossing were much easier than to the Hole-in-the-Rock crossing. From Escalante, the route went down Harris Wash to the Escalante River, up Silver Falls Creek to the Circle Cliffs, then descended Muley Twist Canyon to Halls Creek, thence to the river. On the east side, the route ascended the sand flats and slickrock slopes in the area between Moqui and Lake Canyons, then joined the Hole-in-the-Rock Trail to the east, which led to Bluff.

The ferry is said to have been built with materials from Escalante, some 80 kms away. It consisted of two pine logs with planks spanning the logs. It measured about 3 x 10 meters. Hall operated the ferry from 1881 to 1884. The reason he closed the ferry was the completion of the railroad through eastern Utah in 1883, which eased transportation problems on both sides of the Colorado.

The best sources of information for the historic **Baker Ranch,** now lying below the waters of Lake Powell, comes from a number of papers and studies done by many people and various universities. Some of the research of the recent human history part of Glen Canyon was done by C. Gregory Crampton, and is documented in the *Anthropological Papers of the University of Utah.* These studies were done because of the building of Lake Powell. They of course concentrated their efforts on that part of the land which is below the high water mark of Lake Powell, or 1128 meters elevation.

Halls Creek and the beginning of the Halls Creek narrows.

Much of what is known of the Baker Ranch comes from Crampton's *Anthropological Paper #61.*

Within the Lake Powell Reservoir area there were a few areas put under cultivation in historic times. Baker Ranch on the right side of Halls Creek, 6 miles[10 kms] from Halls Crossing of the Colorado, was one of the largest of these. At one time approximately 100 acres[40 hectares] of pasture, alfalfa and corn were irrigated from waters diverted from the creek--this was before 1936 when Eugene Baker, after whom the place is named, patented 800 acres[about 320 hectares] of land in the vicinity.

The first(white) settler on lower Halls Creek, is believed to have been Charles Hall who maintained a small farm 2 miles[3 kms] above Baker Ranch while operating the ferry at Halls Crossing, 1881-1884. Thomas William Smith(living in Green River, Utah, in 1962 and son of Thomas Smith who made the original location at Baker Ranch), stated that he remembers the old Hall place, which consisted of a log cabin 15 x 15 feet[5 by 5 meters]. He said that Charles Hall would climb over the slickrock slopes of the Waterpocket Fold to a point about 500 feet[150 meters] above the creek bed where he could see the ferry crossing 8 miles[13 kms] away. Smith thought there may have been some way for parties on the opposite side who wished to cross the river, to signal the ferryman. The site of Halls Ranch, which was referred to by name as late as 1922(by other writers), has not been located by this author[Crampton].

Crampton continues, *The second settler in lower Halls Creek, is believed to have been Thomas Smith who located the Baker Ranch site around 1900.* According to Barbara Ekker of Hanksville, it was in 1907, the Thomas Smith family moved there. Smith was a polygamist, with two wives, Eliza and Sarah. In August 1907, all three filed claims on 800 acres[320 hectares] of land on lower Halls Creek, under the Desert Land Act of 1877. This must have been just the place Smith and his wives were looking for; a quiet and isolated placed to live, and away from the law which frowned on a man having two wives.

In the course of time, Smith and family constructed several buildings including two log cabins and one stone structure. After several years of hardship, this property was transferred to Eugene Baker in about 1917. A public land survey of the vicinity was made in 1923. The survey notes reflect the improvements on the ranch, which then consisted of about 3 miles[5 kms] of fencing, one three-room frame house, a one-room log cabin, a one-room rock store-house and a large corral and stockyard. Twenty acres[8 hectares] of land, including fruit trees and alfalfa, were under cultivation at the time.

Crampton visited with a number of people and got first hand accounts from several individuals. One was *Carlyle Baker, son of Eugene Baker, living at Teasdale, Utah, in 1960,* who stated that he spent a number of his younger years at the ranch. During the spring of the year, when storms broke

Part of the narrows of Halls Creek, one of the most spectacular gorges around.

over the Waterpocket Fold, enough water came down Halls Creek before June to irrigate up to 100 acres[40 hectares] of land on both sides of the stream. However, farming was only an adjunct to grazing and the uncertainties of the water supply, the hot climate of the summer months, and the sandy soil led to its abandonment by about 1940. The Bakers later sold the property to other interests who still use the ranch as a grazing headquarters(1962).

The Baker Ranch is now under the waters of Lake Powell, it being one of the last historic sites to be covered. If in the next few years, the lake waters recede only a few meters, it might be possible to see parts of this lost landmark, if they aren't covered by too much silt and mud.

Near the mouth of Halls Creek and the crossing, were several sand bars which were important locations during the Glen Canyon Gold Rush days. On the west side of the Colorado were **Halls Bar,** just upstream, and **Burro Bar,** just down stream from the mouth of the creek. Across the river and down stream, was **Boston Bar.**

Boston Bar was the more important of the three. Operations at this site began in 1889, but it wasn't until 1899-1900 that there was significant work done. During this time period, the Boston Placer Mining Company, a corporation under the organization of Maine residents, A.J. Strouse and Charles Sherwin, invested fairly heavy sums of money into the operation. But of course the venture failed in the end, just like the Stanton Dredge. In place along the river in 1958-59, were pumps and gasoline motors, and older equipment such as a flume, sluice boxes, lumber, iron rails and odds and ends.

Not far from where you leave Halls Crossing Marina and just around the corner from the mouth of Halls Creek Bay, is the narrow and almost hidden inlet to **Lost Eden Canyon.** This inlet has three very narrow branches, the longest of which is about 1 1/2 kms. When the lake is at or near the HWM, there will be no campsites. However, you can get out of your boat in several places and walk along the Navajo slickrock. You could gain access to the southern end of the Waterpocket Fold from inside this inlet, but there are not that many places to tie up your boat.

The Baker Ranch before being covered by Lake Powell(Hamilton Parker foto).

Lake & Annies Canyons, The Schock & Gretchen Bar Trails and Lake Pagahrit

Location and Campsites Lake Canyon is the first major tributary on the east side of Lake Powell as you head south from Bullfrog or Halls Crossing Marinas. Buoy number M89(K142) is near and a buoy marked Lake Canyon, sits at the mouth of the inlet. Lake Canyon Inlet is rather long and narrow. The canyon walls are made of Navajo Sandstone and aren't too high.

Near the middle of the inlet there are several campsites, mainly on the north side. At the head of the inlet and near where Lake Creek enters, there's a very good sandy beach in front of a small alcove with several trees. Right at the upper end there should always be another sandy campsite, regardless of how high the lake water is.

The Schock Trail begins not far below the mouth of Lake Canyon and on the other side of the channel. The buoy nearest the mouth of Annies Canyon is marked M84(K134). Campsites in these parts are limited, because for the most part, the walls of the main channel and the side canyons come right down to the water. The walls are made of Navajo Sandstone. Just east of the beginning of the Schock Trail there are several small inlets in the gradual sloping Navajo. Depending on lake levels, these will make fine campsites. There are even several sandy places for tents.

In the upper end of the north fork of Annies, there's a big falls and alcove, which is another fine campsite. The author was stuck there once for nearly 24 hours because of a howling spring-time wind storm. In the middle fork of Annies, there's also a possible campsite where you can begin hiking.

Routes or Trails If you enjoy visiting Anasazi ruins, you'll enjoy the hike up **Lake Canyon.** It has as many, if not more ruins or archaeology sites, than any other canyon entering the lake. You'll boat past one set of ruins about a km below the HWM. Also, to the left, right at the HWM, and upon an alluvial bench, is another set of ruins. Climb up to this one from the west end of the bench. It's not much to look at.

As you walk up canyon, you'll be wading in the creek much of the time. There are livestock in the drainage from October to June, so there are many cattle trails in and along the stream as well. Use these trails when you can, but in some places you'll have to wade in the stream.

About 2 kms above the HWM, and just as the creek bed is making a couple of gooseneck turns, you'll see high on the western wall, a rather well preserved set of ruins. It's very difficult to reach these now, as the alluvial base has been washed away. About one km above these wall ruins, look for an easy way out of the canyon to the east using cow trails; then walk south again. Nearby, and on the south side of a short shallow drainage is another Anasazi dwelling, this time out on top of the mesa, instead of under an overhang.

From the area of these ruins, you can either walk up stream along the creek bed; or stay on the

The wall ruins in Lake Canyon.

MAP 14, LAKE & ANNIES CANYONS, SCHOCK & GRETCHEN BAR TRAILS, AND LAKE PAGAHRIT

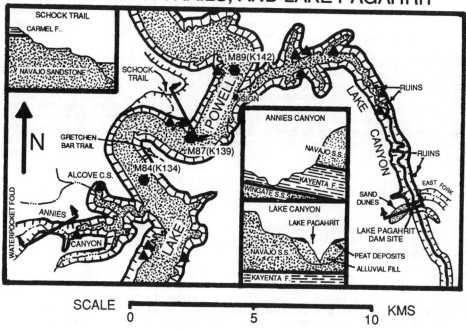

SCALE
0   5   10   KMS

canyon rim. If you stay on the rim, you can reach a high point after less than a km. From this vantage point you can see ahead to where an old lake once was. This was called **Lake Pagahrit**(sometimes called Hermit Lake). The remains of this lake bed is perhaps the most interesting feature in the canyon. More on this below. The author went no further than the old dam site, but there may be other interesting things to see where the upper end of the lake once was. Somewhere in the east fork, and on the mesa top, is a large Anasazi structure called The Fortress. About 1 1/2 or 2 kms up stream from the dam site, is where the Hole-in-the-Rock Trail crosses the drainage.

The **Schock Trail** is said to be an old cattle trail which began at the Baker Ranch(see Map 13), then headed upon the slickrock of the Waterpocket Fold, and finally descended 300 meters to the Colorado just below the mouth of Lake Canyon. However, because of it's steepness over slickrock, it was likely used almost exclusively by prospectors, rather than livestock. According to Crampton's studies on Glen Canyon prior to Lake Powell, the name of the trail is from one W.H. Schock, an old prospector who worked the river bars for 20 years after about 1898.

You'll have to look for the beginning of this trail. It's about 200 meters to the west of the largest of the tiny inlets which can be used for camping, and 700-800 meters west of buoy M87(K139). Park your boat and get out and walk. Look for some steps cut and blasted out in steeper places, and some stone cairns. It first zig zags up to the north, then once on an intermediate Navajo bench, it veers to the northwest. It tops out on the Carmel rim above, then disappears.

In **Annies Canyon**, the only place you can hike is up from the end of the middle fork inlet. At that point the canyon is widening because of the emergence of the Kayenta Formation. Climb the steep talus slope to the left of the creek bed, then head up canyon. As you climb, the canyon broadens, and after about 4 kms you'll reach the top of the Waterpocket Fold. Get to a high point for good views in all directions. The view down on the Navajo bluffs and domes is worth the easy walk.

One last trail which few people know of, is the **Gretchen Bar Trail**. It was built for one purpose according to Crampton's research, and that was to allow a 1930's model Caterpillar tractor down to the river. The Cat was used for mining at the Gretchen Bar(see more below).

This trail is located about one km southeast from the corner of the old river bend, or about 2 kms north of the mouth of Annies Canyon and on the east side of the lake. Look for a large stone cairn just above the HWM, and on a little slickrock ridge jutting out into the lake a few meters. On the south side of this very minor ridge, is an area which has been blasted out to form a narrow roadway. Walk up this and follow the half dozen or so cairns to the east. A bit further up, there's another minor ridge where some work was done. At the very top of a prominent bluff, which can be seen faintly from the lake, is one last cairn. This one has an old metal piece sticking up in the middle--some kind of a machine part. At that point, the route seems to vanish.

Hike Length and Time Needed It's about 6 kms from the HWM to the former dam of Lake Pagahrit. It isn't far and the traveling is mostly easy, but there are many things to see. That's why you'll need most of a day to make the round-trip. The author spent over 4 hours walking to the dam and back, but wishes now he'd spent more time there.

The walk from the water to the Carmel rim where the Schock Trail disappears, is less than 2 kms. Once you locate the trail, you can do the whole thing is about an hour. It's about 4 kms to the top of Annies Canyon, and this hike can be done in maybe 3 hours, round-trip, depending on side trips. The walk to the top of the Gretchen Bar Trail will take 15 minutes, round-trip.

Boots or Shoes For Lake Canyon use wading shoes, but for all the other hikes, any kind of boots or shoes will do.

Water There's a year-round flow in Lake Creek, but there are cattle in the area most of the year, so better not drink water from the creek. Some where above the old dam site are many springs. They should have good drinking water--at the spring source. There are no springs or streams on any of the other hikes, so take your own water.

Main Attractions Anasazi ruins and deposits of the old lake bed. Also, two old and historic miners trails cut into the slickrock, and a easy hike to the top of the Waterpocket Fold, for some fine views.

Hiking Maps USGS or BLM map Navajo Mountain(1:100,000), or Lake Canyon and The Rincon(1:62,500).

Anasazi Ruins and Lake Pagahrit The University of Utah archaeological report on Lake Canyon conducted in 1959, states there were 77 sites observed in or near Lake Canyon. Not all of these were the magnificent cliff dwellings so common in southern Utah canyons; some were mesa top homes and flint sites. There were also an unusually large number of food storage sites observed. Still other sites were from the Navajos or early day cattlemen. Many of the more interesting sites are now under water.

Fowler's survey in 1959, indicated that Lake Canyon was outside the usual settlement pattern as found in other drainages flowing into Glen Canyon. In other canyons, potsherds indicate either Mesa Verde or Kayenta Anasazi cultures exited. But in Lake, there appeared to have been an odd mixture

Just below the dam of the former Lake Pagahrit. The sand dune on the right is what created the lake in the first place.

of both of these cultures into one, leading researchers to believe this was one of the first canyons settled in the region. Anasazi settlements in Lake Canyon spanned about 200 years, from about 1100 to 1300 AD.

Late in the 19th and into the 20th century, there were Navajos in the region, as indicated by some circular pole structures, as well as parts of a buggy, a dutch oven, wire grills and water pipe. These artifacts were found in the area of **Lake Pagahrit.** Apparently the first time white men knew of the lake was in February of 1880, when the Hole-in-the-Rock Party passed that way on their journey to Bluff, on the San Juan River. It was such an inviting place, they camped there for several days to make repairs and rest.

Ever since the Mornons passed through the Pagahrit country, they had cattle grazing through out the years. From about 1880 until 1898, the cattle belonged to the Bluff Pool. Then the Mormons sold out to the Scorup Brothers, Al and Jim. They ran cattle in the region until about 1965. Al Scorup believed overgrazing in the drought years of the mid-1890's began to damage the range, then more grazing continued early in the 20th century. This led to the beginning of an erosional cycle, and the eventual breaching of the lake's dam. It was Jim S. Scorup who witnessed the event. After three days of heavy rains, and on November 1, 1915, the water first started making a cut in the natural dam of the lake and it drained rapidly. Before that day the lake was reported to be about 12 meters deep and nearly one km long. Read more on the cattle industry in the Introduction to this book.

This was the beginning of this latest stage of downcutting of the alluvial benches you see so prominently exposed in the canyon today. All the ruins in the canyon were built while the stream was at that higher level. On top of these benches you'll find dead trees, which last grew when the water table was higher. They would have died sometime after 1915.

Here's what you'll find at Lake Pagahrit today. The dam of the lake was actually created by a slowly moving sand dune. It gradually filled in the canyon and the lake slowly developed. It likely wasn't very deep; instead rather shallow and swampy. You can see on the high benches where the lake once was, deep beds of organic matter. This looks like dead peat, like what you find in Ireland. The canyon is now "V" shaped and the stream runs at bedrock. With time, and if the area is not overused or abused any more, the place should again develop into a lake. It's the authors view that similar abuse or overuse by the Anasazi, may have caused a similar event in their time; resulting in downcutting and the lowering of the watertable. This would have led to the loss of farmland and may have been a major cause for their departure from this canyon and others, around 1275 AD to 1300 AD.

Just below the mouth of Lake Canyon is what river runners used to call **Lake Canyon Rapids.** Actually, it wasn't really rapids, mostly just a fast ride over some ripples. The rapids or ripple, was created by debris washed down and out of Lake Canyon during flash floods. When Stanton passed

A close-up view of the old lake bed of Pagahrit. Looking south from about where the dam was.

through the area in January, 1898, the river was jammed up with ice, and they were lucky to have gotten their boats out without damage being done. The cause of the ice jam was the shallow quiet waters just above the rapids.

Just down stream from the bottom of the Schock Trail, was a place called **Anderson Bar.** Records show it was placer mined as early as 1889. In 1961, near the lower end of this gravel and sand embankment and about 50 meters from the river, was a dugout(log?) cabin consisting mainly of a fireplace chimney built of sandstone slabs and standing about 3 meters high. According to A. L. Chaffin and Crampton, this cabin was another built by W. H. Schock, who was known to have lived in the area in 1898 and again in 1908-09.

Before Lake Powell came to be, one of the more important placer gold mining areas in this region was located just across the river from the mouth of Annies Canyon. It had many names over the years, such as Schock Bar and Anderson Camp, but the best known name was **Gretchen Bar.** It saw considerable placer mining dating from 1889, when three men--Harris, Davis and Vance, located the Hope Placer Mine.

It must have been a pleasant camp. There was a cool spring, with some of the water being piped to a nearby stone cabin. The cabin was built by W. H. Schock, perhaps in the 1890's. Spring water also watered fig, apricot and pomegranate trees, as well as grapes. Crampton reported that when his party inspected the place in 1961, these plants and trees were still alive, and that they picked and ate delicious fruit from a fig tree.

There was all kinds of old mining equipment lying around atop this bar, which included sorting screens, a large boiler-dating from about the turn of the century, sluicing tables, several gasoline motors and pumps, and a 1930's model "Thirty", eight-cylinder Caterpillar tractor, still attached to a Fresno scraper. It had been driven from Blanding, Utah, about 160 kms away, via the old Mormon Hole-in-the-Rock Trail. It was brought in to the west of Lake Canyon, then carefully taken down the slickrock just north of the bar. Several places had to be prepared by blasting the slickrock with dynamite. This is now known as the Gretchen Bar Trail(see more on the trail above).

The normal way the miners got to this site was via Escalante or the Loa areas, down Halls Creek to Baker Ranch, then to the west and upon the Waterpocket Fold along the Black Trail. Finally, the Schock Trail veered to the east and dropped into Glen Canyon not far below the mouth of Lake Canyon. From there the route went down the west bank of the Colorado, and during times of low water, pack horses could make a ford of the river in front of Gretchen Bar.

Part of the old lake bed of Pagahrit, showing the dried up peat and silt deposits.

From the west side looking east at the dried up lake bed of Pagahrit.

Close-up view of the sediments of the former lake bed of Pagahrit.

A nice campsite under an alcove in the north fork of Annies Canyon.

Part of the Gretchen Bar Trail as it enters the lake.

Lake Pagahrit as it was sometime before November 1, 1915.

An ice jam at the mouth of Lake Canyon(Stanton foto, January, 1898).

Slickrock and Iceberg Canyons

Location and Campsites The two canyons on this map are located about half way between Halls Crossing and the mouth of the Escalante River. At the mouth of Slickrock is a buoy marked M81A(K130), and buoy M78(K125) is at the mouth of Iceberg.

Slickrock Canyon has several good sandy campsites at it's upper end. These sites are found on the emerging Kayenta benches. Iceberg Canyon also has a number of campsites, but given it's length, they are rather sparse. Iceberg's campsites tend to be rather small and are surrounded by water and vertical cliffs because the Navajo Sandstone walls come right down to the waters edge in most places. Iceberg Canyon is one of the longest and deepest on the lake. These Navajo walls really soar. Perhaps no other canyon has Navajo walls as high, as vertical, and as spectacular as these.

An interesting feature in Iceberg is the large rockfall and resultant dam across the middle part of the south fork. Huge boulders peeled off the eastern wall and created a dam. If the water level is at or very near the HWM, you can get your boat into the upper end of this inlet; otherwise you're locked out, and you can't walk far into this one. Both Slickrock and Iceberg have minor Anasazi ruins.

Routes or Trails Going up **Slickrock Canyon**, you'll find hiker-made trails, mostly on the north side of the stream. Most of the time the creek will have a small flow of water. The canyon is lined with willows, cottonwoods and gamble oak. There is evidence of beaver, but when the author visited the place, there were no new signs. There are small alcoves on both sides of the canyon, many of which have springs issuing from the bottom of the Navajo Sandstone and/or top of the Kayenta. At the end is a high fall, with a seep beginning at the bottom. This canyon shows no sign of being gutted by recent erosion, as one sees in Lake, Moqui, or other area canyons.

In **Iceberg Canyon,** you only have one rather short hike in the upper end of the main fork. This canyon bottom is littered with downed cottonwood trees, the result of past beaver populations. On the author's visit there were no fresh sign, so beaver apparently move from one canyon to another as food supplies dwindle.

There's a hiker-made trail heading up canyon, mostly on the north side of the year-round flowing stream. It ends at one of the highest falls seen anywhere. The spring water seems to flow out at the contact point between the Navajo and Kayenta Formations. The Navajo Sandstone seems to be at it's thickest in this canyon.

Hike Length and Time Needed You can only walk up Slickrock about 2 1/2 kms. It took the author only 1 hr. 30 min. for the round-trip hike. In Iceberg, you can walk less than 2 kms to the end of the box canyon. The author hurried on this one and did it in 1 hr. 5 min. You should plan on 2 hours for

The rockfall dam in a tributary of Iceberg Canyon(formerly called Wilson Canyon).

MAP 15, SLICKROCK AND ICEBERG CANYONS

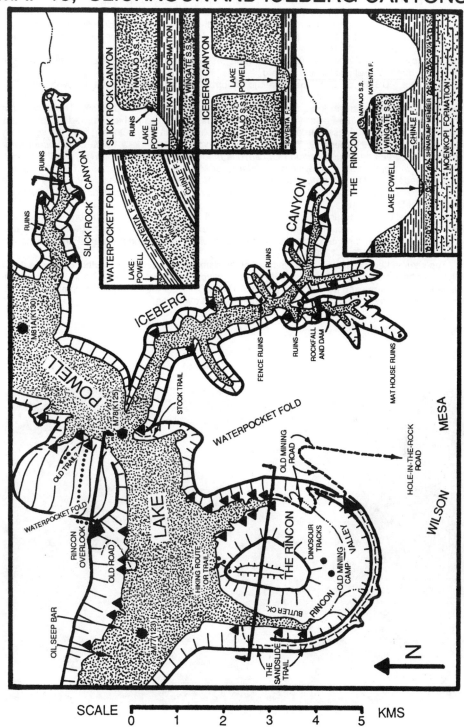

SCALE

0   1   2   3   4   5   KMS

each one. Both of these canyons are short and easy hikes, and worth the effort.

Boots or Shoes There are small streams in both drainages, but you can usually avoid getting wet feet, so any kind of boots or shoes are OK.

Water If you see fresh sign of beaver, better not drink the water unless it's directly from a spring. If there is no new evidence of beaver, then it will likely be drinkable in the upper parts of both canyons. In the future, expect to find more and more human pollution.

Main Attractions Very high Navajo Canyon walls, especially in Iceberg, several Anasazi ruins in each, and a huge rockfall and dam in Iceberg.

Hiking Maps USGS or BLM map Navajo Mountain(1:100,000), or Lake Canyon and The Rincon(1:62,500).

Anasazi Ruins There are at least two well preserved ruins in Slickrock Canyon. These two sites were excavated before Lake Powell time, and researchers found pottery which showed the inhabitants to be about half from the Mesa Verde group; half from the Kayenta clan. Quoting from the University of Utah Anthropological Paper #39, *Within the Glen Canyon Kayenta-Mesa Verde Group boundaries, Slick Rock occupies a unique position. Of canyons tributary to the Colorado River, it is the farthest downstream in which there is a significant evidence of Mesa Verde contact. As in Lake and Moqui Canyons, peoples of the two groups seem to have met and mingled peaceably, if pottery may be legitimately used as a criterion.* These sites were occupied sometime during the 1200's and abandoned before 1300 AD.

In Iceberg, there are parts of three ruins visible, all storage structures. The one called Fence Ruins is a small one, perhaps a granary. Fence was extensively studied because it was a major site. So the author believes the main part of that group of shelters is now under water. Fence Ruins was occupied from about 1250 to 1280 AD.

The site marked Mat House is at the head of the dammed off inlet, so the author didn't see it. It's likely to still be there and possible to see, if you can get your boat past the rockfall dam. Mat House is believed to have been used from about 1230 until 1250 AD.   Near the mouth of the dammed off inlet, there's a small storage structure tucked up underneath an overhang.

Typical scene of the soaring walls in Iceberg Canyon.

One of the better preserved Anasazi ruins on the lake is in Slickrock Canyon.

The inlet of Slickrock Canyon seen from an alcove cave near the canyon rim.

135

The Rincon & Rincon Overlook Hikes

Location and Campsites All these Rincon sites are between buoys marked M77(K123) and M78(K125) and not far northeast of the mouth of the Escalante River. The name rincon is sometimes used in place of *abandoned meander* or *abandoned stream channel*. These all mean the same thing. Rincon is used here to describe a giant abandoned meander of the Colorado River. It once flowed through this circular channel a few million years ago. It may have been forced into that direction or position by the uplift called the Waterpocket Fold.

This fold, sometimes called a monocline, begins far to the north around Thousand Lakes Mountain and the north end of Capitol Reef National Park. It generally ends in this area. As time went on, two parts of a gooseneck bend of the river closed in on each other, and finally a narrow wall was broken down, and the river rushed through into a new channel. This left The Rincon Valley high and dry as we see today. Rincons are common features on the Colorado Plateau, but this is the largest of them all.

On the eastern side of The Rincon you'll find many good campsites. These beaches are made of both the sand and clay from the Navajo and Wingate Sandstones, and the claybeds of the Chinle Formation. There are also several sites on the western arm of The Rincon, along what used to be called Butler Creek. Perhaps the single best site of all sits at the mouth of Iceberg Canyon. It's a big sandy beach, but open to lake-size waves when the wind blows in from the north.

Routes or Trails There are several good hikes in this area. Perhaps the most popular would be the hike around the central butte of **The Rincon**, and into the **Rincon Valley.** You can start on either side, but for this description, let's begin on the east side of The Rincon.

Right in the bottom of the dry creek bed you will see an old abandoned mining road. You can walk this for a ways, but when it turns east, you continue southwest on some cow trails. Lots of cows graze this area from October to June. Further on, and as you're heading west, take note of some of the large Wingate Sandstone boulders to your right. If the sun is right, you can see on the south side of one boulder, some kind of animal tracks, likely those of small dinosaurs. After another 200-300 meters, you'll come to some old abandoned barrels, buckets, etc. This must have been an old 1950's mining camp. The miners came to look for uranium in the Chinle claybeds.

On the west side of The Rincon is the canyon or drainage called Butler Creek. In this area is an old **stock trail** from the rim to the river. Local cowboys called this the **Sandslide.** It used to start, or end, just down stream from the mouth of Butler Creek on the Colorado. Then it must have gone up Butler Creek Canyon a ways, before angling up a sandslide to the west, to the top of the first major terrace, the Kayenta bench. From the top of the Kayenta, it headed south at the same elevation until it either breached the Navajo Sandstone at a point about 2 kms to the south; or cattle could have been

The eastern side of the Rincon Valley looking north. Notice the old mining road along the bottom.

MAP 16, THE RINCON & RINCON OVERLOOK HIKES

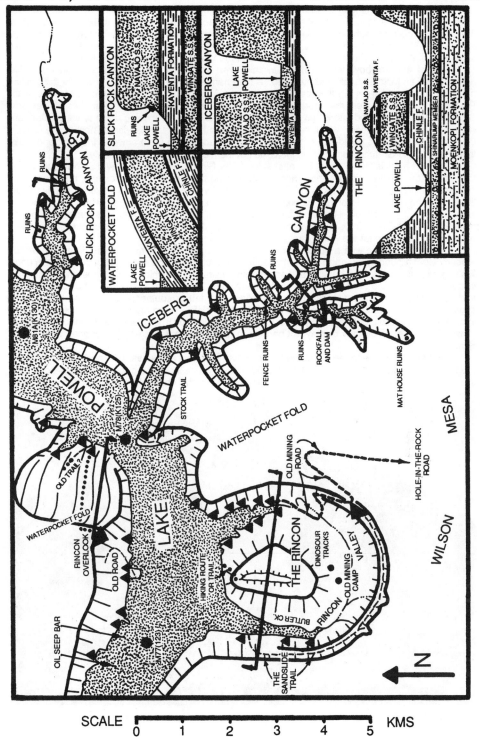

SCALE

0 1 2 3 4 5 KMS

driven on around the same Kayenta bench to where the old mining road now comes out of the Rincon Valley.

This stock trail was long used by cattlemen of San Juan County as a route by which livestock were driven to winter range in the Rincon Valley and adjacent areas, including Iceberg Canyon. After the road was built down the east side of The Rincon, this trail was abandoned. Today, you can't see any trace of the trail but the route is still there. If you hike up to the Kayenta bench, you will have some fine views of the Rincon Valley, the tail end of the Waterpocket Fold and the lake.

One of the cowboys who worked in this area was Clarence Rogers of Blanding. He remembered an incident back in about 1920. A man named John Adams had just bought the grazing rights for this region from big-time cattlemen Jim and Al Scorup. He took 100 head of cows to the Rincon Valley and left them there for the winter. The grass looked good enough for lots of livestock. But when Adams returned late in the spring, his cows had eaten everything down to the ground, and were in very poor condition. When he tried to push them back up the Sandslide, neither the cows or their newly born calves could make it. As a result he had to take them down to the river and move them north to the Gretchen Bar. From there, he got them out of Glen Canyon safely.

The next hike, is to the top of the east side of The Rincon. Above the HWM at the south end of the inlet on the eastern side of The Rincon, is an **old mining road.** Follow it south, then east, as it zig zags up through the broken-down Wingate cliffs until you're on top of the Kayenta ledges. From there, you'll have fine views of The Rincon and lake. If you continue on this road, which is still used up to the point of this overlook, it first heads northeast, then it turns south to meet the remains of the still older Hole-in-the-Rock Trail, dating from 1880. This is the easiest way to reach the rim and is a popular and easy hike for the whole family.

Another short hike with a good view, is one to the top of the central butte in the middle of The Rincon. Boat around to the north side of the butte, and park just to the northeast of the northern ridge. Walk to the southwest, up a boulder and sagebrush covered slope which gets steeper the higher you climb. Higher up, and not far from the big Wingate cliffs, you'll begin to see signs from other hikers and a trail-of-sorts. When you reach the first cliffs, veer left or southeast, and get on a minor little ridge, then go up again. Look for cracks in the top-most cliffs. There are several cracks you can get into, then wander a bit, before exiting to the top. At that point, you'll be on a Kayenta bench, with good views of the lake. You may or may not be able to reach the very top, which is capped with Navajo Sandstone.

Another hike is one to the top of the Waterpocket Fold, just across the lake north of The Rincon. From what the author is calling the **Rincon Overlook,** you will enjoy a good view to the south and the interesting geology of the area. Dock directly across the channel from the mouth of Iceberg

Large boulder in the Rincon Valley showing some kind of prehistoric animal tracks.

Canyon in one of several tiny coves. Simply walk up the inclined slope to the west. You'll be walking on top of Kayenta slickrock all the way. Once you reach a high point of the Fold, turn left, or south, and walk to the rim of the overlook. Below on the Chinle slopes, you'll see an old mining exploration track, and of course, have fine views of The Rincon and the southern extension of the Waterpocket Fold.

When the author first made this hike up to the top of the Fold, he was unaware of an old **stock trail** up to the top in about the same area as his own route. This is how Crampton describes it. *This trail begins on the west side of the river, opposite the mouth of Iceberg Canyon, and ascends the steep eastern slope of the Waterpocket Fold. This trail, reportedly used by prospectors and by Indians before them, probably joins with the Black Trail[Baker Ranch--Escalante River Trail] at some point on the crest of the Waterpocket Fold.*

On another trip the author again went part way up the slope to check out this trail. He did find a couple of cairns, but no other sign. Since it's not too steep, horses could have used any one of many routes. However, way up on top there are Navajo bluffs, which would channel all traffic into one or another narrow corridor. In one of these locations, it's possible one might find evidence of a real trail. This leaves room for someone to explore.

Hike Length and Time Needed To walk around The Rincon, from lake to lake, is to walk about 5 kms. This round-trip hike can be done in a couple of hours. It's about 3 kms to the top of the mesa on the southeast side of The Rincon, and this too will take about two hours round-trip.

In 15 minutes you can walk from the lake up the Sandslide to the Kayenta bench on the west side of The Rincon. In about half a day, one could walk up this old stock trail, and come down the road on the east side, then return to the boat. This would be somewhere near 12 kms round-trip.

To the top of the butte in the middle of The Rincon is less than a km, and will take about an hour for most people. The hike up to the Rincon Overlook is about 2 kms, and will take less than two hours, round-trip.

Boots or Shoes Any dry weather type of boots or shoes will be fine for all hikes.

Water There are no springs or streams in this immediate area, so take your own water.

Main Attractions Some fine views of some unusual geologic features, and a number of very good short hikes for the whole family.

Hiking Maps USGS or BLM map Navajo Mountain(1:100,000), or The Rincon(1:62,500).

Historical Sites The old mining road mentioned above has an interesting history according to Crampton's research. Sometime after World War II, the Hole-in-the-Rock Trail through Clay Hills Pass was replaced by a new road built by an oil company, which extended it to the top of Nokai Dome. This was very close to an overlook of the San Juan River. A few years later, beginning on July 4, 1957, a

The Sandslide, on the west side of The Rincon. It's formerly an old stock route to the rim.

uranium company with Texas interests(a man named Howell), began repairing the Nokai Dome Road, then extended it to the west along the old Hole-in-the-Rock Trail. From on top of Grey Mesa, the road went north to the east side of The Rincon then dropped down to the river. It reached the river to the northeast of the center butte of The Rincon.

Before the lake covered the area, one of the most unusual sites in Glen Canyon was **Oil Seep Bar.** This area was just northwest of The Rincon and on the north side of the river. Just a few meters above the river were several natural oil seeps. Some travelers called them oil springs. Because of the remote location, no commercial drilling took place there until after World War I. In 1920-21, there were a number of places in southeastern Utah under investigation for possible oil drilling, and The Rincon was one area of interest.

Under the supervision of a Frank Bennett, who had been involved in various gold mining ventures in Glen Canyon since 1897, the Henry Mountains Oil Company drilled four wells at this site, which was sometimes called Bennett's Oil Field. Two of the wells, about 10 meters apart, were drilled in the seep area and a third, about 100 meters to the east. The fourth was drilled about 1 1/2 kms east of the seeps and just below the present day HWM of the lake.

Operations began in July, 1920. Five tons of oil drilling equipment, consisting of an Armstrong rig and a wooden frame, a large wooden bullwheel, a gasoline engine, and drill stems and bits, were freighted by team from Richfield, Utah, to Halls Crossing. There rafts were built and the equipment and supplies were floated down river 32 kms to the drilling site. In November of the same year, part of the Stanton Dredge, marooned near Stanton Canyon, was dismantled and rafted down to Oil Seep Bar and used to build living quarters for workmen.

Later supplies were brought in by boat from Halls Crossing or by pack horses over the Black Trail from Baker Ranch(the Black Trail went south along the top of the Waterpocket Fold, then dropped down into Bowns Canyon, contoured along the Kayenta bench within Glen Canyon and south to the mouth of the Escalante River). From near the mouth of Bowns Canyon, they blasted out a trail down from the Kayenta bench and into the lower end of Bowns, then out Long Canyon, and finally along the north side of the Colorado River to Oil Seep Bar(see Map 17 on Long and Bowns Canyons for a look at Bennett's Oil Field Trail).

The oil wells proved unprofitable, as the flow was sluggish, and the operation shut down in 1921. When Crampton visited the site in 1961 a number of artifacts were found, including bits, drill stems, scrapers, three small cabins, and a wagon. The drilling rig was later moved to Gretchen Bar and used for other things, and finally parts of it ended up at Hite.

Walking through a crack near the rim of the butte in the center of The Rincon.

The Rincon Butte. The route up through the cliffs in on the upper right side.

A view of the lake and The Rincon from the Rincon Overlook.

Long & Bowns Canyons and the Black Trail

Location and Campsites Long and Bowns Canyons share a common mouth or opening into Lake Powell. Just as you enter the lower end of Long, you turn to the left and enter Bowns Inlet. Near the mouth of the inlet and in the main channel should be a buoy marked M74(K118). These two canyons form the first drainage you'll find to the north, or up-lake from the Escalante River Arm.

You find very few campsites in this part of Lake Powell. The reason is, the Wingate or Navajo Sandstone walls rise vertically right from the water. However, just to the west of the mouth of this inlet are a couple of campsite possibilities on the Kayenta bench. These places exist as the lake channel runs to the south, and the Wingate dips under the water leaving the Kayenta benches exposed at lake level. There are also springs coming out of the Navajo-Kayenta contact.

At the very end of each inlet, you should always find one sandy campsite. The author camped in upper Bowns Inlet on a sandy ledge, but a sad story came from that site. While hiking up Bowns Canyon one afternoon, ravens gobbled up 3 loaves of bread sitting in his boat--so beware, and cover things up well.

One thing unique about these canyons, there were until September of 1988, wild horses and cattle in both. Actually, the best term to use instead of wild or semi wild, would be feral cattle or horses. This means they escaped captivity in recent years. These animals can enter/exit this canyon complex in only one place, via the Black Trail in the East Fork of Bowns. From there, they move into Long Canyon via the Kayenta bench, which is above the lake and Wingate falls. Read more about this below.

Routes or Trails In **Bowns Canyon,** it's possible you may have trouble getting up the drainage if the lake levels are very low(it's possible there could be some falls to climb). But normally, it shouldn't be a problem.

If you have trouble getting into the canyon at the very end of the inlet, head back out about 400 meters, and on the left, or northwest, look for the remains of the **Bennett's Oil Field Trail.** It makes about two zigs and a zag up the rocky talus slope, then heads up to the right against the upper Wingate wall, and into a short drainage. At the point where the trail crosses a minor dry creek bed, it has been blasted out with dynamite. Above that, it disappears in the creek bed. About 100 meters beyond the blasted site, you can bench-walk the Kayenta into lower Bowns(or Long Canyon).

Normally you will park your boat in a narrow slickrock canyon at the end of Bowns Canyon Inlet, and walk up beside a small stream. About 200 meters above the HWM, you will come to a nice little two meter high waterfall and plunge pool. Beyond that, in the first km or so of the hike, you'll have a number of large boulders to get around, but above that it's wide open and easy walking. There will be a

From the Black Trail, looking down on the head of the inlet to Bowns Canyon.

MAP 17, LONG & BOWNS CANYONS AND THE BLACK TRAIL

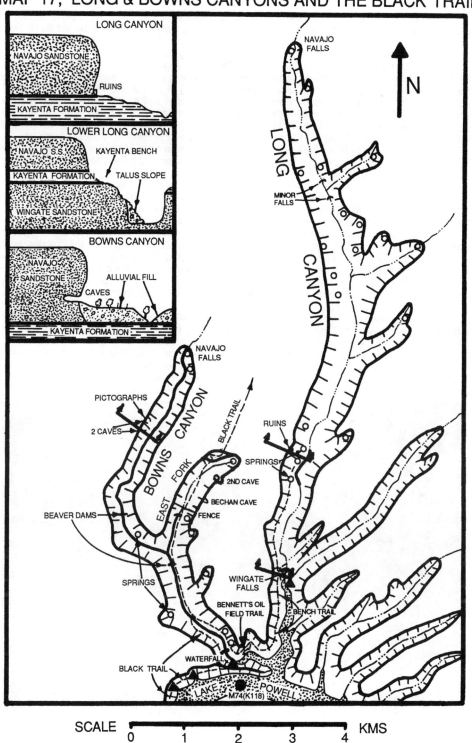

LONG CANYON

NAVAJO SANDSTONE

RUINS

KAYENTA FORMATION

LOWER LONG CANYON

NAVAJO S.S.   KAYENTA BENCH

KAYENTA FORMATION   TALUS SLOPE

WINGATE SANDSTONE

BOWNS CANYON

NAVAJO SANDSTONE   ALLUVIAL FILL

CAVES

KAYENTA FORMATION

NAVAJO FALLS

N

LONG CANYON

MINOR FALLS

NAVAJO FALLS

PICTOGRAPHS

2 CAVES

BOWNS CANYON

BLACK TRAIL

RUINS

SPRINGS

2ND CAVE

BECHAN CAVE

EAST FORK

FENCE

BEAVER DAMS

SPRINGS

WINGATE FALLS

BENNETT'S OIL FIELD TRAIL

BENCH TRAIL

WATERFALL

BLACK TRAIL

LAKE POWELL
M74(K118)

SCALE

0   1   2   3   4   KMS

143

small stream of water in this canyon on a year-round basis, all the way to the upper end of the main fork.

At about the time you get out of the part with large boulders, you will be on the Kayenta bench. At that point you can get onto this bench on the west side, and walk along part of the old Black Trail, which heads out to the main channel and towards the Escalante River. This trail is discussed more below. You can also turn to the right, and bench-walk into Long Canyon.

About 3 kms above the HWM in lower Bowns, the East Fork enters on the right. As you walk up the bottom of the East Fork drainage, you will have a tiny running stream for about a km. At about the point where there's a falls, which will usually be the beginning of the running water, you can get out easily on to the low Kayenta bench on either side. No matter which side you walk up, you will encounter an old fence made of cedar trees, which has to date back to very near the turn of the 20th century. It may have been built by Will Bowns, who was known to have run cattle in the canyon between 1909 and 1913. It stretches from one side of the canyon to the other, about half way up.

If you stay on the right, or east side, you will notice a large cave not far beyond the old cedar fence. This is Bechan Cave, where researchers have found what they believe to be mammoth dung about 12,000 years old. Read more on this cave below.

Just up canyon another 300 meters and again on the right, or east side, is another large cave. This one has no name, but it's nearly as big as Bechan Cave. There's a small spring below the entrance, and the little alcove where it's located, has been fenced off to form a corral or holding pen for livestock. This cedar tree and stone fence must also date back to early in the 20th century.

As you near the upper end of the canyon, the main part of the drainage veers to the right or northeast, and ends in a large alcove with a minor spring below. In this area, if you will look due north, or to the left a bit, you can see on the lower part of the Navajo slickrock, a pile of old cedar posts or trees. This is at the bottom of the most gentle slope in the canyon, and is the lower end of a stock trail which was built by Will Bowns. This is part of the Black Trail(discussed below), and is the only way livestock can enter either Bowns or Long Canyons. In several places along this part of the Black Trail, steps have been cut or blasted out of the rock.

Now back to the main fork of Bowns Canyon. As you walk up the drainage on trails made by the wild horses, you'll see a small spring on the right side and less than a km further is a large beaver dam. It had a very active beaver population upon the author's visit in 1988.

As you go up Bowns you can walk along side the stream, or get up onto a soil or alluvial bench. This bench, seen in many canyons entering Lake Powell, once was the floor of the canyon, where the Anasazi or Fremont Indians must have had gardens, and where until recently, many trees grew. The downcutting you see began early in the 20th century, very likely not too many years after the

The waterfall in lower Bowns Canyon.

144

introduction of livestock. Because of this downcutting, the water table dropped, thus a forest of dead trees is seen high and dry in places on this bench. Most people believe over grazing to be the reason for the recent and rapid erosion.

In the upper end of Bowns, and on the left or west side, are a number of alcoves and caves. Two of the caves are interesting. In the first, the author found a large stone with half a dozen metate grooves on top. In the second cave, some eroded pictographs were observed. At the end of this dead-end canyon are a couple of high falls and alcove springs. There seems to be plenty of running water in this fork of Bowns on a year-round basis.

Now for **Long Canyon.** Just above the HWM in Long Canyon Inlet, you'll find a big Wingate falls and a small stream flowing from beneath. It's a blocking falls, but about 100 meters below the falls and on the left, or west side, is a talus slope. Walk up this steep slope to the terrace above, then bench-walk to the north and into the upper canyon. This bench is either at the bottom of the Kayenta, or the top part of the Wingate Sandstone.

Inside Long Canyon, you don't find the same alluvial benches as you find in Bowns. Instead the Kayenta benches are exposed, giving the canyon a slightly different look. It's easy walking right along the mostly dry creek bed, or you can walk on either bench and along the wild horse trails. There is some running water in the lower end, but not nearly as much as in Bowns. You will however, find a number of small springs in the many alcoves which line each side of the drainage. The water seeps out at the bottom of the Navajo Sandstone.

Until 1988 there were wild horses in Long too, along with at least one Anasazi ruin, as shown on the map. This one is under an overhang and has been trampled by cattle and horses. The author has walked all the way up canyon on the west side, then returned via the dry creek bed. If you explore the short side canyons on the east side, you could find something interesting. There are many green places at the upper ends of each alcove, indicating plenty of spring water.

Another way into Long Canyon is via the Kayenta bench which connects it with lower Bowns. The author once docked at the bottom of Bennett's Oil Field Trail, climbed up on the Kayenta, then bench-walked around the corner into Long via what was obvious in places, a man-made trail. The author surmises, this **Bench Trail** was also built by Will Bowns in the same time frame as the other man-made features in Bowns Canyon. From this bench you'll have a fine view down on the Wingate falls at the head of Long Canyon Inlet.

Hike Length and Time Needed Bowns Canyon is about 8 kms long. It should take all day to see both forks and do some exploring. Long Canyon is rather long; about 12 kms from the Wingate falls to the upper end and the Navajo falls. If you enjoy exploring while hiking, and there are lots of places to explore, then plan on a full days hike.

Part of the Bennett's Oil Field Trail where it was blasted out of solid sandstone in the lower end of Bowns Canyon.

Boots or Shoes In Bowns Canyon, you can make better time if you do some wading, so wading shoes would be best. In Long Canyon, you'll be walking on a lot of Kayenta slickrock, so any kind of boots or shoes are OK.

Water If the NPS wild horse and cattle roundup proves to have been successful, the water quality in either canyon should be much better than before, but it's best not to drink from the streams in either canyon. Expect to find beaver in Bowns at all times. However, there are many springs in both drainages. Drinking the water directly from a spring should be safe.

Main Attractions Two green desert canyons(especially Bowns), interesting caves, waterfalls, and Anasazi ruins and pictographs.

Hiking Maps USGS or BLM map Navajo Mountain(1:100,000), or The Rincon(1:62,500).

The Black Trail and Will Bowns, Wild Horses, and Bechan Cave Of all the trails in the Glen Canyon region, the **Black Trail** might have the most interesting history. It began along the Hole-in-the-Rock Road near the head of Clear Creek. It then went east, just north of Clear Creek Canyon, to the rim of the Escalante River. There it must have zig zagged down the Navajo slickrock to the canyon just north of the mouth of Clear Creek. After running down the Escalante for 3 kms, it veered left, or east, and went up to and along the Kayenta bench, which is just below the Navajo walls. This bench is now under water near the lower end of the Escalante.

At the mouth of the Escalante, it continued to contour along the Kayenta bench to the east, then north for about 11 kms, to just below the mouth of Long Canyon. It then went around the corner and into lower Bowns Canyon, still on the same bench. A third the way up Bowns, it headed north into the East Fork, and out on top of the Waterpocket Fold along the west side of upper Long Canyon. It continued north along the crest of the Fold, until somewhere above the Baker Ranch, then descended to the ranch on Halls Creek.

The reason it got the name Black Trail, is because just east of the mouth of the Escalante River, is a small alcove with the inscription, *J W Black, Feb. 2, 1896,* written in charcoal. It's not a certainty, but this may have been put there by a John Black, long time resident of Escalante and Boulder, who was born in 1871. Others have referred to the same route as the *Baker Ranch-Escalante Trail.*

According to Crampton's research on Glen Canyon, the creek in Long Canyon was at one time called Navajo Creek. Bowns Canyon gets it's name from an old cattleman who had a ranch on Sandy Creek, just west of Mt. Ellen in the Henry Mountains. **William(Will) Bowns** used to winter cattle in these two canyons, during the years from about 1909 to 1913, but maybe earlier.

Bowns originally brought cattle into the area via the Escalante River Canyon, but sometime later he built the trail down into the East Fork of Bowns. At the same time, he must have built the cedar fences and the Bench Trail connecting Bowns and Long Canyons. After that time, he brought cattle in

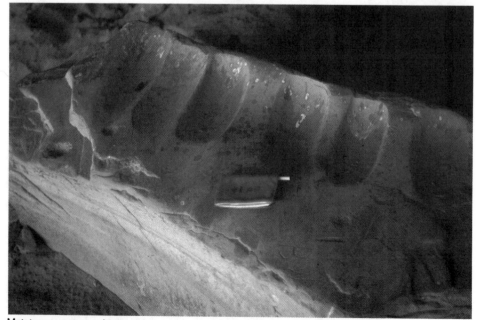

Metate grooves on a large rock in a cave in upper Bowns Canyon.

via the Black Trail described above. This new route allowed him to take cattle in or out of these canyons via the top of the Waterpocket Fold to the Baker Ranch, then along the eastern base of the Fold, which was an easier drive from his Sandy Ranch.

In the beginning, Bowns called this drainage Meadow Canyon. That must have been before all the erosion took place, which has left the canyon half gutted today.

During the summer of 1988, the National Park Service made the decision to remove the **wild horses and cattle** in Bowns and Long Canyons. These animals were left-overs from the Eugene Baker herd(Baker Ranch on Halls Creek) dating back to the 1930's(according to Max Jackson). The herd had multiplied to the point they were threatening the ecology in the entire region. They had eaten down the vegetation and made hundreds of trails, creating the possibility of even more soil erosion.

So in the last days of September, 1988, a crew from the Kane County Sheriffs office was sent in to have a roundup. This land is administered by the NPS, but it was the duty of the Kane County Sheriff, Max Jackson, to remove the animals.

Several days before the roundup, a crew of four men were in lower Bowns preparing the place for entrapment. First, a trail was made down through the boulders to the head of the inlet, where the animals were to be finally caught. The crew also fixed bright colored ribbons in places where the animals might get out of the trap.

On Saturday, October 1, the roundup began. One helicopter was used to locate and drive the horses and cattle out of upper Bowns and off the mesa top, down to the lower end of Bowns Canyon. In the lower end, and on either side bench, were four wranglers on horse back. In the end, 7 head of cattle and 5 horses were trapped and removed to Bullfrog Marina by a World War II landing craft. During the chase, one of the riders had an accident and his horse broke a leg. It was later destroyed. Two horses, a mare(female) and her foal(colt), managed to escape into Long Canyon. If it later proves that the colt is a male, then another roundup will be necessary.

One of the alcoves in Bowns Canyon is called **Bechan Cave.** This cave is just another alcove, just like thousands of others on the Colorado Plateau, but researchers found mammoth dung inside this one.

It all started in November of 1982 when a team of NPS people entered Bowns Canyon to do a grazing survey. They found the cave and noticed someone had dug holes in the floor; obviously a pot hunter looking for Anasazi or Fremont artifacts. In the bottom of these small pits, they noticed a blanket of dung, which later proved interesting. Incidentally, few if any human artifacts have been found there, although some parts of the cave were used as an Indian campsite.

In February of 1983, a crew of NPS people and others from the University of Utah and Utah State University went to the site and did some digging of their own. They found the cave to be about 52

Bechan Cave in the East Fork of Bowns Canyon.

meters deep, 31 meters wide at the mouth, and about 9 meters in height. The cave is well lit during the afternoons, because it faces the southwest. Because of the steep slope right in front of the entrance, there was no cattle or horse manure found.

In the test pits dug, they found a dung blanket about 1/3 of a meter deep, with some manure piles in their original shape. Some of these **boluses** measured 23 x 17 x 9 cms(9 x 7 x 2.5 inches). Two of the boluses closely resembled those of African elephant dung. These later proved to be(with carbon 14 dating) 11,670 year old plus or minus 300 years, and 12,900 years old plus or minus 160 years. In the same dig, they found other dung which closely resembled that of elk and perhaps mountain goat or sheep.

In March and May of 1983, part of the same crew returned to do more digging. Their findings were later published by the Carnegie Museum of Natural History, Special Publication No. 8, Pittsburgh, 1984. It is titled *The Pleistocene Dung Blanket of Bechan Cave, Utah.*

In their digging they failed to find any bones of significances, although they did find bones of small mammals. Packrats had used the cave as well for at least 12,000 years. In the same blanket, dung from ground sloth was also found in abundance, as well as hair that closely resembled mammoth. In more recent layers above the dung, some charcoal was found, but it was dated quite recently.

Examination of pollen showed a different type of vegetation and climate during that period of time. Found was pollen from water birch, blue spruce, elderberry, snowberry, currant, sedges and cattail. These are not found in the immediate area today, although they are found not far to the north in the Henry Mountains.

The dating of material found in the cave closely approximates that of other finds here in North America. Both the Columbian mammoth and the Shasta ground sloths disappeared from the continent about 11,000 years ago.

One thing that has puzzled the author as well as the researchers is, how did these large mammals actually get into the cave? The front is presently very steep, which prevented livestock from entering. Apparently there was a larger sand dune in front of the cave during mammoth times. It's also interesting to speculate on how they could have gotten into the canyon itself. It's possible they could have come up from lower Bowns and the Colorado River, but today(before Lake Powell) it would be a little difficult. Perhaps in those days any falls or cliffs in the Wingate Sandstone may have been covered with soil, making that route different than we saw it just before Lake Powell. They also may have come down the slickrock in the same area where Will Bowns later made his entry trail. But some parts of that route are a little steep, perhaps too steep for cattle or horses, without some slight modification of the grade.

From the top of the Black Trail looking down into the East Fork of Bowns. Navajo Mtn. in the distance.

Stud Piles of manure(stallion territorial markers) in Long Canyon.

Looking north and down on the dry falls at the upper end of the inlet of Long Canyon.

Explorer, Fence and Cow Canyons

Location and Campsites Included here are three tributaries of the Escalante River. All enter from the east, and all are in the upper or northern end of the Escalante Arm of the lake. It's in this upper end of the Escalante the geologic beds are seen rising out of the water. Because the benches of the Kayenta Formation are emerging, there are more campsites available than down canyon. You will find a number of small and often sandy sites along the upper Escalante, as well as at least one good site in the upper end of each canyon inlet.

The upper most end of the **Escalante River Arm,** that part north of Cow and Fence Canyons, often times is full of very muddy water. Therefore, this area isn't normally considered a hiking area, at least with boater access. When the lake levels are at the HWM, the inlet extends north to the mouth of Coyote Gulch. But very slowly, the mud and sand brought down the Escalante River are filling in and making mud flats and shallow waters. The author boated up to within 5 kms of the mouth of Coyote Gulch, and it was becoming very shallow there. There is a fair amount of driftwood about, therefore there are not many boaters in this far upper end. So all in all, this is generally not a pleasant place to visit.

If you're interested in exploring the canyons above the HWM, consult Kelsey's book, *Canyon Hiking Guide to the Colorado Plateau,* or better still, Rudi Lambrechtse's book, *Hiking the Escalante.* Coyote Gulch is one of the best canyons in the Escalante River System.

Routes or Trails Like all inlets of the Escalante, **Explorer Canyon Inlet** is fairly long and narrow. Explorer is also one of the more interesting drainages to visit in the Escalante. Right at the HWM you can find a small spring on each side of the creek, which makes a good place to stock up on water. It's there you find the beginning of a hiker-made trail running up canyon. You'll have to use it, because the creek bed has a number of beaver ponds and is choked with water-loving plants.

The main trail is on the left or north side of the creek. It winds its way up and down and through oak brush, and for the most part is atop the alluvial bench deposits in the canyon bottom. About 2/3 the way up, look to your left, and you should see the interesting Zane Grey Arch in the upper part of the Kayenta Formation.

From where you can see the arch, the trail winds around a buttress, and after about 75-100 meters, you'll see a good panel of petroglyphs on your left. The lower part has figures of humans with big horn sheep heads and horns. Higher on the wall are big horn sheep. This is one of the more unusual petroglyphs the author has seen. From this panel, walk along the trail another 50 meters or less, and you'll see another single petroglyph on the left. Beyond this, the trail runs up to the springs at the bottom of the big falls which blocks the way to the mesa above.

Fence and Cow Canyons both share a common mouth, which is deep and narrow. The

Unusual petroglyphs in Explorer Canyon.

150

MAP 18, EXPLORER, FENCE & COW CANYONS

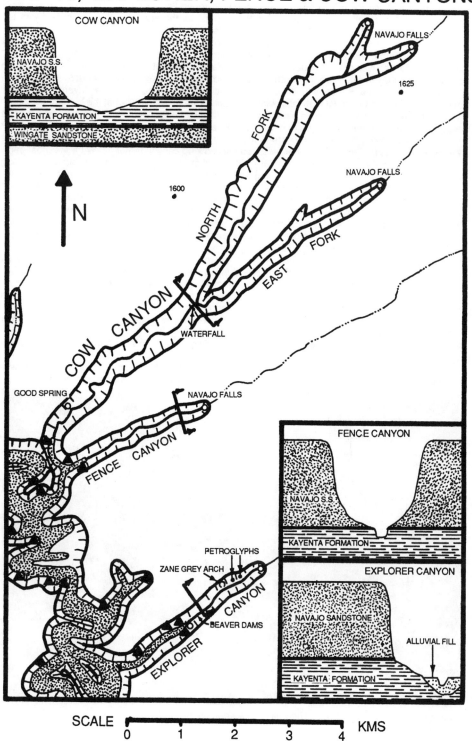

COW CANYON
NAVAJO S.S.
KAYENTA FORMATION
WINGATE SANDSTONE

N

NAVAJO FALLS
1625

1600

NORTH FORK

NAVAJO FALLS

EAST FORK

COW CANYON

WATERFALL

GOOD SPRING

NAVAJO FALLS

FENCE CANYON

FENCE CANYON
NAVAJO S.S.
KAYENTA FORMATION

PETROGLYPHS
ZANE GREY ARCH
CANYON
BEAVER DAMS
EXPLORER

EXPLORER CANYON
NAVAJO SANDSTONE
ALLUVIAL FILL
KAYENTA FORMATION

SCALE
0 1 2 3 4 KMS

151

Navajo walls rise to great heights at this point of the Escalante Canyon. Fence is the shorter canyon of the two, and as you hike up stream, you'll be walking along Kayenta benches. The author used a series of deer trails on the left, or north side, of the year-round flowing stream, but he could see trails on the other side as well. You'll have to use these trails, as the stream bottom is choked with tall grass, willows, trees, and in places small beaver ponds.

Fence and Cow Canyons share what appears to be a captive deer herd. The author saw 5 head of deer in Fence; that's why there are so many trails around. There seems to be plenty of food and it doesn't look to be over grazed, but it's likely the deer can't get out of the Fence-Cow Canyon complex unless they swim. Perhaps when the lake levels are low, they could walk out?

At the upper end of Fence, you will see a deep little groove in the top of the Kayenta Formation. Not far above this are the usual high falls, with good spring water seeping out at the bottom.

Of the three canyons discussed here, Cow Canyon is by far the longest. It has the same look as Fence, with the Kayenta benches along the bottom, and a year-round flowing stream choked with brush and water-loving plants. There aren't too many hikers going up this one, and the deer trails aren't as evident as in Fence. None-the-less, you can walk up canyon rather easily for the most part.

It would be best to do this hike in cooler weather, when you feel more comfortable wearing long pants. This would save your legs from being scratched while wading through tall grass and around willows and beaver ponds. In some places you can walk right up the open stream bed; in other places you have to bushwhack a little. Just below the confluence of the North and East Forks is an interesting waterfall pouring over a Kayenta ledge. As this book goes to press, Max Jackson, the Sheriff who rounded up the wild horses and cattle in Bowns Canyon, told the author the helicopter pilot told him he thought some of those animals were going down into the head of Cow Canyon. This leaves room for someone to explore.

Hike Length and Time Needed The hike up Explorer is only about 2 kms from the HWM to the falls. The author did this one in 1 hr. 15 min. round-trip. Fence Canyon is only slightly longer, maybe 3 kms to the falls. The author got to just below the headwall and returned, in 1 hr. 10 min. Cow Canyon is much longer, the North Fork being about 12 or 13 kms long. To hike this one will take all day. Best to do this hike in spring or fall, then you'll be wearing long pants, which will make the trip more enjoyable. The author walked up the East Fork to a point where he could see the falls at the end, then returned; all in 3 hr. 15 min.

Boots or Shoes In Cow Canyon you better take wading shoes. In Fence and Explorer, you can avoid wading, so any kind of shoes will do.

Water There are year-round streams in each canyon, but also beaver in all three, so try to avoid drinking water from the streams in the lower ends of the canyons. Drink from springs or the upper

Looking down Explorer Canyon. The trail can be seen on the right.

valley creeks. There's a good spring with a large flow, about a km up Cow Canyon on the left.
Main Attractions Deep Navajo Sandstone canyons, small streams and green valleys, and an arch and good petroglyphs in Explorer Canyon.
Hiking Maps USGS or BLM map Navajo Mountain(1:100,000), or The Rincon(1:62,500).

Another of the petroglyphs in Explorer Canyon.

A waterfall at the junction of East and North Forks of Cow Canyon.

The junction of East and North Forks of Cow Canyon. A waterfall is on the lower right.

A view of Navajo Mountain from the lower end of the Escalante River Arm of the lake.

Part of the Black Trail built by Will Bowns, in the East Fork of Bowns Canyon.

Looking down Long Canyon with Navajo Mountain in the background.

155

Fortymile Gulch, Willow Creek, & Bishop Canyon

Location and Campsites This map features Willow Creek and all of its tributaries, which include Fortymile Gulch, Willow Gulch(on some maps it's named Sooner Gulch), North Fork of Willow Creek(the author's name), and Bishop Canyon. All these tributaries empty into the middle part of the Escalante River Arm of the lake and from the west side. In 1988, there was a sign at the mouth of this very long and narrow inlet.

There are several campsites in Willow Creek Inlet; all small, but all sandy. There should always be a sandy campsite at the end of navigation into each of the three inlets; Willow Creek, North Fork, and Bishop Canyon.

Routes or Trails Right at the upper end of **Willow Creek** Inlet, you will see a low bench on the north side of the water. Get up on it and look along the main canyon wall for a panel of petroglyphs. From there you can walk up Willow Creek, which has a fairly good sized year-round stream of water. After only a km or so(from the HWM) is a junction. To the left is **Willow Gulch.** Walk up this drainage a short distance and into some pretty good narrows. Not far beyond is the interesting Broken Bow Arch on the right. It was so named because someone once found a broken bow beneath it. It measures 28 by 30 meters. It was years ago when the author visited this part of the canyon from the road, and the arch symbol may not be placed properly on the map, but it's there somewhere. Beyond, you can walk unobstructed to the Hole-in-the-Rock Road, which connects Escalante with the Hole-in-the-Rock Trail to the south.

If you turn north into **Fortymile Gulch,** instead of going up Willow, you will again be wading in a small stream. There are some springs and narrows all the way through this canyon. There are some boulders blocking the creek bed in a place or two, but you can walk all the way up this drainage and exit through Carcass Wash to the Hole-in-the-Rock Road. The best part is in the lower end. There was a truck accident in Carcass Wash in 1963, which is discussed below.

The inlet leading into the **North Fork** is short. In the beginning, the walk is up through tall cane-like grass, so it's best to walk right in the small creek bed. Further up, it's easier walking without the cane grass. As you walk up canyon, the Navajo walls get higher and higher. In the lower part, there are old sign of beaver, but nothing new in 1988. At the upper end, there's a fork. If you take the right fork, you'll walk 300 meters into a deep, dark and narrow box ending. The left fork is where the author momentarily trapped five deer. This is yet another captive deer herd, unless they know how to swim. However, the vegetation appeared healthy, so they weren't eating themselves into starvation in 1988.

Bishop Canyon is one of the more spectacular around. For the author, boating up canyon was slow, because of driftwood. This condition may be seasonal, or just common to this particular canyon.

Water seeping out of a wall in the lower part of Fortymile Canyon.

156

MAP 19, FORTYMILE GULCH, WILLOW CK., & BISHOP CANYON

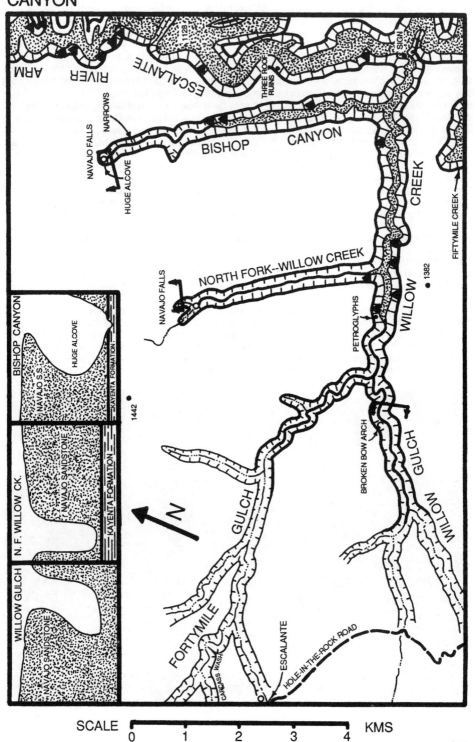

SCALE 0 1 2 3 4 KMS

157

This may be the reason not too many people visit Bishop. But it's worth the time and effort to get there, as it's an interesting canyon.

As you walk up Bishop, the Navajo walls get higher and higher, and its depth compares with Sevenmile and Iceberg Canyons. Along most of the hiking part of the canyon it appears the year-round flowing stream is running on Kayenta bedrock. In the bottom of the canyon is a groove which has been cut by raging flood waters. Near the upper end, there's a short section which is narrow(in this Kayenta groove), so you'll either have to wade, or spread your legs and wall-walk above the stream. It's easy. At the very end is one of the largest alcoves the author has seen. It's worth the walk. Under the dry falls is the beginning of the stream flow. No sign of beaver in this box canyon, but they seem to come and go into different canyons, depending on food supplies.

Hike Length and Time Needed It's about 10 kms up Willow Creek and Gulch, to the the Hole-in-the-Rock Road. Round-trip will take most people 4 or 5 hours. In Fortymile Gulch, you can walk for as long as you like, but it's the lower end that's worth seeing. The upper part is less interesting.

It's about 4 or 5 kms to the end of North Fork. The author did this one in 1 hr. 40 min. You'll want two to three hours. There's only about 2 kms of walking in Bishop Canyon, and this can be done in a couple of hours, round-trip. The author did it in 1 hr. 30 min.

Boots or Shoes Use wading boots or shoes in all canyons.

Water No sign of beaver in Bishop, so you can drink it from any place, but at the source would be safest. North Fork water should be safe higher up, at or near the source. Drink from springs only in Willow and Fortymile Gulches. There are cattle coming down part way in each of these drainages from October to June.

Main Attractions Very deep, well watered, and narrow canyons. Also, petroglyphs and Broken Bow Arch.

Hiking Maps USGS or BLM map Navajo Mountain(1:100,000), or The Rincon(1:62,500).

Boy Scout Tragedy Right where the Hole-in-the-Rock Road crosses Carcass Wash, was the scene of one the worst accidents in southern Utah history. That's where 13 boy scouts died on June 10, 1963.

A group of scouts and scout masters had made there way from Salt Lake, Ogden and Provo, to Escalante by bus on their way to the Colorado River at the Hole-in-the-Rock Trail. The plan was to board a large open-bed truck and drive the Hole-in-the-Rock Road to where the trail began on the rim of the canyon. Then they were to walk down to the river, where they would meet boaters who started at Hite(this was just before the lake began to fill). They then were to float down the Colorado.

As the road crosses Carcass Wash, it dips down, then runs up a steep grade to the rim on the

The upper end of the North Fork of Willow Creek.

other side. As the truck was climbing the grade, the driver apparently tried to shift to a lower gear but missed, and the truck stalled. He tried to use the brakes to prevent it from rolling backwards, but they didn't hold. He then tried to steer the truck back down the steep grade, but missed the curve half way down, and it rolled over a 10 meter high embankment, eventually landing on its side. Since most of the scouts were in the back, many were thrown out and some were crushed as the truck rolled over once. Twelve were dead on the spot, and another died later.

After the accident, two boys headed up the road toward Escalante for help. Soon they met a couple of local ranchers mending fences. One drove to town to sound the alarm. Men from the BLM, Forest Service, and Sheriffs office, and even tourists and a number of local towns people joined the rescue. Later, someone drove toward the river, where one of the boaters was a doctor. Eventually several station wagons went to the scene and hauled the injured to the hospital in Panguitch. The nightmere ended when parents and relatives of the dead and wounded came to claim their own. So ended one of the worst tradgedies in southern Utah history.

One of the narrow places in the upper end of Bishop Canyon.

Fiftymile Ck., Davis Gulch, Clear & Indian Creek Canyons

Location and Campsites These four canyons, Fiftymile, Davis, Clear and Indian Creeks, are all part of the Escalante River system. As you enter the Escalante and boat north, these are the first four canyons on the left, or west(Indian Creek Inlet is not shown on this map). These waterways or inlets, are some of the narrowest and most fotogenic of all canyons on the lake.

It's in this part of the Escalante Arm that campsites are the hardest to find. It's all Navajo slickrock rising sheer out of the water, except for just a few sandy beaches, most of which are found at the head of each inlet. Clear Creek and Indian Creek Inlets have no campsites at all, with Davis and Fiftymile having about half a dozen each. The number of sites and their size will depend on lake levels.

Routes or Trails The upper end of **Clear Creek Inlet** is very narrow, but some house boats get into it--just barely. Some have left scratch marks on the walls at one point where their roofs have scraped. Right at the end is a cool shaded overhang, then a little narrow place where you get out of your boat to walk up canyon. If water levels are low, you may be blocked by a falls right at the water line. About 100 meters above the HWM is a waterfall. Bypass this one on the left, and walk another 300 meters to where the hiking ends under a another big overhang where a large pool exists. Many hikers reach this point, as this is one of the shortest, but most popular hikes around.

Before Lake Powell, **Davis Gulch** was one of the most fascinating canyons leading into the Escalante. Some of the better parts are now under water. The inlet is very long, narrow and sinuous. About half way up is La Gorce Arch. If the lake is full, the water almost reaches the bottom part of it. Just beyond the arch, and on the right or northwest, is a small Anasazi structure? At the very end of the inlet, are a couple of fine campsites.

As you hike up canyon, about 200 meters above the HWM, you see on the right, or northwest, a sloping ridge coming down to the bottom lands. This is the first of two natural exits out of the canyon. About 150 meters beyond this one, look to the right again, and next to the hiker-made trail is an old wooden pole corral lying in ruins. Immediately behind this is the **Davis Gulch Cattle Trail.** It has steps cut out of the slickrock in the bottom part. As you go up, look for cairns marking the upper part of the trail.

The corral at the bottom of this trail was evidently the last camping place of a young naturalist-artist by the name of **Everett Ruess,** who disappeared in 1934 without a trace. His mules and camp were found, but no trace of him. The events of his disappearance has become one of the big legends in southern Utah.

In between these two natural exits, and on the walls behind the oak brush on the northwest side of the canyon, you'll find a rather long panel of good petroglyphs. These are likely Fremont etchings,

The narrows of Fiftymile Canyon.

MAP 20, FIFTYMILE CK., DAVIS G. & CLEAR CK.

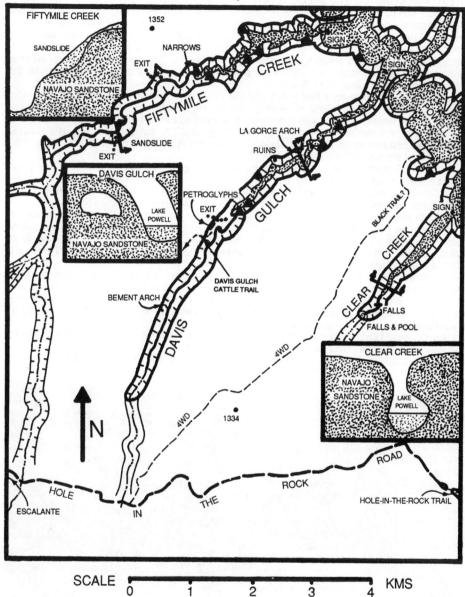

FIFTYMILE CREEK

1352

SANDSLIDE

NARROWS

EXIT

CREEK

NAVAJO SANDSTONE

FIFTYMILE

SANDSLIDE

EXIT

SIGN

SIGN

LAKE

POWELL

1182

LA GORCE ARCH

RUINS

DAVIS GULCH

PETROGLYPHS

GULCH

LAKE POWELL

EXIT

BLACK TRAIL?

SIGN

NAVAJO SANDSTONE

CREEK

DAVIS GULCH CATTLE TRAIL

CLEAR

BEMENT ARCH

DAVIS

FALLS

FALLS & POOL

4WD

CLEAR CREEK

NAVAJO SANDSTONE

LAKE POWELL

N

4WD

1334

ROAD

HOLE

ROCK

ESCALANTE

IN

THE

HOLE-IN-THE-ROCK TRAIL

SCALE 0 1 2 3 4 KMS

as they often made such panels along important routes or trails.

As you go up canyon beyond the cattle trail, the hikers path fades, and you'll be walking mostly in the shallow stream 3 to 5 cms deep. There are active beaver colonies in this part. They burrow under the banks, instead of making dams and ponds. Three kms above the cattle trail is Bement Arch. Above this arch the canyon narrows, and you can walk only about another two kms before it constricts to nothing and there's finally a falls at the end(no route out).

As you walk the area near Bement Arch, notice the alluvial or soil banks about 6 or 8 meters high. The erosion or down-cutting began about 1900, likely the result of overgrazing. There are no cattle in

161

the canyon today.

Fiftymile Creek Canyon Inlet is another long, narrow and sinuous waterway, with half a dozen small campsites. Just above the HWM, the canyon really constricts, and you have a fine narrows section, where you'll wade in what could be at times, deep water. The author found it to be knee deep. Beyond this, the drainage opens a bit and the walking is very easy. This canyon has running water in the lower half, but it doesn't have the amount of vegetation as does Davis Gulch. This drainage seems to be more prone to flash flooding than Davis, and the creek bed is swept clean of debris and is lined with cobble stones. It's possible Fiftymile was not used for habitation by the Anasazi or Fremonts, as was Davis Gulch.

Less than a km above the HWM in Fiftymile Canyon, there's a small canyon coming down from the right. Enter this, then climb over some ledges on the left, and you can exit along an old deer trail. About 1 1/2 kms beyond this first exit is a sandslide coming down from the left, or south. At either side of this slide, you can walk up to the rim. West of this sandslide, the canyon slowly opens and is more shallow. Two kms above the sandslide is where the year-round water begins to flow. If you like, you can walk all the way to the Hole-in-the-Rock Road.

In the Escalante River Arm of Lake Powell, most of the canyons have some kind of hiking, but one that doesn't is **Indian Creek**. This canyon is now a short inlet only about a km long. The sheer Navajo Sandstone walls rise directly out of the water and it ends in a big alcove where the flood waters fall into the lake during stormy weather. There are no campsites in this canyon.

Hike Length and Time Needed You can only walk up Clear Creek about half a km, which will take but a few minutes. In Davis Gulch, you can walk about 5 kms up stream. About half a day should be enough time to see this one. The author spent 3 hours there, but went only as far as Bement Arch. It's about another half day in Fiftymile Creek, depending on how far you walk. It's about 5 kms up to where the water begins to flow.

Boots or Shoes For Fiftymile and Davis, use wading type shoes. For Clear Creek it doesn't matter.

Water The water comes and goes in Fiftymile. From places where it first seeps out of the creek bed, it should be good to drink. No beaver or cattle in Fiftymile. In Davis, better find a spring to drink from, as there are beaver in the lower parts of the creek. Clear Creek flows for a very short distance, but it's likely polluted by so much human traffic.

Main Attractions Long, narrow and sinuous waterways, deep narrow canyons, some petroglyphs, a historic trail, sandy campsites, and at times too many people.

Hiking Maps USGS or BLM map Navajo Mountain(1:100,000), or The Rincon(1:62,500).

Looking down into Fiftymile Canyon from the top of the sandslide.

La Gorce Arch in the middle part of the Davis Gulch Inlet.

The Davis Gulch stock trail, with the old corral to the left.

163

The narrows and an undercut in the upper part of Davis Gulch.

Davis Gulch from the canyon rim, with the Kaiparowits Plateau in the far background.

Bement Arch in the upper part of Davis Gulch.

Right at the end of the inlet of Clear Creek Canyon.

Ribbon & Cottonwood Canyons, and the Hole-in-the-Rock & Jackass Bench Trails

Location and Campsites There are four hikes covered on this map, all within a short distance of each other, and all just down lake from the mouth of the Escalante River Arm. Near the Jackass Bench Trail and Ribbon Canyon are buoys numbered M68(K109) and M67(K107). In front of Hole-in-the-Rock Bay is buoy M66(K106), while just down lake from the mouth of Cottonwood Canyon is buoy M63A(K101).

This is one of the most popular areas on the lake for camping; at least it was being heavily used upon the author's visit. Lots of water skiers too. In Ribbon Canyon there are several small campsites and one large, sandy one. Most of the other campsites are in Cottonwood Canyon. The Kayenta benches are exposed in Cottonwood, plus there are high Navajo Sandstone cliffs nearby. The combination of these two formations has created many sandy beaches and small coves.

Routes and Trails The **Jackass Bench Trail** was a constructed pack and livestock trail from the rim of Glen Canyon down to Jackass Bench, which is now submerged in water. Jackass Bench was about 50 meters above the Colorado River and was made of the Kayenta Formation, which is above the Wingate and below the Navajo Sandstone. The bench was used for grazing livestock in 1879 by the Hole-in-the-Rock Party, and by subsequent residents at the Hole.

Crampton believes this trail may have been built by the Hoskaninni Mining Company, as part of the assessment work to keep their claims alive and valid. Apparently, the company had intended to build a road from the mouth of Hole-in-the-Rock Creek, up along Jackass Bench, thence to the rim in the same area as the present trail. But they didn't get that far. This trail however, proved easier than the old Hole Trail.

The Jackass Bench Trail had steps picked out of the Navajo slickrock. It wound its way up to the rim, then turned left and after 3 kms met the Hole-in-the-Rock Road coming down from Escalante. Parts of it are still there today. Steps can be seen coming out of the water about 2 kms northeast, or up-lake, from the mouth of Hole-in-the-Rock Bay. There's no place to anchor right at the steps, so boat to the northeast about 100 meters to a small inlet. From there, you can walk up on the slickrock parallel to the lake until you see about four series of steps. Not far above the lake, the slope is more gentle, and there are only scattered cairns to mark the way. If you can't follow the cairns, just head up to the west and near the rim, veer to the left. Once on top, you'll have excellent views down lake with Navajo Mountain in the background. It's an easy walk from there to the top of the Hole-in-the-Rock Trail.

Ribbon Canyon is a short side drainage which makes a fun hike. Going up canyon, you'll be walking along slickrock from the Kayenta Formation. In several places there's running water, but it's a

Camping scene in the upper end of Ribbon Canyon Inlet.

166

MAP 21, RIBBON & COTTONWOOD CANYONS AND HOLE-IN-THE-ROCK & JACKASS BENCH TRAILS

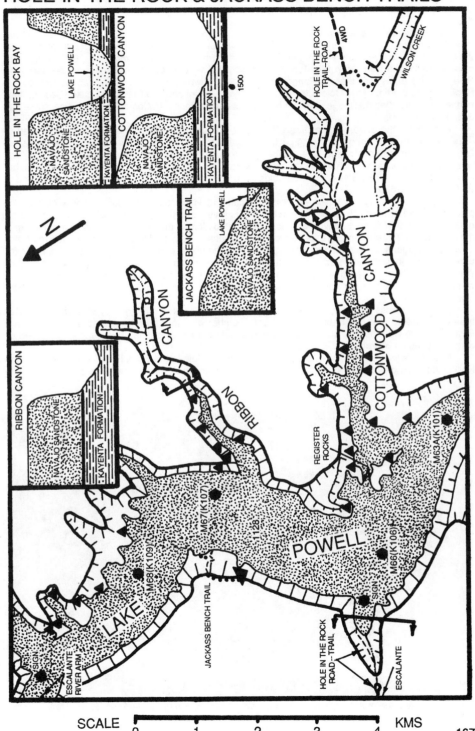

HOLE IN THE ROCK BAY

LAKE POWELL

NAVAJO SANDSTONE

KAYENTA FORMATION

COTTONWOOD CANYON

NAVAJO SANDSTONE

KAYENTA FORMATION

1500

HOLE IN THE ROCK TRAIL–ROAD

4WD

WILSON CREEK

N

JACKASS BENCH TRAIL

LAKE POWELL

NAVAJO SANDSTONE

CANYON

RIBBON CANYON

NAVAJO SANDSTONE

KAYENTA FORMATION

COTTONWOOD CANYON

RIBBON

REGISTER ROCKS

M63A(K101)

M67(K107)

1128

POWELL

M66(K106)

M68(K109)/2

SIGN

LAKE

JACKASS BENCH TRAIL

HOLE IN THE ROCK ROAD – TRAIL

ESCALANTE

SIGN

ESCALANTE RIVER ARM

SCALE   0   1   2   3   4   KMS

167

small stream. The higher you go, the steeper and more difficult it is to walk. In the upper ends of each of the two major forks, there are some large boulders, trees and ledges to slow you down. This is the fourth canyon in which the author recalls seeing a captive deer herd. There seems no way out of this box canyon but to swim out through the inlet. It'll be interesting to see how long they stay in this drainage.

One of the most daring and difficult journeys of the American west is told in the story of the **Hole-in-the-Rock Party.** Their expedition began in southwest Utah, with volunteer Mormons from the Cedar City, Parowan and Paragonah areas. The journey began on October 22, 1879. They were officially called the **San Juan Mission Party,** and were sent to build a settlement on the San Juan River. Their journey took them to Panguitch, Escalante, down what is today known as the Hole-in-the-Rock Road to the rim of the Colorado, across the river, up Cottonwood Canyon to Lake Pagahrit, then northeast to near Natural Bridges Natural Monument and southeast to Comb Wash, then on to the San Juan River at Bluff.

Altogether, there were more than 230 people in about 83 wagons, along with 1000 head of livestock. There had been a scouting party sent out, which had taken an easier but longer route via Lee's Ferry, but they decided to take a short-cut into unknown country. As it turned out, the journey was over 320 kms long, much of which was roadless. The trip was to last 6 weeks or thereabouts, but it took nearly 6 months instead. Three babies were born along the way. The lead wagons arrived at Bluff on April 6, 1880.

The part of the journey which was most difficult and which took the most road building, was the place which we now call **Hole-in-the-Rock.** This is a very steep ravine, cleft, slot or crack in the rim of Glen Canyon. The short canyon was actually created along a minor geologic fault. From the rim to the river was just over a km, but it had a drop of 300 meters. They had to dig and blast out a road wide enough for wagons. The route went straight down in the upper part, then it angled to the left. In the upper sections they drilled holes in the sandstone, inserted poles, then laid brush and rocks on top of that. Wagons were taken down one at a time. Wheels were locked, and men on ropes held the wagons back in the steeper parts. The average grade was said to be 25%, while the steepest part was about 45%!

In order to cross the river, the Mormon Church(which sponsored the group) sent Charles T. Hall from Escalante to the river to build a ferryboat. Lumber was sent from Escalante and a boat large enough for two wagons was built. There was no cable or rope across the river, and only one set of oars was used for power.

Not all of what you see there today was made by the Hole-in-the-Rock Party. In 1899-1900, the Hoskaninni Mining Company built steps in the upper section which made it easier for men or horses to

Lake Powell and the mouth of Ribbon Canyon, seen from the top of the Jackass Bench Trail.

168

walk down. After that time no more wagons were taken down through the Hole. Several large boulders have since fallen into the slot and erosion has taken a toll. Today, one wonders how wagons could have been taken down through it. When you arrive, dock on the right, or north side of the bay. From there, you can walk up on part of the old road. Near the top you'll likely have to walk on all fours to get up the steeper parts.

Much of the road which took so much time to make is now under water. You can pick up the route though, as it went between Register Rocks on the east side of the river. If the water is at or near the HWM, you can boat between these two tall rocks, as seen on the map. From there the party went up Cottonwood Canyon which required more road building. In the upper sections near the rim is where they once again had to blast their way through.

When you first start walking up **Cottonwood Canyon,** you'll likely pick up this old road or trail on the right, or south side of the creek bed. Once you get on it, it's then easy to follow. After a little more than a km, the road begins to climb up the hillside on the right. There it becomes very visible as it heads up a dugway. For the most part, the old wagon road runs up a kind of hogsback or ridge, but at the same time runs along the bottom of shallow drainages, until it reaches the top of Wilson Mesa.

Along the way where the road runs across slickrock, you can still see ruts and grooves in the solid sandstone. On top you'll arrive at the end of the hiking part of the old trail. Beyond is the old road, but which is presently used by 4WD's(they start from Highway 276, about half way between Hall's Crossing Marina and Highway 95). At that point are signs, stopping motor vehicles from going down toward the lake, and the most interesting part of this historic trail. From the end of this 4WD road, you can walk down Wilson Creek into the San Juan River Arm of Lake Powell. More about this on Map 27.

Hike Length and Time Needed The hike to the rim along the Jackass Bench Trail is about one km. Most people can do this round-trip hike in less than an hour; the author did it in 40 min. In Ribbon Canyon, you can walk about 3 kms, which should take about 2 to 3 hours, round-trip. The author took less than two hours.

Up the Hole-in-the-Rock Trail, on the west side of the lake, is less than a km, and most people can do this in an hour or two. Some will take longer if they want to rim-walk for better views of the lake. From the HWM to the top of the trail in Cottonwood Canyon, is about 3 kms, one way. The author did it in just over an hour and a half, but you may want 2 to 3 hours, round-trip.

Boots or Shoes There is no wading in any of these canyons, so any boots or shoes will do.

Water The water would likely be good to drink anywhere in Ribbon Canyon, although the higher up canyon you go, the better the water. There's one real good bubbling spring near the head of the main canyon.

Steps cut in the Navajo Sandstone in the lower part of the Jackass Bench Trail.

There may be a very minor seep near the top of the Hole-in-the-Rock Trail, but with so many people around, it's surely polluted. There's a year-round stream in Cottonwood Canyon, but it's grazed by Melvin Dalton's cattle during the period from October until June. If you can drink from a spring, OK; otherwise best to take you own water.

Main Attractions Good views of the lake and Navajo Mountain, a box canyon with a captive deer herd, and an old historic wagon road or trail. Also, one of the better areas on the lake for camping in Cottonwood Canyon.

Hiking Maps USGS or BLM map Navajo Mountain(1:100,000), or The Rincon and Navajo Mtn.(1:62,500).

Later History For about one year after the Hole-in-the-Rock Party passed through, this was the normal route used between the people on the San Juan River and the Mormon settlements to the west. But it was a rough road, and Charles T. Hall didn't get much business. So he moved his ferry up stream to Halls Crossing and opened an easier route there in 1881.

Meanwhile, Kumen Jones, the last person of the original Hole-in-the-Rock group to pass through the Hole route, reported that a William Hyde had set up a trading post on the river to do business with the Utes, Piutes and Navajos, who began to use the trail themselves to reach the Mormon settlements west of the Colorado. Stories tell of outlaws and cattle rustlers using the route as well.

During the Glen Canyon Gold Rush days, this route was also a boon to prospectors. In 1888, J. R. Neilson, an enterprising miner, with the help of several hired hands, packed several tons of supplies down to the river where he constructed a large double decked boat measuring about 6 x 12 meters. It took four men one month to ferry all the supplies to the river along the trail. The boat was built with living quarters for four men and machinery for placer mining, along with a kitchen, and carpenter and blacksmith shops.

In December of 1888, the barge was complete. It had no power, and could only float down stream. It was guided by two sweeps, one at either end. The first stop for the craft was about 14 kms down stream, at a place Crampton believes was near the mouth of Music Temple Canyon. There they began operations. The gravel and sand were first screened twice, and the fine material placed in a stirring tub. From there it was washed over mercury coated amalgamators. The amalgam was supposed to collect the fine particles of gold, but apparently without success.

The operation was then moved to a point about 16 kms below the mouth of the San Juan for two months; again without success. Finally, it's believed they sailed on down to Lee's Ferry where the boat was presumably abandoned.

It was the **Hoskaninni Company** which spent the most time and money in the area of the Hole-in-the-Rock. In 1898, the company sent Robert B. Stanton down Glen Canyon, where he staked and

A great view of Navajo Mountain seen from the top of the Jackass Bench Trail.

re-claimed the entire length of the canyon with 145 claims. But by law, it was necessary to perform assessment work on the claims each year in order to hold them and prevent others from *claim-jumping*. Under Stanton, four groups of men were sent out into Glen Canyon to build trails and roads, and prepare various locations for future mining work.

One of the groups was sent to the Hole-in-the-Rock. Nathaniel Galloway took 26 men to the Hole and established camp in the fall of 1899. They lugged 3800 kgs of supplies down the Hole Trail to the river on the backs of men. To do that, they modified the trail with cut steps, to make it easier for men to walk down. During this same period of time, which was from October 1899, until January 1900, they built the better trail up to the canyon rim from Jackass Bench.

They also started a road up on Jackass Bench, as well as a trail down stream along the river on the west bank for about 1 1/2 kms. All in all, they made many minor trails along the river from just below the mouth of the San Juan, to nearly the mouth of the Escalante River in the north. Galloway's men may also have built several stone structures at the bottom of the trail. But all this work was for nothing, because when it was learned that Stanton's Dredge up in the Bullfrog Creek region, couldn't separate the fine gold dust from the sand, the company folded. That was in about May of 1901. The dredge and all the equipment were eventually sold to J. T. Raleigh for $200.

After the Hoskaninni Company left the Hole, two fellows name Henry Newell Cowles and Joseph T. Hall(no relation to Charles T. Hall) opened a trading post at the mouth of Hole-in-the-Rock Creek on the Colorado. They built a small stone cabin at the bottom end of the little creek, and referred to as Fort Hall or Hall's Trading Post. They used the creek water for drinking and for irrigating a small garden.

Hall and Cowles had a good business with the Indians from about mid-1900 until mid-1902. They hired two helpers, one Navajo, one Piute, to help ferry customers across the river and to lug down supplies from the newly built Jackass Bench Trail. The Indians, who were Utes, Piutes and Navajos, would trade sheep and goat hides, wool, and hand-woven blankets; for sugar, meat, tobacco, yardage, knives, hardware and livestock.

After these traders left, the route was used only sporadically throughout the years by Navajos who occasionally traded with the Mormon settlements to the west. Since the early days of this century, not much was going on there, but with the tourist boom after the building of Glen Canyon Dam, the place is visited daily by dozens of boaters and by people who drive down the Hole-in-the-Rock Road from Escalante.

A sign at the mouth of Hole-in-the-Rock Bay. The trail is seen in the background.

Steps cut in the Hole-in-the-Rock Trail. These were probably cut by the Hoskaninni Mining Company, not the Hole-in-the-Rock Party.

From the top of the Hole-in-the-Rock Trail looking southeast toward Cottonwood Canyon across the lake.

The Hole-in-the-Rock Trail near the head of Cottonwood Canyon on the east side of the lake.

Telefoto view down Cottonwood Canyon, across Lake Powell and up Hole-in-the-Rock Canyon.

Llewellyn Gulch & Reflection, Hidden Passage & Music Temple Canyons

Location and Campsites All of these canyons are very near the confluence of the San Juan River Arm of the lake. Llewellyn Gulch is north of the confluence and near buoy M63(K101), while the mouth of Reflection Canyon is near buoy M57(K91). On the Navajo Mountain metric map(1:100,000 scale), Reflection Canyon is called Cottonwood Gulch. The mouth of the San Juan River Arm runs east from near buoy M57(K91). Both Hidden Passage and Music Temple Canyons are just below the mouth of the San Juan River.

This is one of the few places in the main channel of Lake Powell where good campsites exist. Most of the campsites are located between Llewellyn and Reflection Canyons. These sites are there because of the geology. The rocks have been raised to the point that some of the Kayenta benches are exposed. This, and the weathering Navajo Sandstone cliffs nearby, combine to create a number of sandy beaches.

Llewellyn Gulch Inlet also has a number of good sandy campsites in its middle and upper end. Sometime during the winter of 1987-88, a part of the canyon wall crashed, creating a large rockfall at the upper end of the inlet. The NPS has placed a warning sign nearby.

Reflection Inlet is another Navajo Sandstone job, with walls rising directly out of the water. There are a couple of small campsites in the middle of the inlet, and at the end of each channel there are good sandy sites. At the end of the main fork there is one almost continuous beach for nearly 300 meters. The author camped there along with half a dozen other boating groups. There are no campsite in Hidden Passage, but there should be two in Music Temple Canyon.

Routes or Trails As you start up **Llewellyn Gulch,** on the left and behind the dam created by the rockfall, is the upper and now blocked-off part of the waterway. The author once stood on the banks of this pond and watched a rather tame beaver swim back and fourth for several minutes.

To begin the hike, walk along the top of the bench on the right, or north side of the upper pond. Just above the HWM, and along the bottom of the Navajo cliff on the right, is the first of three panels of petroglyphs in the canyon. Immediately around the corner and on the left, or south side, is a sandslide. Go up this slide, and near the top you'll find the remains of an old cattle trail. This is the first of two stock trails entering the canyon.

From the first trail, walk along the bench on the north side of the stream. You can use hiker-made trails. After 200 meters or so, is the second panel of petroglyphs on the right or north side. After this one, and perhaps another 200-300 meters further up canyon is the third panel of petroglyphs, again on the right side. Just beyond this last panel and on the left, or south side, and at

Camping scene in the middle part of the inlet to Llewellyn Gulch.

MAP 22, LLEWELLYN GULCH AND REFLECTION, HIDDEN PASSAGE & MUSIC TEMPLE CANYONS

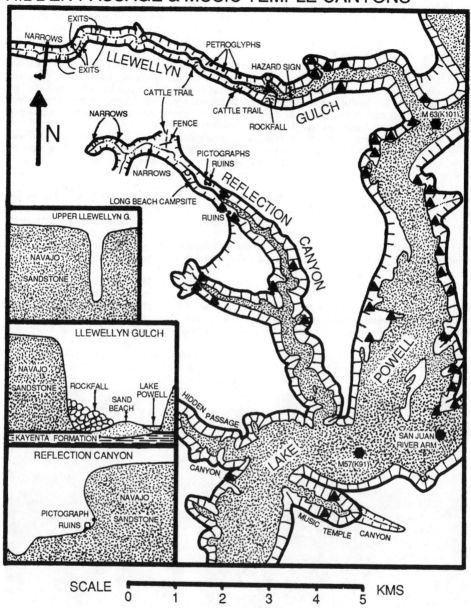

SCALE 0 1 2 3 4 5 KMS

a tight bend of the canyon is the second cattle trail. This one has steps picked out of the Navajo slickrock.

Above this trail, the canyon constricts and after another km it begins to be very narrow. This is where the stream first begins to flow. It appears to be a year-round stream in this drainage. The author continued up these very good narrows for 2 to 3 kms, but simply got tired of walking through this slot canyon. He never did reach the end. In the upper part, above where the water begins to flow, the author counted two exits out to the north, or right hand side(the first of which has steps cut, perhaps by a miner), and five exits to the south, or left side of the canyon. For someone who hasn't seen a good slot canyon before, this is a good one--one of the best leading into Lake Powell.

Reflection Canyon is another place worth visiting. Right at the upper end of the inlet is a long sandy beach. At the beginning of this beach area look to the left, or south side, and high on the wall in a small alcove is an Anasazi or Fremont ruin. You can't get up to it now. It was likely easy to reach when built, but subsequent flooding and erosion has washed away the bench below(it's possible too that the builders used ladders?).

Going up canyon, you'll be wading in a stream or be walking upon a sandy bench made of alluvial fill. Less than half a km above the HWM, and on the right, or northeast side of the stream, you'll see up against the wall and under an overhang, another set of ruins. This one has been damaged by cattle. Just to the left on the wall is one of the few pictographs(painted on) seen in the Glen Canyon area. At first the author thought it could be fake, but it's seems similar to pictographs in other canyons in the region. Someone has shot bullets into part of it.

A km above these ruins the canyon opens up for a short distance. At that point you can walk out of the canyon bottom on an old stock trail to the right and through a gate in a short barbed wire fence. Just to the left of the fence is a short and shallow set of narrows. You can walk around this section. Further up and near the end of the canyon is still another slot and blocking falls in the Navajo Sandstone.

Hike Length and Time Needed You can walk up Llewellyn Gulch about 7 kms. Most people would want about 5 or 6 hours to see everything in the canyon. The author did it in 3 1/2 hours, round-trip. You can walk about 4 kms up Reflection Canyon easily in half a day. The author's visit lasted 2 hrs. 20 min.

Boots or Shoes There's water in the lower end of both canyons, but you can normally avoid wading in Reflection, unless you want to wade through potholes in the slot parts of the canyon. You'll have to use wading boots or shoes in Llewellyn.

Water There were no fresh signs of cattle or beaver in Reflection in 1988, so that water would likely be good to drink, at least where it seeps out of the creek bed higher up. If you see cattle(winter months only--October to June), beware. There haven't been any cattle in Llewellyn for years, so it should have good water higher in the canyon. There are beaver in the lower end of Llewellyn.

Main Attractions Anasazi or Fremont ruins, pictographs and petroglyphs, and very good narrow or slot canyons.

Hiking Maps USGS or BLM map Navajo Mountain(1:100,000), or Navajo Mtn.(1:62,500).

J.W. Powell's Report Just below the mouth of Reflection Canyon is another drainage entering Glen Canyon from the east. Here's what Powell had to say about it for August 1, 1869. *On entering,*

Narrows in the upper end of Llewellyn Gulch. One of the best narrows hikes around.

we find a little grove of box-elder and cottonwood trees, and turning to the right, we find ourselves in a vast chamber, carved out of the rock. At the upper end there is a clear, deep pool of water, bordered with verdure. Standing by the side of this, we can see the grove at the entrance. The chamber is more than 200 feet[60 meters] high, 500 feet[150 meters] long, and 200 feet[60 meters] wide. Through the ceiling, and on through the rocks for a thousand feet[300 meters] above, there is a narrow, winding skylight; and this is all carved out by a little stream which runs only during the few showers that fall now and then in this arid country..... The rock at the ceiling is hard, the rock below, very soft and friable; and having cut through the upper and harder portion down into the lower and softer, the stream has washed out these friable sandstones; and thus the chamber has been excavated.

Here we bring our camp. When "Old Shady" sings us a song at night, we are pleased to find that this hollow in the rock is filled with sweet sounds. It was doubtless made for an academy of music by its storm-born architect; so we name it **Music Temple[Canyon].**

Music Temple Canyon now is a short but narrow inlet, which opens a bit in the upper end, to make a couple of campsites. Right at the very end of the inlet, the walls come very close together, not allowing boats to enter. The energetic hiker may try swimming this last part. It looked like there might be some short hiking possibilities if you can get out of the extreme narrow part. You might even try parking your boat out in the broader parts of the inlet and walking over the slickrock and re-entering the upper canyon from above.

Directly across the main channel from Music Temple is **Hidden Passage Canyon.** This is another very narrow waterway in the Navajo Sandstone. It has no campsites and no hiking possibilities. There are however, a couple of very deep and narrow side canyons which might make good anchorages, or a fine place to have a lunch in the middle of a hot summer day.

Camping beaches in the upper end of the inlet to Reflection Canyon.

Mikes & Copper Canyons and Castle Creek, Johnies Hole & Nokai Dome

Location and Campsites Both of these hiking areas, Mikes Canyon and Castle Creek, and the hike to the top of Nokai Dome and Johnies Hole, are in the upper end of the San Juan River Arm. The best way to reach this area, is to launch at the new San Juan Marina, located at the bottom end of Piute Farms Wash, very near the upper end of the San Juan Arm of the lake.

This marina and bay is slowly silting in, so the present plan is to move it to Copper Canyon, across the lake from the mouth of Castle Creek. This move is expected to take place in about 1990-91. Read more about this launch site under Marinas in the introduction of this book.

There are many good campsites on either side of the present marina, and in the inlet to Mikes Canyon. Also, in and near the short bay of Castle Creek are some good sandy camping beaches. Just south of this mapped area is the mouth of Copper Canyon. It too has several good sites, but there may be cattle and semi-wild donkeys roaming around the shore line at times. Also, Navajos in 4WD vehicles make it to the region of the lake to fish.

Routes and Trails Mikes Canyon is a long drainage which begins just south of Highway 276. It has a main fork and a left or west fork. It seems the left fork would be of most interest to hikers. For most of the year, this is a dry canyon, so you walk right up the dry creek bed. The way is free of obstacles, and the walking is generally easy. The formation you'll be walking through is the Chinle Formation. As you walk along, notice all the petrified wood. Most of the petrified wood you see on the Colorado Plateau comes from this formation.

In places you'll see the faded remains of an old mining exploration track weaving its way up the canyon bottom. In places you can walk on this. When you reach the fork in the canyon, walk into the left fork. It continues for a number of kms, becoming narrower and narrower. It's a deep canyon with impressive Wingate walls. At its end there is likely a big headwall. In past years, Mikes Canyon has been used for winter grazing of livestock.

The best hike here is up **Castle Creek,** another very long drainage. It begins as Steer Pasture Canyon far to the northeast and to the north of Highway 276. Only the lower end, including a tributary valley called **Johnies Hole,** is covered here.

In the lower end of Castle Creek, the walking is a little slow in places. There are some boulders, falls and willows in the canyon bottom, as several sections of it has a year-round flow of water. There are also cattle in the canyon, so there are some cow trails to follow in places. It's the lower end below the first two waterfalls, which has these very minor obstacles. Pass the first waterfall on the right, then as you approach the second, look up to the left for the trail on the west side of the canyon which

The first waterfall you'll come to as you hike up Castle Creek Canyon.

178

MAP 23, MIKES CANYON, CASTLE CK. AND JOHNIES HOLE & NOKAI DOME

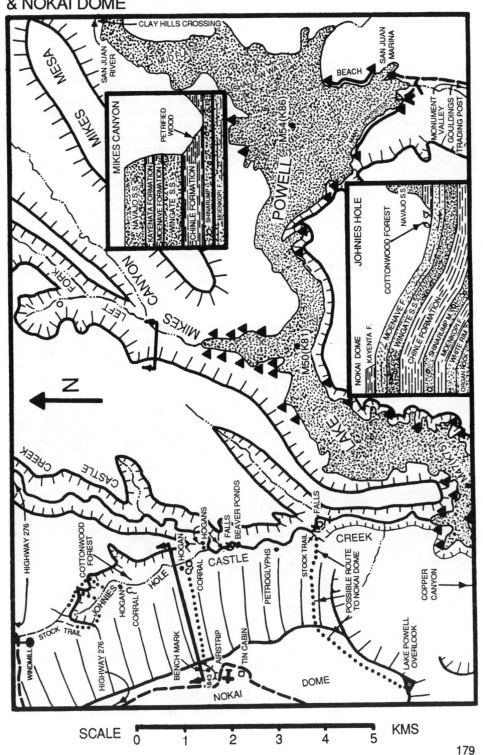

SCALE

0   1   2   3   4   5   KMS

takes hikers around this obstacle. Above the falls, the going is easier, and the creek bed may be dry at times. In the author's two trips to this canyon, it had running water once, but the next time it was bone dry.

Just above the second falls, is an old stock trail zig zagging up the slope to the left, or west. This short trail provides a way up to a small grazing area on the southeast side of Nokai Dome.

A km above the second falls and on the left, is an old Navajo or Piute camp of some kind. On a nearby rock are some recent Navajo petroglyphs. After another km, you'll come to a sizeable beaver pond with willows. Get out of the willow bottoms on the left, and look for cattle trails leading up on a bench. This trail bypasses another big Wingate waterfall just above the beaver pond.

Just beyond this third waterfall and on the right is a boulder with a very recent Navajo petroglyph reading, *Old Navajo Land*. This is obviously a *protestglyph*, dating from sometime this century when the BLM ran Navajos out of this canyon and back onto their national lands to the south. At this same point the valley changes, and from there on up, there are good grazing areas, cottonwood trees, a number of abandoned Navajo or possibly Piute homes, sweat houses and corrals.

Right at the junction of Castle Creek and Johnies Hole Valley, and up on a bench are some Indian structures. The author went up into Johnies Hole on two occasions instead of up Castle Creek(which could be an interesting canyon). Many kms up Castle Creek are a number of Anasazi ruins, which are very near the highway leading to Halls Crossing.

Johnies Hole is an oasis in the desert. It's a wide little valley with a small forest of mostly cottonwoods, but with some tall gamble oak and cedar trees. Upon the author's first visit, there was some running water in places. The second trip it was bone dry, except for one minor seep in about the middle of the valley.

There are several corrals and round log structures, which Stan Jones says were built by Piutes. However, Carl Mahon, a former BLM ranger out of Monticello, told the author he used to run Navajos and their flocks of sheep and goats out of the area on a regular basis up until the building of the Glen Canyon Dam. So it's likely at least some of these structures were built by Navajo herdsmen. Some appear to date from early this century, perhaps from about the first World War. Others are more recent, probably built after World War II.

There's supposed to be an old stock trail leading down into Johnies Hole from the north. The author made one trip there just to find it. He never did find a real man-made trail, but there are a couple of routes out of the upper end of the Hole, as shown on the map. The one furthest north is the easiest route out. On top are several stone cairns marking a route due north to an old windmill and stock tank located on the Nokai Dome Road. After that trip, the author was told by Melvin Dalton, the man who presently has grazing rights to this region, that the trail actually is on the west side of the upper part of

Protestglyph along the trail in Castle Creek Canyon, not far to the south of Johnies Hole.

Johnies Hole. This leaves room for some exploration.

An interesting side trip is to walk from Johnies Hole, to the top of **Nokai Dome.** From the lower end of of the Hole, simply start walking west up the sloping slickrock, which is likely the Moenave Formation. It's an easy walk and the slope isn't too steep. Near the top, you'll have to route-find up through some ledges, but that's easy too. If you go to the top of the little Kayenta bench at 1843 meters, you'll have fine views in all directions.

On top, find and follow the old oil exploration road south, and you'll come to an airstrip, a small tin cabin and the old oil drilling site. This road was build by an oil company sometime after World War II. For some good views of the lake, walk 3 or 4 kms south to the rim on this same road. The author hasn't walked the road south from the tin cabin, but a NPS ranger had it shown on his map. It runs out to very near the rim or overlook. Possibly an easier and shorter route to the rim exists from about where you pass the first two waterfalls in lower Castle Creek. The author hasn't used this, but there appears to be no major obstacles.

Hike Length and Time Needed You can walk for many kms into either fork of Mikes Canyon, but the petrified wood in the lower end might be more interesting than a long hike. It's about 10 kms from the lake to the middle of Johnies Hole and another 3 kms to the tin cabin on Nokai Dome. To do this hike will take all day. To hike to Johnies Hole and back will be about half a day for most hikers.

Boots or Shoes There's a stream in Castle Creek, but you can avoid getting your feet wet, so any kind of shoes are OK. Rugged hiking boots would be best if you plan to hike up to the top of Nokai Dome. Mikes Canyon is dry.

Water There were some minor seeps in Mikes Canyon upon the author's visit, but they were seasonal. It appeared there were springs higher up in Mikes left fork. There are good springs just above and below the second waterfall in lower Castle; your best source. There are cattle in all parts of Castle Creek from October to June, so creek water is suspect.

Main Attractions Petrified wood, waterfalls, beaver ponds, old Piute or Navajo ruins, and good views from Nokai Dome.

Hiking Maps USGS or BLM map Navajo Mountain(1:100,000), or Lake Canyon and Clay Hills(1:62,500).

Historical Sites--Upper San Juan River Arm Located at the eastern end of the navigable part of the San Juan Arm is **Piute Farms Wash and Bay**. This is the head of navigation as far as boaters are concerned. In the northeastern corner of the bay, and 3 or 4 kms down lake from Clay Hill Crossing, the river has silted up the bay to the point that even the inflatable rafts coming down river have to use oars until they're within about 3 kms of the San Juan Marina. This was the situation in the summer of 1988.

Looking southwest from the east rim of Johnies Hole toward the eastern slope of Nokai Dome.

Clay Hill Crossing is where the San Juan River emerges from a deep canyon and enters the open main body of the lake, at about M58(K93). This is the river distance from the mouth of the San Juan. The HWM actually extends up canyon about 20 more kms almost to the mouth of Grand Gulch, but it's impossible for boats to get up that far. Rubber rafts can barely float down when the water in the river is high.

This crossing was surely an old Indian route, but in more recent times the Navajo's used it when they were at war with the United States, during the years 1846-1864. A 1860 map by Egloffstein called it *Navajo Crossing*. This would have been a natural route for the Indians if they were heading for the Colorado River, via either White or Red Canyons.

The first extensive use of the Clay Hill Crossing by white men undoubtedly came with the San Juan Gold Rush, which began in 1892-93, and lasted for about 10 years. It was in this region that 200 mining claims were staked out between October and December of 1892 by the Gabel Mining District. One of the men who created the company was J. P. Williams, the same miner who built the Williams Trail near the mouth of Nokai Canyon.

Much later in history, and during the uranium boom days of the 1950's, a better road was built to the crossing. From there, another road was built along the south side of Mikes Mesa and to the mouth of Mikes Canyon.

The name **Piute Farms** comes from a broad open area at the mouth of Piute Farms Wash in pre-Lake Powell days. This area was originally settled by Piutes who farmed about 40-60 hectares(100-150 acres). They were living there when the Navajo's were at war with the USA. Because of those problems, there was a good deal of mixing of the tribes in the San Juan River region.

Just before the waters of Lake Powell covered the farms, Crampton reported a dozen peach and three or four apple trees growing, but no one lived there permanently. There were also half a dozen hogans, a sweathouse and one new Carter water pump. The pump was used to lift water from the San Juan to the farms when the river was low. It appears that during May and June, they may have used river water to irrigate, without pumping.

On the northeast corner or toe of Monitor Mesa, just above the lake northwest of the San Juan Marina, is the **Whirlwind Mine.** This uranium mine is located in the Shinarump Member(a conglomerate) of the Chinle Formation. According to Cal Black of Blanding, the ore was discovered in the 1940's, but the first uranium was shipped in 1950. It was worked periodically until 1960. Look for this one after you have traveled northwest of San Juan Marina about 2 kms(look south, high on the cliffs).

As you head west from the Piute Farms Bay, and at about M52(K83), look to the south and you'll see the remains of an old hand-built road. This wagon road or trail goes up and down along the shore line, occasionally rising to just above the HWM. It apparently was built during the San Juan Gold

Some kind of Navajo or Piute shelter in the lower end of Johnies Hole.

182

Rush. Crampton believes it was built as part of the assessment work, which was required to maintain active claims.

One of the easiest ways to enter the San Juan River Valley from the south before Lake Powell, was through **Copper Canyon**. The name undoubtedly derives from the discovery of copper deposits along the upper courses of the canyon, and at the base of Hoskaninni Mesa west of Oljeto in Monument Valley. It is quite probable that these deposits gave rise to the legend of the lost Merrick-Mitchell Silver Mine that drew prospectors, including Cass Hite, into the vicinity in about 1881. Copper, together with uranium, is found in vegetal fossil channel structures in the Chinle Formation.

The legend of the lost Merrick-Mitchell Mine started when two prospectors(who may or may not have found the place) by the names of James Merrick and Ernest Mitchell, were killed by Indians in Monument Valley in March, 1880. When their bodies were later examined, silver samples were found. This led to the belief that Merrick and Mitchell had found the reported Navajo silver mine. This was the single most important event which started the Glen Canyon Gold Rush beginning in 1884, and later the San Juan Gold Rush in 1892-93.

Some time during the San Juan Gold Rush of the 1890's, a road was built from Oljeto Trading Post down into Copper Canyon to the San Juan River, a distance of about 35 kms. About 6 kms above the mouth of Copper, the road left the wash and topped out on the east rim of the canyon. It then descended to the river and ended at **Williams Bar**, about 3 kms upstream, or east, from the mouth of the Copper Canyon. Williams Bar was located at about M49(K78), while the mouth of Copper Canyon entered the river at M47(K75). These distances are the mileage(kilomage) from the mouth of the San Juan River where it emptied into the Colorado River. There are no buoys in the San Juan Arm of the lake.

Williams Bar was one of the major placer gold mining sites along the San Juan River during the gold rush of 1892-93, and later. The site seems to be identified prominently with the name of J. P. Williams, one of the organizers of the Gabel Mining District, who also had many of the claims in the area of Clay Hill Crossing. Williams in 1884-85, had prospected the Navajo Mountain area looking for the Merrick-Mitchell Mine, during which time his party is reported to have seen Rainbow Bridge. In 1890 he was on the San Juan River.

In 1892, J. P. Williams was carrying on trade with the Navajo Indians, presumably at a location on the San Juan River. On file in the Recorder's Office, San Juan County, Utah, is the original day book kept by Williams. It showed entries or transactions with Indians and whites from April 22, 1892 to November in 1893. The same book recorded the events on Williams Bar. The first official claim recorded in the Williams Mining District was the *Plum Bob*. At one time, Williams had a steam boiler, evidently to run a pump, which was fixed to a barge. All this was at a place he called **Williamsburg**.

In 1960 when Crampton visited this place, they found a stone house about 300 meters from the river. It was built up against a cliff, which formed one wall. The house measured about 4 x 6 meters, and had a fireplace and one door. Less than a km upstream, was the foundation of another stone house, measuring about 6 by 7 meters. Some sources believed it was built by Charles H. Spencer before 1908. If this is true, it was the first of at least four different sites this mining engineer developed in the Glen Canyon region in a 7 or 8 year period. This must have been Spencer's first of four total failures at gold mining.

From the mouth of Copper Canyon another road headed to the west. It stayed up above the river and atop the Shinarump bench all the way to Nokai Canyon. This road is used by Navajos today driving 4WD pickup trucks. From the bay at the mouth of Nokai, one branch was called Spencer Road, and ran further west to end at Spencer Camp. Another road ran to Zahn Camp. Read more on Spencer and Zahn on Map 24.

Spencer Road, Williams Trail and Nokai Canyon

Location and Campsites The old road and trail covered on this map are located south of Zahn Bay, which is about in the middle of the San Juan River Arm of Lake Powell. There are no buoys in the San Juan Arm, so the old river mileage/kilomage is used here to show relative distances. The mouth of Nokai Canyon is M44(K70), and Spencer Camp is about M38(K61) from the mouth of the San Juan River. These two places are the two beginning points you can hike from. Both of these hikes are on Navajo Nation lands.

In this region are a number of good campsites. The best ones are in the bay or inlet to Nokai Canyon. These are sandy, but in some places the water is shallow leading to the shore line. Right where the normally dry Nokai Creek enters is a big sandy delta. Be aware, there may be semi-wild Navajo donkeys around this bay, and they can be noisy as hell at night especially if one of the females is in heat, as was the case on one of the author's visits.

On the south side of Zahn Bay are a number of sites, but some are clay, rather than sandy beaches. The islands in the bay may also provide good campsites, and there are places at the western end of the Spencer Road for a camp. One word of caution when camping at the mouth of Nokai Canyon and where the Spencer Road enters the lake. With lots of donkeys and other livestock in these two areas, and all the manure lying around, expect to see a lot more flies than in other areas.

Routes or Trails As you boat into **Nokai Canyon Inlet,** look to the southwest and upon the inclined slope made of the Shinarump Member of the Chinle Formation. High above you can see an old wagon road zig zagging it's way up toward the cliffs beyond. This is the **Spencer Road.** Park somewhere along the southwest shore of the bay. You may have to look around for the beginning of this road, but the further up you go, the easier it will be to find it. There are Navajo donkeys and cattle in the area, and they use this old track. In areas where the road itself has faded, the livestock have usually created their own trail in its place.

About two kms from the HWM in Nokai Bay, you will see to the left, and running south, the beginning of an old trail built by a miner named Williams. At about that point, the Spencer Road is running due west and still climbing. Not far above this junction, the road runs atop landslide debris from the big walls to the south, which are made up mostly of Wingate Sandstone. Up to that point, the road is on top of the Shinarump Member of the Chinle Formation. There is lots of petrified wood in this part of the Chinle.

From a high point, the road then runs to the west and northwest, and for the most part along the rim of the Shinarump bench. From the half way point the road gradually descends. In some places it's hard to see, but there will always be livestock tracks to mark the way. The northwest end of the road gradually merges into the lake at about M39(K62). You can start at either end of this track, and

The Williams Trail as it zig zags up through the Wingate Sandstone cliffs.

184

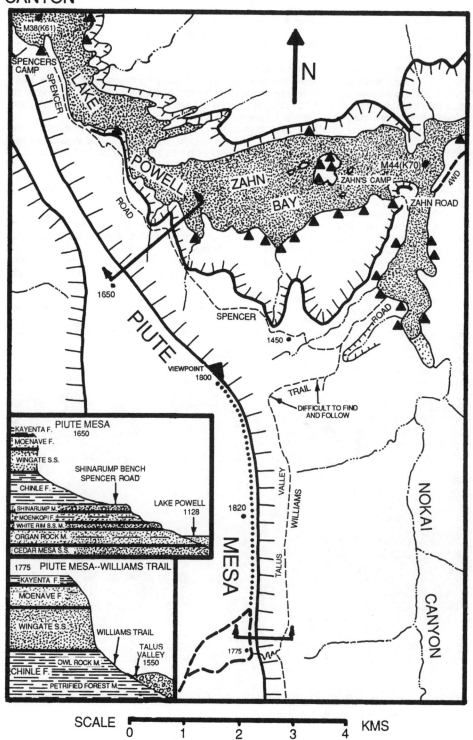

M38(K61)

SPENCERS CAMP

SPENCER

LAKE

POWELL

ZAHN

BAY

N

M44(K70)

ZAHN'S CAMP

ZAHN ROAD

4WD

ROAD

1650

PIUTE

SPENCER

1450

ROAD

VIEWPOINT
1800

TRAIL

DIFFICULT TO FIND
AND FOLLOW

KAYENTA F.
MOENAVE F.
WINGATE S.S.

PIUTE MESA
1650

SHINARUMP BENCH
SPENCER ROAD

CHINLE F.

LAKE POWELL
1128

SHINARUMP M.
MOENKOPI F.
WHITE RIM S.S. M.
ORGAN ROCK M.

CEDAR MESA S.S.

1820

1775   PIUTE MESA--WILLIAMS TRAIL

KAYENTA F.

MOENAVE F.

WINGATE S.S.

WILLIAMS TRAIL

TALUS
VALLEY
1550

OWL ROCK M.

CHINLE F.

PETRIFIED FOREST M.

1775

MESA

VALLEY

WILLIAMS

TALUS

NOKAI

CANYON

SCALE

0   1   2   3   4   KMS

185

walk toward the middle, as did the author. The part of road most interesting to visit is near Nokai Bay. It's the highest part and it affords the best views of the lake and country-side, including the exposed geology of the south side of Nokai Dome.

The **Williams Trail** takes off from the Spencer Road about 2 kms above the southwest side of the bay or inlet to Nokai Canyon. As you walk up Spencer Road, look to the left and you should see a shallow canyon or drainage. Just above the head of this mini-canyon about 100 meters is where the Williams Trail heads south.

This trail is man-made, but in places it's hard to find and follow. The author lost it twice; going and coming, in the area between the head of the mini-canyon and the soaring Wingate cliffs of Piute Mesa. The main thing to remember is, it runs north-south along the foot of the Wingate cliffs and in what the author calls the Talus Valley. This little valley is a nearly flat region used for grazing. You can surely find and follow it there, but in the sagebrush it's sometimes hard to see.

At the southern end of this valley, the trail veers up to the right, then it's easier to locate. In this part as it begins to steepen, it was dug out with pick and shovel and it's still clearly visible and used often by some hikers and livestock. When the trail reaches the bottom of a break in the Wingate cliff it's clear that hardrock miners built this one. Parts of it have been blasted out of the rock as it zig zags up through the cliffs. It's been said that it was originally built by J. P. Williams, a miner during the San Juan Gold Rush. But the author believes it's also very likely some work was done on this part of the trail during the Depression days of the 1930's by the CCC crews.

As it starts to zig zag up the face, look to the south. and you'll see another trail coming north to meet the one you're on. That trail is apparently connected to the Wetherill Trail about 12 kms to the south. When you finally reach the rim of Piute Mesa, the trail ends. At that point is an old road, which you could follow to the west and to Navajo Mtn. Trading Post. This road also runs along the rim to the north for about a km. If you'd like good views of the lake and the exposed geology of the Nokai Dome, rim-walk to the north another 5 kms. The elevation of the viewpoint shown is about 1800 meters, while the lake is 1128 at the HWM.

Hike Length and Time Needed The length of the Spencer Road is about 12 or 13 kms. It would take all day to walk from one end to the other and back, but the recommended hike is from Nokai Bay to a high point in the middle, and return. The Williams Trail runs for about 7 or 8 kms. Add two kms along the first part of the Spencer Road, and it's about 10 kms to the top of the mesa and the end of this historic trail.

Boots or Shoes Any dry weather hiking boots or shoes.

Water There are no springs anywhere near, so take your own water.

Main Attractions Two historic old trails and some great views of the geology of Nokai Dome from

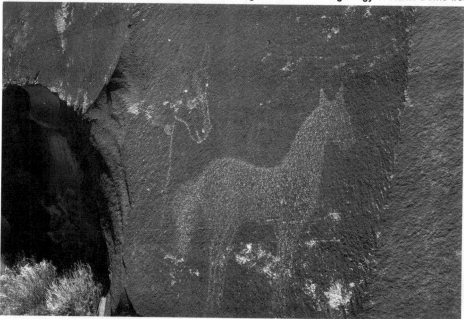

Recent Navajo etchings along the Williams Trail.

Piute Mesa.
Hiking Maps USGS or BLM map Navajo Mountain(1:100,000), or No Mans Mesa(1:62,500).
History of the Spencer Road and Williams Trail This story begins late in 1892 with the San Juan Gold Rush. One of the principal parties who got this one off the ground was a J. P. Williams. In April of 1892, he was carrying on some kind of trade with the Navajos from a place on the San Juan River. Presumably that location was just east of the mouth of Copper Canyon, around M46(K73). This was for a time called Williamsburg. It was on one of the most productive gold mining sites in the canyon, a place called Williams Bar.

Williams, according to Crampton and Charles H. Spencer, was the man who built this trail from the mouth of Nokai Canyon to the top of Piute Mesa. No explanations were given as to why it was originally built, but when Spencer came along, his crews used it to reach the top of the mesa where they cut cedar trees, then threw them over the cliff and used them in his own operations at Spencer Camp. Williams may have done the same thing.

Another chapter of San Juan history was written by the Zahn brothers of Los Angeles. The five brothers; Oscar, Otto, Paul, Hector and Oswald, did much of the development work at a place called Zahn's Camp. It was actually begun by T. R. Gabel, who organized the Gabel Mining District in this region in 1892. For many years it was referred to as Gabel Camp, but the Zahns bought him out later, along with various other interests in about 1902.

The five Zahn brothers, along with their mother, organized the Zahn and Baldwin Mining Company. They poured big money into the site, which already included a boiler and other machinery. They drove wagon loads of pipe and new equipment from Flagstaff, a distance of 300 kms. They also rafted machinery down the San Juan from Piute Farms.

The Zahns operated this placer mining outfit until the end of World War I before pulling out. They never made much profit, but one of their most famous accomplishments took place in September of 1915 when they drove a new Franklin automobile from Los Angeles to Zahn's Camp. On the return trip when they were driving out of Nokai Canyon, they broke the transmission and had to be pulled to Oljeto by John Wetherill and two teams of horses. You can still see part of what remains of Zahn's Road. Near the mouth of Nokai Bay, park and walk along the hill side to the west. Their road goes over a little divide and is clearly visible in several places. See the site on the map.

One of the more dynamic figures in the history of both the San Juan River and Glen Canyon, was Charles H. Spencer. Spencer was a big dreamer and even greater promoter. He originally came to the Glen Canyon-San Juan country in about 1900, but in 1909 he built this route now called Spencer Road. He set up a mining operation on the river near M38(K61). The road was built with pick and shovel by Navajos and Piutes. It rose from the canyon bottom to a hogsback about 300 meters

A view to the northeast from a high point along the Spencer Road.

187

above the river, then returned to the river with grades up to 25%.

Spencer Camp, or Camp Ibex as he called it, was set up near the river where great Wingate boulders were in abundance. His dream was to separate gold from the Wingate Sandstone. The machinery consisted of a Sampson Crusher, powered by a single cylinder Otto gasoline engine. They installed sorting screens and an amalgamating table. They also used a steam boiler for power. They obtained part of their firewood from the top of Piute Mesa. In the area of the viewpoint shown on the map, you may see stumps of trees which, according to Crampton, was the location where they felled the trees and threw them over the cliff. They also stretched a cable across the river to catch and haul in driftwood.

Spencer operated his crushing mill using 10 hired men in June, 1909, and again in the winter of 1909-10, but this scheme was a failure. Spencer abandoned Camp Ibex in the spring of 1910, when he heard of gold being discovered in the Chinle claybeds at Lee's Ferry. He was at Lee's Ferry for a couple of years, using up thousands of investors dollars. While there, he devised a scheme to haul coal from Warm Creek to Lee's Ferry in a paddle wheeled steamboat. The coal was to be used to power a steam boiler to help extract the gold from the clay. Things failed there too. He then ended his illustrious career at Pahreah, Utah, in about 1915.

Looking north from the rim of Piute Mesa toward the southern exposure of Nokai Dome.

Petrified wood along the Spencer Road. It comes mostly from the Shinarump Member of the Chinle Formation.

Spencer Camp as it looked in February of 1910(Spencer foto).

Great Bend Canyons and Neskahi & Piute Canyons

Location and Campsites The canyons included on this map are around a huge gooseneck bend in about the middle of the San Juan River Arm called the Great Bend. The author found this section to be fairly popular with boaters, but there are very few visitors compared to the canyons between Wahweap and Rainbow Bridge. The Bend has some of the best scenery on the lake. Very few boaters go further up the San Juan Arm.

Campsites are a little scarce in these parts. However, there are several Kayenta slickrock type sites on the inside of the bend along the main channel, and for the most part, camping places exist in the upper end of each canyon or inlet. Most of those in the little alcoves are sandy and very pleasant. Note the number of springs on the outside of the bend. Water seeps out from the contact point of the Navajo Sandstone above, and the Kayenta Formation below.

The main channel is very narrow in this section. On the right hand side of this map, you will see the Wingate walls rising from waters edge, but it slowly submerges to the northwest and takes a dive under Grey Mesa. Neskahi and Piute Canyons are discussed below

Routes or Trails The longest canyon on this map is what Crampton and the old river runners used to call Navajo Canyon. However, Carl Mahon, big game guide and former BLM employee out of Monticello, along with all the local cattlemen always called the drainage **San Juan Canyon.** Presently, and during times of high water, the lake makes it two separate canyons. The author camped right at the HWM at the upper end of the inlet to East Fork on a sandy beach; one of the best little campsites he had on Lake Powell.

Whether you want to hike in the East or the West Fork of San Juan Canyon, you'll have to start at the same place, right at the bottom end of the East Fork. The reason for this is a dry fall in the lower end of the West Fork.

Just at the HWM in the East Fork is a good little seep with cold water. Just above the spring, the canyon is full of house-size boulders. All this debris covers up any falls or dropoffs, allowing you to get up through the Wingate Sandstone easily. After perhaps a half a km, you leave this *boulder alley* and the canyon all of a sudden opens up. At that point you can walk up either canyon. For the sake of simplicity, this description will take the hiker up West and down East Fork. This is the recommended hike, if you are fit and have the time to take an all day walk.

Once you get to the top of boulder alley in the lower end of East Fork, make a 180 degree turn to the left and work your way up on top of the Kayenta bench. This bench is in both canyons, and you can walk on it from one to the other. This seems the only way into **West Fork,** unless you dock out in the main channel somewhere and walk from there.

Once you've turned the corner and have entered the lower end of West Fork, it will be necessary

An old cowboy trail in the upper end of the West Fork of San Juan Canyon.

190

MAP 25, THE GREAT BEND CANYONS

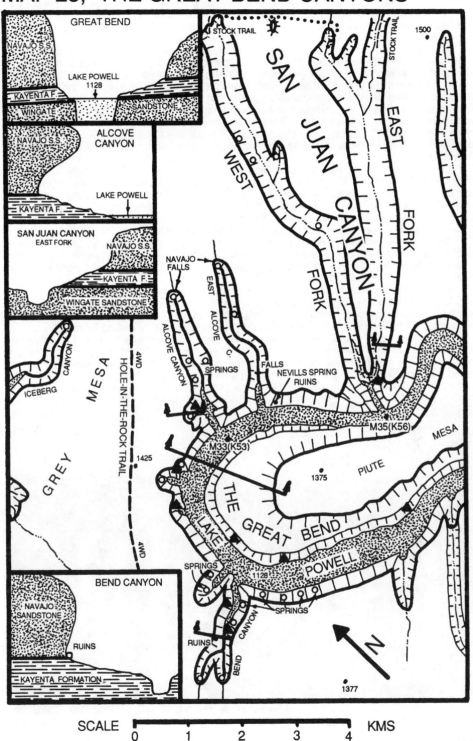

GREAT BEND

NAVAJO S.S.

LAKE POWELL
1128

KAYENTA F.

WINGATE   SANDSTONE

ALCOVE
CANYON

NAVAJO S.S.

LAKE POWELL

KAYENTA F.

SAN JUAN CANYON
EAST FORK

NAVAJO S.S.

KAYENTA F.

WINGATE SANDSTONE

STOCK TRAIL

1500

SAN

JUAN

WEST   CANYON

EAST

FORK   FORK

NAVAJO
FALLS

EAST

ALCOVE

C.

ALCOVE CANYON   SPRINGS   FALLS

NEVILLS SPRING
RUINS

CANYON

ICEBERG

MESA

4WD

HOLE-IN-THE-ROCK TRAIL

GREY   MESA

1425

M33(K53)

M35(K56)

MESA

PIUTE

1375

THE

LAKE   GREAT   BEND

POWELL

SPRINGS

1128

SPRINGS

BEND CANYON

NAVAJO
SANDSTONE

RUINS

RUINS

BEND   CANYON

KAYENTA FORMATION

4WD

N

1377

SCALE   0   1   2   3   4   KMS

191

to stay on the Kayenta bench for one or two kms, before the terrain allows you to actually walk in the bottom of the usually dry creek bed. As you then walk along the bottom of the canyon, there will be a number of places where willows, cottonwood trees and other water-loving plants grow. Upon the author's visit, on the first of October, 1988, there was no running water anywhere, but he did find springs or seeps in 3 or 4 places. In wetter times you should find lots more water.

After walking a total of about 10 kms, you'll come to the end of the canyon. It would be a box, but some time in the early days of San Juan County settlement, cattlemen built a **stock trail** down from the top of the Navajo rim. To find it, go right to the upper end where you'll find the usual blocking falls. Just to the left of it and back down canyon 300 meters on the west side, is a break in the Navajo wall. It's the only place anyone has a chance of getting out and should be easy to locate. It's been blasted out in a place or two, and you can see fresh scrape marks on the slickrock, as this trail is still used occasionally by cowboys today. However, the trail is too steep for cattle so they are taken down into the East Fork, then they make their way into the West Fork via the Kayenta bench just described. This according to Monticello stockman Melvin Dalton, who grazes cattle in these canyons from October to June.

Once you get on top, look for stone cairns marking the route up along a minor ridge to the northeast a ways. Not far above, the cairns seem to vanish and you're on your own. At that point, turn right 90 degrees, and head southeast past the top of the dry falls. Continue southeast and to the left of a fairly prominent little butte. Just past this butte, you'll begin to drop down into the drainage of the **East Fork**. You will then have to route-find south down into the canyon, then up the other side, while looking for another route over the upper Navajo falls in that drainage.

The author entered the upper end of East Fork not far below the big Navajo falls, but there is another easier way down in if you were to walk further to the south. The author didn't take the time to explore every nook and cranny, but there is a walk-in route in an upper east fork, approximately as shown on the map--according to Dalton.

From the head of East Fork, it's about 7 kms back down to the boulder alley and the lake. There should be a number of potholes along the upper and middle sections of the drainage and in the Kayenta slickrock; but don't count on water being in them all the time. In wetter times there will be a seep or two. The lower end of East Fork is very dry and sandy, but easy walking otherwise.

Just to the east of Alcove Canyon is another drainage which could be it's twin. The author has named it **East Alcove Canyon** for convenience. Along the main channel and just to the east, or right side, of the mouth of East Alcove is a shallow indentation. Before Lake Powell, river runners called this place Nevills Spring, but the main spring is now under water. Presently, it has some wet dirt and greenery, but no water. On a ledge to the left is a small Anasazi granary still in good condition.

Looking southwest from the upper end of East Fork of San Juan Canyon. Navajo Mtn. in the background.

East Alcove has a short inlet, but had no campsites when the author visited the place. Just above the HWM is a short waterfall, which you can get around easily. As you go up canyon, you'll see a developing hiker's trail in places. The canyon has what appears to be a year-round flowing stream, with lots of tall grasses and trees. It's another green oasis in the desert. There are several alcoves in the canyon, each of which seems to have a small seep or spring. The author saw no fresh sign of beaver, so the water is likely good drinking especially if you get it from a spring. There are no cattle or deer in the canyon at present, but in the past it was used for grazing by Navajo livestock.

In Crampton's research of the San Juan River before Lake Powell, he found there was a man-made stock trail leading out of the main channel and up through the Wingate to the Kayenta bench between Alcove and East Alcove. This allowed cattle to enter the upper parts of each drainage. The Wingate is now covered by water and the trail lost. There was another trail up to the wide bench on the inside of the Great Bend curve as well. As of the early 1960's, this was also used as a Navajo pasture.

Alcove Canyon is so named because just inside the inlet and on the left, or west, is one of the biggest alcoves around. Actually, there are many large alcoves on the outside curve of the Great Bend, so this one isn't as unique as it otherwise might be. Walking up Alcove, you'll see several other alcoves on both sides of the drainage, each with a minor spring. There is running water, likely the year-round, but it could dry up at times. This canyon is green with all kinds of water-loving plants. The author saw no sign of beaver, but they seem to come and go into various Lake Powell canyons throughout the year. When they finish the food supply in one place they simply swim to another canyon. The only campsite the author saw was at the bottom of the biggest alcove mentioned above.

The last of the Great Bend canyons has no official name, so the author is calling it simply **Bend Canyon.** It's on the western side of the Bend, and is similar in geology and appearance to the Twin Alcove Canyons just to the north. This one however, has two upper forks, both of which are box canyons. The inlet to Bend Canyon has several good springs which flow down into the lake. Early one morning, the author observed a beaver washing itself on the shore line below one spring. He seemed to ignore the noisy motor boat. Up this canyon there are more sign of beaver, indicating a sizable population.

As you walk up canyon, get up onto the Kayenta bench to the right, or north side, and scan the walls. There is one fallen down cliff dwelling under a shallow overhang. Along the canyon bottom are several minor waterfalls, a year-round stream, and big alcoves at the head of each fork.

Hike Length and Time Needed If you were to walk up either fork of San Juan Canyon and return the same way it would likely take 5 or 6 hours round-trip. But if you make the loop-hike as suggested, plan on an all day hike. Alcove and East Alcove are both about 2 kms long, and you can walk up to

Small storage granary just above the now drowned Nevills Spring.

the end of each and back, in an hour or two. Bend Canyon is slightly shorter, but has more to see, so it's another hike of an hour or two.

Boots or Shoes   What streams there are in these canyons are small and you likely won't get your feet wet, so any kind of boots or shoes are OK.

Water Each canyon(with the exception of East Fork of San Juan) has springs, and if you take water directly from a spring, you shouldn't have any trouble. The author as usual, sampled water from each canyon, and didn't get a belly ache.

Main Attractions   Very high canyon walls, short but deep side canyons, lots of springs, at least two small ruins, great scenery and not too many people.

Hiking Maps   USGS or BLM map Navajo Mountain(1:100,000), or Lake Canyon and No Mans Mesa(1:62,500).

Other Nearby Canyons   In the area due south of the Great Bend, which is down-lake, there is a large open bay, the largest open body of water in the San Juan Arm. Entering this bay are two drainages. The first is **Neskahi Wash,** which entered the San Juan River at M24(K38). This is a short drainage, which in its lower parts has lots of landslide debris and the Chinle clay beds exposed at the shore line. The gentle slope makes for some campsites, but there are few if any sandy beaches. Instead, they're mostly clay-type sites.

Entering this large expanse of water on the southwest corner is **Piute Canyon**. This is a very long tributary to the San Juan, and it drains all of the eastern slopes of Navajo Mountain. It entered the river at M21(K34). It has had several different names throughout the years, but whatever may have been the first name applied to this canyon by the white men, it marked the practical lower limit of prospecting during the gold rush days. Below Piute Canyon, there were practically no lateral gravel deposits to be seen until Glen Canyon, 34 kms below.

The present-day inlet to Piute Canyon has a gentle slope from the shore line and a number of good campsites. The Chinle clays are exposed, but there are also some sandy areas. In this bay, you may see Navajo livestock grazing. There's a 4WD type road running down to the lake from Navajo Mtn. Trading Post. This was likely first built during the 1950's uranium boom, when miners were out scratching the Chinle beds. Along the shore line, you can find lots of petrified wood from the same Chinle Formation, and on the west side of the bay somewhere are some large boulders with petroglyphs(as shown on Stan Jones' map).

Small fox in East Alcove Canyon.

One of many huge alcoves seen along the outer wall of the Great Bend curve.

Waterfall and alcove in the upper part of Great Bend Canyon.

Deep, Desha & Trail Canyons

Location and Campsites The three canyons on this map are located in the lower end of the San Juan River Arm. Using old river distances from the Colorado, we find the mouth of Trail Canyon is near M13(K21); Desha Creek is at about M15(K24); and Deep Canyon is at about M18(K29). There are no buoys in the San Juan Arm of the lake. These drainages are all on the Navajo Nation.

This is another part of the lake where campsites are scarce. But there should be at least one sandy camping place at the head of each inlet or bay. The country these canyons drain is very sandy, so with every storm, more sand is deposited where the flood waters enter the lake. There are several other small sites in the main channel as well, usually on the Chinle bench. But much of the main channel has Wingate walls rising directly out of the water.

Routes or Trails The **Deep Canyon Inlet** is not so long, but is moderately narrow. The sheer walls rising from the water are Wingate Sandstone. Right at the end of the inlet where Deep Creek enters, there should always be a sandy bench that's high and dry and hopefully large enough for a tent. But the inlet is very narrow at that location. There is a stream in this canyon and it surely flows year-round, but it's small enough so you can avoid wading.

As you walk up canyon, you'll immediately see lots of tracks of horses, donkeys and cattle. There are at least two trails which allow livestock to enter and exit the canyon. These are located about half way up canyon on the right, or west side. This drainage is not very deep, so hikers can climb out in a number of places besides at the trails.

Not far above where the livestock trails are found, there's a major junction in the canyon. The tributary coming from the right, or west, has a waterfall not far above. Below the fall is a pool of water, where beaver have burrowed under the bank to make their home. The main canyon is the one to the left. Not far above the junction is a very good spring coming out of a crack in the wall. This is where the stream begins to flow and where you can safely tank up on water. This is where the author stopped. The canyon looks less interesting above the spring.

Desha Creek or Canyon is one the author has visited from both ends. The first time he came down from the Navajo Mtn. Trading Post, and is familiar with it's upper end. The inlet to Desha is similar to that of Deep Canyon. It has sheer Wingate walls rising from the water, except at its upper end, where there should be several sandy campsites.

Immediately above the HWM and just around the corner is a small beaver pond, then a couple of waterfalls pouring over the Wingate Sandstone. At the bottom of the lower falls is a nice pool. To get around these obstacles, regress about 75 meters and look to the east. There's a hikers trail up to the top of the ledge at a point where a side canyon enters. Climb upon the top of the Wingate(or perhaps on a bench of the Moenave?), and walk south to a point beyond the second or upper falls. Then look

Waterfall and pool in the lower Desha Canyon.

MAP 26, DEEP, DESHA & TRAIL CANYONS

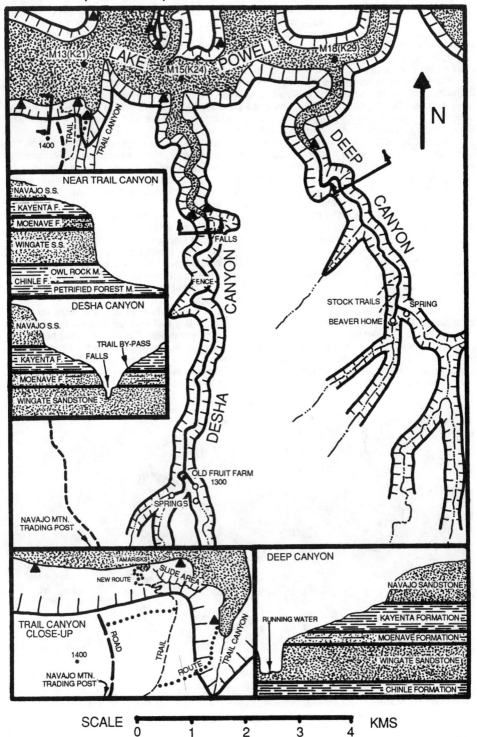

LAKE POWELL

M13(K21)
M15(K24)
M18(K29)

N

TRAIL
TRAIL CANYON
1400

DEEP CANYON

NEAR TRAIL CANYON
NAVAJO S.S.
KAYENTA F.
MOENAVE F.
WINGATE S.S.
OWL ROCK M.
CHINLE F.
PETRIFIED FOREST M.

FALLS
FENCE

DESHA CANYON
NAVAJO S.S.
TRAIL BY-PASS
KAYENTA F.   FALLS
MOENAVE F.
WINGATE SANDSTONE

DESHA CANYON

STOCK TRAILS   SPRING
BEAVER HOME

DESHA

OLD FRUIT FARM
1300

SPRINGS

NAVAJO MTN.
TRADING POST

TAMARISKS
SLIDE AREA
NEW ROUTE

TRAIL CANYON CLOSE-UP
ROAD
TRAIL
ROUTE
1400
NAVAJO MTN.
TRADING POST
TRAIL CANYON

DEEP CANYON
NAVAJO SANDSTONE
RUNNING WATER
KAYENTA FORMATION
MOENAVE FORMATION
WINGATE SANDSTONE
CHINLE FORMATION

SCALE   0   1   2   3   4   KMS

for a way down into the creek bed once again.

Above the falls and for a distance of about a km, the year-round creek flows on top of Wingate slickrock. In places it has cut small potholes, ravines and other erosional features in the sandstone. Just above this part is an old wooden fence across the canyon to keep livestock out of the lower end. From this point on up, the canyon is better suited for grazing. If you walk up from the fence about 4 or 5 kms, you'll come to an area with a number of old fruit trees and irrigated fields. Just above the fruit farm in the right hand, or western drainage, is where some good springs are located, which feed the small creek. This upper end of the canyon is heavily grazed by Navajo livestock.

The last hike is up an old Anasazi, and more recently a Navajo livestock trail, near **Trail Canyon.** Trail Canyon is very short with steep terraced walls. There are large boulders lining the dry creek bottom. There probably will be one good campsite in the upper part of the bay. From that campsite you could get to the rim of the canyon by walking up along the right, or west side, but there's some climbing *on all fours.* An interesting route anyone can climb.

The trail for which Trail Canyon is named, is actually around the corner to the west and on the north facing wall. This route has been used since Anasazi times, but more recently by Navajos. In the years after the Mormons built the Hole-in-the-Rock Trail, they would go down this trail, ford the San Juan a km or two above the mouth of Trail Canyon, then head up the trail in Wilson Creek. This would put them at the top of Wilson Mesa and on the Hole-in-the-Rock route to the Colorado. From the Colorado, they would go on to the Mormon settlements to trade.

This same trail was used by miners during the 1892-93 San Juan Gold Rush, and later during the uranium boom days of the 1950's. In the years prior to Lake Powell, the Navajos used the trail to reach the San Juan River bottoms between Cha and Desha Canyon, where they herded livestock. According to Crampton and his study of the Glen Canyon area, it was improved by the government CCC crews during the Depression days of the 1930's. Whoever worked on the trail did a good job, as it's almost wide enough for a 4WD vehicle. However, in 1982(according to Stan Jones), there was a landslide which wiped out the lower half of the trail. It seems that the rising lake waters lubricated the clay beds of the Chinle Formation, which allowed the slippage.

Since the landslide, people using the trail have started to develop an alternate route up to the lower part of the cliff face. From a point where Trail Canyon Bay and the main channel meet, boat to the west about 400 meters where there's a large grove of tamarisks. Dock there. Just behind the tamarisks is what appears to be a fault or landslide scarp, so at first angle up to the right or to the southwest; then when past the scarp, veer left and walk up to the southeast. Eventually, you'll meet and can use one of several minor hiker-made trails. Once you reach the base of the Wingate wall, a more heavily used trail is found. Walk east a few meters until you meet the middle part of the

Looking northeast at the San Juan Arm from the top of the trail near Trail Canyon.

constructed Trail Canyon Trail. After about three more switchbacks, you're on top. From there you can get on a road and walk to Navajo Mtn. Trading Post.

Hike Length and Time Needed It's about 5 kms to the large spring in Deep Canyon. This round-trip hike can be done in 2-3 hours. From the HWM to the old fruit farm in Desha is about 8 kms. You will need at least half a day to do this hike, maybe longer. From the lake to the top of the cliffs beside Trail Canyon is only about a km. Most can do this one in an hour or two.

Boots or Shoes Normally you can keep your feet dry in Deep or Desha Canyons, but they have a year-round flow of water, so consider wading shoes. Use a more rugged hiking boot for the climb up the old trail near Trail Canyon.

Water Because there's lots of livestock in all canyons, drink water only from springs in Deep or Desha Canyons. Trail Canyon is dry.

Main Attractions Waterfalls, old livestock trails, and good views of the lake and Navajo Mountain on the Navajo Nation lands.

Hiking Maps USGS or BLM map Navajo Mountain(1:100,000), or Navajo Mtn. and No Mans Mesa(1:62,500).

From the top of the trail near Trail Canyon one has good views of Navajo Mountain to the south.

199

Wilson Creek Canyon

Location and Campsites Wilson Creek drains into the San Juan River Arm of the lake at about M13(K21). This figure comes from the old river mileage or kilomage. The canyon heads northwest, and ends immediately next to the upper end of Cottonwood Canyon, right where the 4WD part of the Hole-in-the-Rock Trail ends.

There are only three small possible campsites within the Wilson Creek Bay. Upon the author's visit, there was one boat anchored with two ropes right at the end of the bay where the creek flows over a waterfall. There appears to be room for one small tent near this waterfall.

Routes or Trails If you go to the end of the bay, you will be confronted with a short waterfall, so you must go a different route to get above the Wingate cliffs. Long before Lake Powell days, there was first an old **Indian trail,** then later, a **cattle trail** into Wilson Canyon. Crampton's report states: *Just above the mouth of the canyon a stock trail starts at the river's edge and ascends the irregular walls of Wilson Canyon in switchbacks and steep pitches to top out on a ledge about 400 feet(125 meters) above the San Juan.* Today, that trail is lost under water, but you can still see it in places further up the canyon.

The author never did find the exact location where the trail reached the rim, but if you dock in a little bay on the right side, you can walk up through what appears to be the top of the Moenave, to the same area where this old trail was located. From there, walk along the bench almost due north. You may or may not see a trail, but it doesn't matter; just head up canyon on the right hand side. After less than a km, there's a stock trail leading down into the entrenched part of the drainage. Actually, you can get down into the stream bed at a number of locations further up.

The mostly dry creek bed is easy to walk in all the way. There are about four small seeps, which may or may not have water the year-round. As you near the upper end of the canyon the walls close in, but are not as high. Watch to the right side, and you will see a stock trail ascending a low bench. This takes cattle around a short waterfall right at the end of the canyon. Not far beyond, it opens up and you're near the top of Wilson Mesa. When you reach a point where you can see down to the west, veer to the right, and after another 200 meters or so you'll come to the end of the 4WD part of the old Hole-in-the-Rock Trail. An idea for the adventurous hiker; walk up Wilson while someone takes your boat around to the end of Cottonwood Canyon Bay, and meet it there by walking down Cottonwood.

Hike Length and Time Needed It's only about 5 kms from the lake to the end of the vehicle-used part of the Hole-in-the-Rock Trail. This means about 3 to 4 hours round-trip for the average hiker. The author made it in 2 hrs. 40 min.

Boots or Shoes Any dry weather boots or shoes are OK.

Water There's good water in the bottom end, but you'll have to go out of you way to get it. There are cattle in the canyon from October to June, so caution should be taken with the seep water higher up.

The head of the Wilson Creek Canyon Inlet. Note the small waterfall on the right.

MAP 27, WILSON CREEK CANYON

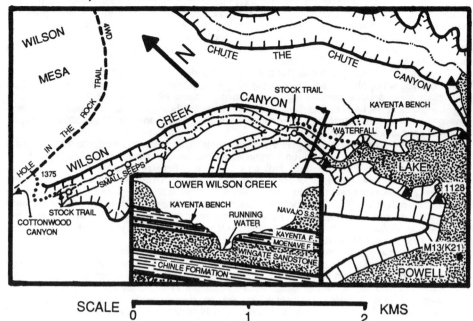

SCALE

0   1   2   KMS

The seeps could dry up at times, so best to take your own.
Main Attractions An old Indian and cattle trail, and the historic Hole-in-the-Rock Trail.
Hiking Maps USGS or BLM map Navajo Mountain(1:100,000), or Navajo Mtn.(1:62,500).

The lower end of Wilson Creek Canyon has a small year-round flowing stream.

Nasja, Bald Rock and Cha Canyons

Location and Campsites The three canyons on this map are among the most interesting in the San Juan River Arm of Lake Powell. All three canyons, Nasja, Bald Rock and Cha, drain the north slope of Navajo Mountain before making their way to the lake. All three are in the lower end of the San Juan, on the south side of the lake and on Navajo Nation lands. The mouth of Nasja, which is shared with Bald Rock Canyon, is located at the old river mileage(kilomage) M6(K10), while the mouth of Cha is M11.6(K18) above the mouth of the San Juan.

There are not too many campsites in these parts, but right at the end of the inlet to Bald Rock Canyon is a nice sandy place or two, under a big Wingate pourover. If the lake is low, there might be a similar place under another Wingate alcove at the head of Nasja Inlet. There will always be several sandy campsites at the head of Cha Canyon Bay. Perhaps the best campsite and one large enough for several boats, is just around the corner and to the west of the mouth of the Nasja-Bald Rock Inlet. It's labeled *good sandy beach* on the map.

Routes or Trails Cha Canyon is likely the most spectacular canyon draining into the San Juan. As you boat into the bay, there will be several campsites on either side in the Chinle claybeds. Starting up canyon, you'll find livestock trails on either side of the sizeable stream. The tracks are mostly those of semi-wild horses or donkeys belonging to Navajo herdsmen. About a km above the HWM, there's a fork in the canyon and a wide open place. The author found an old corral and some large boulders with recent Navajo petroglyphs. Crampton and other researchers have found evidence that this area, as well as areas now covered by Lake Powell, had been used first by Anasazi, then about 1900, by Piutes and Navajos. If you take the time to look around you might find something interesting near this canyon junction.

As you continue up canyon, there will be more livestock trails and cottonwood trees. Soon you'll come to a nice waterfall where the creek flows over a limestone layer of the Chinle Formation. Look for a trail on the right, or west side. Not far above this one is still another waterfall and subsequent pool. Pass this one on the left, or east. Above these two falls, the canyon constricts and the Wingate walls close in. Further along there will be large boulders in the canyon bottom, and the going becomes a bit slow. There are old sign of beaver and wild horses, but nothing new. Incidentally the Navajo word for beaver is *Cha*.

Above the areas with the boulders, the canyon makes a turn to the west, and becomes narrow. There you must get out of the bottom and bench-walk on the left side above more falls and narrows. Around another couple of more turns in the canyon, you'll have to wade a bit, then get up on the right, or west side, where an old faded trail has been made up through a talus slope to the Kayenta bench above.

The first waterfall you come to as you hike up Cha Canyon.

MAP 28, NASJA, BALD ROCK & CHA CANYONS

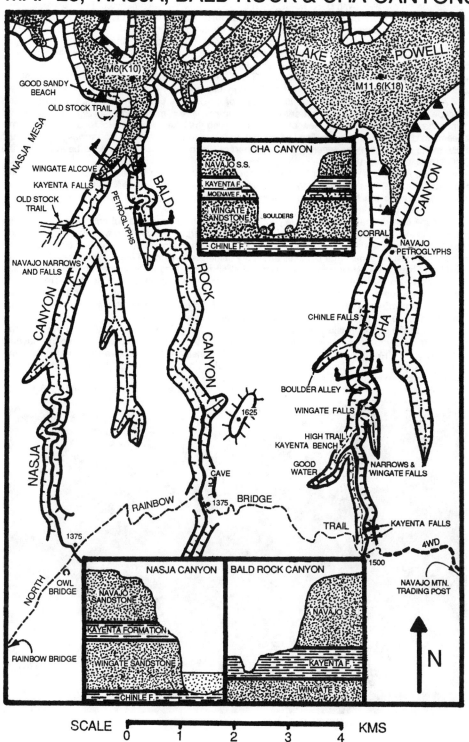

LAKE POWELL

M6(K10)

M11.6(K18)

GOOD SANDY BEACH

OLD STOCK TRAIL

NASJA MESA

WINGATE ALCOVE

KAYENTA FALLS

OLD STOCK TRAIL

PETROGLYPHS

BALD

ROCK

CANYON

CHA CANYON
NAVAJO S.S.
KAYENTA F.
MOENAVE F.
WINGATE SANDSTONE
BOULDERS
CHINLE F.

CORRAL

NAVAJO PETROGLYPHS

NAVAJO NARROWS AND FALLS

CANYON

CHINLE FALLS

CHA

CANYON

1625

BOULDER ALLEY

WINGATE FALLS

NASJA

HIGH TRAIL
KAYENTA BENCH

GOOD WATER

NARROWS & WINGATE FALLS

CAVE

RAINBOW   1375   BRIDGE

TRAIL

KAYENTA FALLS

4WD

1375

1500

NORTH

OWL BRIDGE

NASJA CANYON
NAVAJO SANDSTONE
KAYENTA FORMATION
WINGATE SANDSTONE
CHINLE F.

BALD ROCK CANYON
NAVAJO S.S.
KAYENTA F.
WINGATE S.S.

NAVAJO MTN. TRADING POST

N

RAINBOW BRIDGE

SCALE

0   1   2   3   4

KMS

This takes you high above some Wingate narrows and still more waterfalls. This trail goes into a side canyon on the west(with good water), then cuts back into the main canyon. From there, the trail is used more and more by cattle until you meet the **North Rainbow Bridge Trail.** This rather good trail skirts the north side of Navajo Mountain, running from the Navajo Mtn. Trading Post to Rainbow Bridge(the first part of which is a sandy road, from the trading post to near Cha Canyon).

Just before entering the inlet to Nasja and Bald Rock Canyons, you have a chance to get upon the rim for some fine views of the lake via an old **stock trail.** To do this, boat to the sandy beach just west of the mouth of Nasja-Bald Rock Inlet. Dock there and walk along the bench to the east just above the water line. There are several hiker trails in this area.

As you near the corner, look up to the right for an obvious break in the cliffs. Walk up in that direction, and as you near the first set of cliffs, you can see a man-made trail zig zagging up. It rounds the corner to the left and heads south overlooking the lake and inlet. Not far around the corner it seems to disappear, as it's heading to the southwest and towards Nasja Mesa. It was probably built at the same time as the one entering the lower part of Nasja Canyon. It may have been built by the CCC crews in the mid-1930's.

As you near the end of the inlet in **Bald Rock Canyon,** look to the left, or east side, and you'll see a route(or trail) up through the top of the Wingate. From there you walk up the mostly dry creek bed all the way to the North Rainbow Bridge Trail. Along the way you'll be walking on Kayenta slickrock much of the time.

Around the first major bend, look to your right and you may see some petroglyphs on a wall. The petroglyphs indicate this is an old Anasazi trail or route. Further up, you'll be walking inside a shallow section of Kayenta narrows. Before it gets too deep, you'll have to get out and onto a bench on either side as there will be some large potholes and a dry fall further on. In the upper portions of the canyon, you'll likely find some running water. This small stream gets bigger the further up you go. Finally, you'll once again reach the North Rainbow Bridge Trail. If you walk up the Rainbow Trail a short distance to the east, it ascends a steep dugway in rather spectacular fashion. At the top of that slope, you'll have some fine views of the upper end of the canyon which is the most beautiful part. This is right under Navajo Mountain as it begins its steep rise.

Right at the end of Nasja Inlet, is a shaded grotto. To get above this, regress to the northeast 150 meters and you'll see a break in the Wingate wall on the south side. Climb up onto the Kayenta bench and bench-walk back into **Nasja Canyon.** Just inside the canyon, you'll immediately come to a short Kayenta falls, which you can skirt to the left. From there on up, you'll be surrounded by Navajo Sandstone walls.

This canyon has some trees, but no willows or other greenery, and no running water. Big floods

The head of the inlet to Bald Rock Canyon.

can roar down this wide open drainage. If you stay in the main channel of Nasja, you can only walk about 3 kms before you come to a place with some narrows, a large pool and falls. If you could somehow get above this, it could be an interesting walk. The author is guessing as to the running water in the upper end of Nasja, as shown on the map. There is some kind of water at the Rainbow Trail, but the upper end of the canyon is unknown to the author because of the falls.

You can still reach the North Rainbow Bridge Trail via Nasja Canyon however. About a km above the Kayenta falls look to the right, or west, and where the canyon walls are low you can see another old **stock trail** running up through the low bench. It's hard to see, because some oak brush has grown up in the canyon at the very bottom of the trail, but once you get above the 3 meter-high bench it's clearly visible. The trail, marked with several cairns, runs to the west inside a shallow drainage, then seems to head southwest. The author lost it, but he continued in the same direction, and eventually topped out and could see a route up along the west side of the canyon. It appeared that someone with an entire day to hike, could walk up the west side of Nasja to the Rainbow Trail. The author never did explore the eastern fork of Nasja, but it appeared to lead to nowhere.

Hike Length and Time Needed It seems to be about 10 kms from the HWM to the North Rainbow Bridge Trail in Cha Canyon. This isn't far, but you'll have to route-find in places, so it's a slow hike. Plan to take most of a day to do this one. The author did it in just under 5 hours, round-trip.

From the lake to the same Rainbow Trail in Bald Rock Canyon, is about 10 kms. This hike is in an open canyon, with easy and fast walking. The author made it to the trail and back in 3 hrs. 40 min. You might consider taking a lunch and spend as much as 6 or 7 hours. You can see Nasja and the beginnings of the old stock trail in just a couple of hours, but to reach the Rainbow Trail, plan on an all day hike.

Boots or Shoes In Cha Canyon, better take wading shoes; while in Bald Rock and Nasja Canyons, you can wear any kind of boots or shoes.

Water Best not to drink the water in Cha Creek, but higher up, and in the little west fork, there is clear spring water without the danger of beaver or cattle to pollute it. There are at times some livestock in upper Bald Rock, but the source is very near and there are several fresh springs near the Rainbow Trail, so this seems a good source of water. The author drank pothole water in Nasja Canyon, but that was right after a storm. Count on Nasja being a dry canyon except for some water near the Rainbow Trail, which this author hasn't confirmed(second hand information).

Main Attractions Cha is a wild and wooly canyon, with narrows and several waterfalls. The upper end of Bald Rock above the Rainbow Trail is very spectacular, and there is a route-finding experience out of Nasja along the old stock trail.

Hiking Maps USGS or BLM map Navajo Mountain(1:100,000), or Navajo Mtn.(1:62,500).

The upper end of Bald Rock Canyon as seen from the North Rainbow Bridge Trail.

The Kayenta Falls just inside the lower end of Nasja Canyon.

Part of an old stock trail in the lower end of Nasja Canyon.

The upper-most campsite in Oak Canyon.

End of the extremely narrow inlet to Secret Canyon.

Oak, Secret, Forbidding, Cliff & Rainbow Bridge Canyons

Location and Campsites The canyons on this map are located near the middle part of the lake and not too far to the southwest, or down lake, from the mouth of the San Juan Arm. Because of Rainbow Bridge National Monument, this is one of the most crowded sections of the lake--at least during the day time. This is when tour boats with tourists, many of whom are foreign, make their way to the world's largest natural bridge. Then everyone leaves the area at night time and it's much like any other part of the lake.

This is another part of the lake without many campsites; the exception being Oak Canyon and the area just to the west of its mouth in the main channel. Right at the upper end of both Forbidding and Secret Canyons, there should always be one good site. Because of the heavy traffic in Rainbow Bridge Canyon, there is no overnight camping allowed there(besides, there are no campsites there anyway).

On USGS maps, the Oak Canyon on this map is un-named, while what is being called Secret Canyon on all boaters maps and in this book, is called Oak Canyon on the same USGS maps. It seems that all boaters maps of the area go by the names which appear on this map.

The apparent reason for the difference is that before Lake Powell, the present Oak and Secret Canyons shared a common mouth. At the mouth it was called Oak Canyon. But when the lake inundated the area, the present-day Oak Canyon was more easily visible; therefore it kept the name Oak. At the same time, the rising waters of the lake made the mouth of the much longer drainage(the real Oak Canyon) less visible; in fact rather obscure. Therefore, a new name was adopted for what we now call Secret Canyon.

Routes or Trails One of the more popular canyons in this part of the lake is **Oak Canyon.** It's popular mainly because of several sandy beaches in the upper end of the inlet which combined are 300-400 meters long. The place is very sandy, because the surrounding countryside is topped by the Navajo Sandstone. As it weathers, it's blown down into this canyon by the prevailing southwest winds.

Oak Canyon is a very short drainage, less than a km long above the HWM. There are hiker-made trails winding along the brushy canyon bottom up to the head of the canyon, and to several green and cool alcoves on the south side. This is where water pours off the Navajo bluffs and domes during rainstorms. There is a little seep or flow of water coming out of most of these little alcoves as a result. There were some fairly fresh sign of beaver in the lower end upon the author's visit.

Perhaps the best hike in this little canyon is to walk up from the little waterfall right at the HWM and to the first minor ridge coming down from the right, or south. Get up next to it, and look for steps cut in the slickrock. Some are obviously Anasazi built; others have been cut more recently with a

Rainbow Bridge is the largest natural bridge in the world.

MAP 29, OAK, SECRET, FORBIDDING, CLIFF & RAINBOW BRIDGE CANYONS

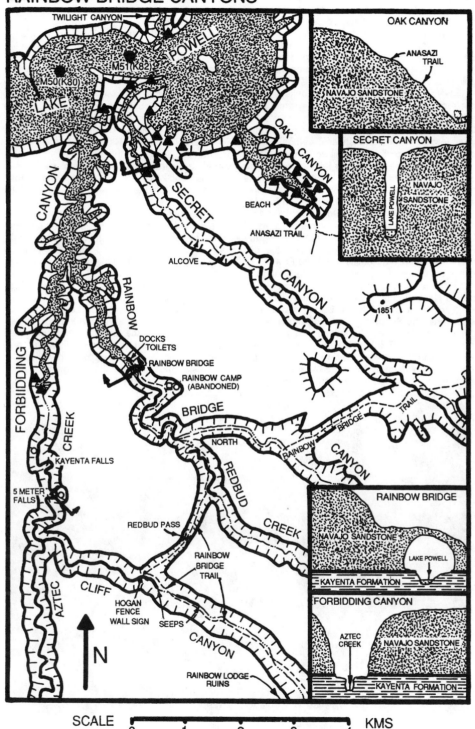

OAK CANYON

ANASAZI TRAIL

NAVAJO SANDSTONE

SECRET CANYON

LAKE POWELL

NAVAJO SANDSTONE

TWILIGHT CANYON

POWELL

M51(K82)

M50(K80)

LAKE

CANYON

OAK CANYON

SECRET

BEACH

ANASAZI TRAIL

ALCOVE

CANYON

1851

RAINBOW

DOCKS TOILETS

RAINBOW BRIDGE

RAINBOW CAMP (ABANDONED)

FORBIDDING

CREEK

KAYENTA FALLS

5 METER FALLS

BRIDGE

NORTH

RAINBOW BRIDGE TRAIL

RAINBOW CANYON

REDBUD CREEK

REDBUD PASS

RAINBOW BRIDGE TRAIL

AZTEC CLIFF

HOGAN FENCE WALL SIGN

SEEPS

CANYON

N

RAINBOW LODGE RUINS

RAINBOW BRIDGE

NAVAJO SANDSTONE

LAKE POWELL

KAYENTA FORMATION

FORBIDDING CANYON

AZTEC CREEK

NAVAJO SANDSTONE

KAYENTA FORMATION

SCALE
0 1 2 3 4 KMS

209

sharp metal instrument, like a miners pick. Head up and to the south and you'll run into half a dozen places where steps have been cut in the steeper sections. On top you'll see several stone cairns, but they don't seem to lead anywhere. However, one could surely walk to the south and southeast and end up in upper Secret Canyon or on the North Rainbow Bridge Trail.

One of the narrowest inlets around is in the back end of **Secret Canyon.** Right at the end it's about as tight as regular sized boats can go through, and the walls are about as high as the Navajo Sandstone walls get. There's one good but small campsite right at the end of the inlet. As you begin to hike up canyon, it gradually becomes wider. There are several large alcoves on the right hand side going up.

Semi-wild Navajo horses and donkeys sometimes come down into this lower part of the canyon, but sometimes there isn't any running water in the last 3 or 4 kms. Above this dry part, you begin to see potholes with water, then running water as you go further up-canyon. The upper end has a nice little year-round flowing stream. After 7 or 8 kms, you'll come to an area with lots of cottonwood trees, gamble oak brush, and several campsites. This is where the **North Rainbow Bridge Trail** passes. It's a heavily used trail and easy to find and follow. You can't miss this one.

The only times the author felt in danger of having his boat overturned by waves were the times he went to see Rainbow Bridge. Other boaters were going at about *Warp II* speed through the narrow channel and those pyramid waves don't stop vibrating for 10 or 15 minutes. Please slow down a little when you reach **Rainbow Bridge Canyon Inlet!**

There are toilets at the Rainbow Bridge docks, then everyone must walk about 200 meters on a floating path before the shore line is reached. There is a road-like trail leading up to beneath the bridge. It continues on up canyon, first along the Kayenta bench, then right in the stream bed itself. About half a km above the bridge and on the left under a big overhang, is the old tourist campsite. It was used up until the building of Lake Powell. Under the alcove is a small spring, along with a small cabin, old bed springs, and other artifacts of a bygone era.

In recent years it has been learned that a Piute Indian named Mikes Boy saw Rainbow Bridge before Nasja Begay. When two white discovery parties were searching for the Bridge in August of 1909, one was led by Nasja Begay and one by Mikes Boy. Later, the two joined forces and re-discovered the Bridge together on August 14. Some of the prominent white men in the group were John Wetherill, Byron Cummings and William B. Douglass. This was the first time white men had *reportedly* seen Rainbow Bridge. It is 88 meters high, 84 meters wide, and at it's smallest part, only 13 meters thick. On May 30, l910, President Taft, proclaimed Rainbow Bridge a national monument.

About a decade before, Mikes Boy had shown Nasja Begay where the Bridge was after discovering it himself while herding horses. Three quarters of a century later, the National Park Service honored the Piute, now known as Jim Mike, with a ceremony at Rainbow Bridge. In 1977, Jim

From the docks one can see Rainbow Bridge and Navajo Mountain.

Mike died at 105 years of age, and was buried in Blanding Utah.

In July, 1922, John Wetherill and Charles Bernheimer opened the first trail to Rainbow Bridge. In those days, all tourists visiting this national monument came down the Rainbow Bridge Trail, which started on the south side of Navajo Mountain at the now abandoned Rainbow Lodge. The distance is 21 kms.

From the lake, this trail runs up Rainbow Bridge and Redbud Canyons, then veers south over Redbud Pass and down into and up Cliff Canyon. It's still a good trail even today. It ends where Rainbow Lodge once stood, where only foundations now mark the spot. There's still another trail out of this area called the North Rainbow Bridge Trail. It skirts the north side of Navajo Mountain, and connects with roads to reach the Navajo Mtn. Trading Post.

By about 1964, the normal route to Rainbow Bridge was from Lake Powell. Today, hundreds visit it daily(in the summer season). At the high water level, which is at 1128 meters, the lake extends under the bridge and up the canyon about half a km.

An adventurous party of hikers could start walking from the Bridge, head up along the North Rainbow Bridge Trail to the stream in Secret Canyon, then walk down Secret to the lake, where someone could pick them up in a boat. The same round-trip type hike can be made from the bridge into the lower part of Cliff Canyon, then down along Aztec Creek to the lake where a non-hiker could take the boat.

The last drainage covered here is **Forbidding Canyon,** through which **Aztec Creek** flows. This is a very long drainage with its beginnings far to the south of Navajo Mountain. The author has been in the upper end and found running water, cottonwood trees, and grazing cattle. This discussion covers just the lower part, the only section of interest to most boaters. At the very end of the long and winding inlet is a large alcove or overhang. Beneath it and just up canyon, you should find a number of good sandy campsites.

As you hike up stream, you'll notice a groove down the middle of the drainage. This is where the stream has cut into the upper part of the Kayenta Formation. In places this complicates hiking just a little. At times you'll be boxed into an area with waterfalls or large potholes. and you'll have to regress a ways, and climb upon the Kayenta bench. But it also makes the hike more exciting. Otherwise, the walking is easy and fast with no brush to slow you down. There are trees and waterfalls in places.

There doesn't seem to be running water in the very bottom of the canyon, but after a km or less, you will come to a stream which appears to be year-round. In this area on the right side, is a spring with good drinking water. About 3 kms or so above the HWM, you may find another spring on the left. Just beyond this spring is a nice 5 meter high waterfall and large swimming pool. Get around this minor obstacle on the right side. Another km above this waterfall, **Cliff Canyon Creek** enters from the left, or east. While you can go up Aztec Creek for many kms, you can also go up Cliff Canyon, and

Plaque at the base of Rainbow Bridge honoring Mikes Boy as the one who guided the first confirmed white mans visit to the bridge.

211

meet the Rainbow Bridge Trail, then walk over Redbud Pass and down to Rainbow Bridge.

Hike Length and Time Needed You can only walk for a few minutes into Oak Canyon, then it's a quick and easy walk to the benchland above. About an hour is all it will take. It's 7 or 8 kms from the HWM in Secret Canyon to the North Rainbow Bridge Trail. This will take most people 6 or 7 hours, round-trip. The author did it in 4 1/2 hours. You can walk as far and as long as you like up Rainbow Bridge or Redbud Canyons. If you walk up Forbidding Canyon, it's about 7 kms to the Rainbow Bridge Trail in Cliff Canyon. Most will need 4 or 5 hours for this round-trip hike. The author did this one in 3 hrs. 20 min.

Boots or Shoes Best to use wading type shoes in all canyons, except Oak.

Water It will likely be good water in Oak, unless you see fresh sign of beaver. Secret Canyon water is suspect, unless you hike above the Rainbow Trail. There may be cattle in its upper part. The spring at the old tourist camp near the bridge gives good water and no cattle get down that low in the canyon. Treat Aztec Creek water, but water in Cliff Canyon may be good, although there are old signs of livestock there too.

Main Attractions The biggest natural bridge in the world, an Anasazi Trail(Oak Canyon), wilderness canyons few people visit, and long narrow inlets.

Hiking Maps USGS or BLM map Navajo Mountain(1:100,000), or Navajo Mtn.(1:62,500)

Campsite at the upper end of Secret Canyon Inlet.

This foto was taken where the North Rainbow Bridge Trail crosses Secret Canyon.

The docks just below Rainbow Bridge.

Twilight and Anasazi Canyons

Location and Campsites Twilight Canyon is the name boaters know this drainage by, but on the USGS metric map Navajo Mountain, the place is called Navajo Valley. Actually both names can apply for this same area, as there's a narrow slot canyon in the middle of a larger valley complex. Before Lake Powell, river runners knew this place as both Twilight and Boulder Canyon. This drainage is located not far to the southwest of the mouth of the San Juan River Arm. Near the mouth of the inlet should be a buoy marked M51(K82).

There are not many campsites in this part of the lake, but there are several inside Oak Canyon and more to the west of its mouth in the main channel. There may be two small sites as well in Anasazi Canyon. The author counted only three small sites inside Twilight Inlet. The best site might be a sandy beach near the upper end of the left hand fork. The other two, and possibly three sites, are near the upper end of the main inlet channel.

Routes or Trails From the lake you'll be walking up a long narrow corridor cut into the Navajo Sandstone. Twilight Canyon is a cobblestone-filled drainage with very few places to exit. The width of the slot might average 5 meters, but in many places it's less than that. Not many people go into these narrows.

After about 5 kms, you'll come to a place where boulders and other debris has clogged the drainage. At that point, regress a short distance and climb up a talus slope to the east side of the slot. Once out of the narrows, you can see a horseshoe shaped circle of cliffs on all sides. To your left, or west, is the Kaiparowits Plateau. An intermediate level one bench above is called the Navajo Bench(on USGS maps). With time and route-finding, you can likely walk to the head of Navajo Valley, then veer to the west and head up a large talus slope. Once above this, you'll again have to route-find up the steeper part of the Kaiparowits. Surely somewhere along that line of cliffs is a route to the top.

Anasazi Canyon has a long and very narrow inlet, but it appears there are no hiking possibilities. The Navajo Sandstone canyon walls rise straight out of the water. You could try swimming into the very end of the main inlet which is too narrow for boats, but the author found lots of driftwood there. The boat ride into this canyon might be worth the time, as it's a pretty one.

Hike Length and Time Needed Inside Twilight Canyon you can only walk about 5 kms. To hike this and return, will take about 3 hours(the author did it in 2 1/2 hours). But you can exit the slot canyon and perhaps get to the top of the Kaiparowits. That's about 12 kms one way, and would take all day.

Boots or Shoes It's a dry canyon, so any boots or shoes will do.

Water There are no springs in this canyon, so take your own water.

Typical scene in the narrows of Twilight Canyon.

MAP 30, TWILIGHT & ANASAZI CANYONS

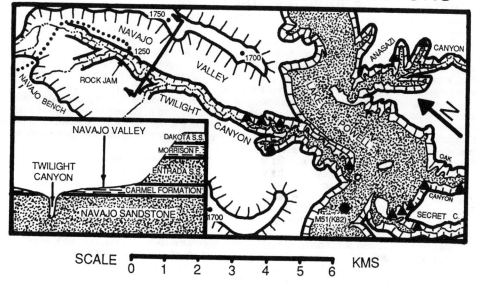

SCALE
0 1 2 3 4 5 6 KMS

Main Attractions One of the best slot canyon hikes on the lake, but it does lack the really narrow one-meter-wide sections.
Hiking Maps USGS or BLM maps Navajo Mountain and Smoky Mountain(1:100,000), or Navajo Mtn. and Cummings Mesa(1:62,500).

A waterfall about 5 meters high along Aztec Creek(Forbidding Canyon).

Cascade, Driftwood, Balanced Rock and Dangling Rope Canyons, & the Klondike Trail

Location and Campsites The four canyons and one historic trail on this map are all located just to the west of the mouth of Forbidding Canyon(where Rainbow Bridge is located) on the north side of the lake. They are all short canyons which drain the southern slopes of the Kaiparowits Plateau(often called Fiftymile Mountain). If you like narrow waterways and tight slot-type canyons, this is the place to go. With all the soaring cliffs, this is one of the most scenic places on Lake Powell. Also on this map is the Dangling Rope Marina, the only fuel stop on the lake with boater access only. Read more on the marina below and in the Introduction of this book.

This is another area with few campsites. The inlet with the most is probably Dangling Rope, followed by Balanced Rock Bay. There is usually one small campsite at the very end of each of these very narrow inlets. There are more sites just to the south of this map on the south side drainages, such as in Cathedral, Mountain Sheep and Wetherill Canyons. If you don't need a beach to crash on, then there are many slickrock anchorages.

Routes or Trails **Cascade Canyon** Inlet is one of the longer and narrowest on the lake, beating anything in the Escalante River system. It's very winding and at the upper end, just wide enough for an average boat to pass through. At the very end right at the HWM is a pile of driftwood. Some of these are large tree trunks, and it's interesting to speculate as to where they could have originated. The author thinks they must have come from some of the springs just under the rim of the Kaiparowits. At times reeds from bullrushes are also seen in the inlet, indicating a spring source somewhere up canyon or on the plateau.

Cascade is also one of the narrowest hiking canyons on the lake. You can only walk and climb for about one km, before you come to high falls at the end of two tributaries. But to get that far, you must climb over some narrow falls and chokestones. To do this it's necessary to use pressure holds. For example, put your back on one wall, and your feet and hands on the other. If the walls are just less than a meter apart, this is an easy trick. This is not a good canyon to be in if the weather is threatening.

Driftwood Canyon is still another extremely deep and narrow slot. The waterway leading into it is winding with high Navajo walls, just like Cascade Canyon. The author once saw a large boat full of tourists having their lunch in the shade at mid-day just inside the left fork near the end of the inlet. Take the right fork as you near the upper end. This part is 600-700 meters in length, and maybe 4 meters wide or less, on average. In the extreme upper end it narrows down to 2 or 2 1/2 meters.

Right at the very end of the inlet is an area covered with driftwood, thus the name. If the water level is high, you can get through this awful looking floating mess by using an oar to push logs out of

Using pressure holds to gain access to the upper part of Cascade Canyon.

MAP 31, CASCADE, DRIFTWOOD, BALANCED ROCK & DANGLING ROPE CANYONS & THE KLONDIKE TRAIL

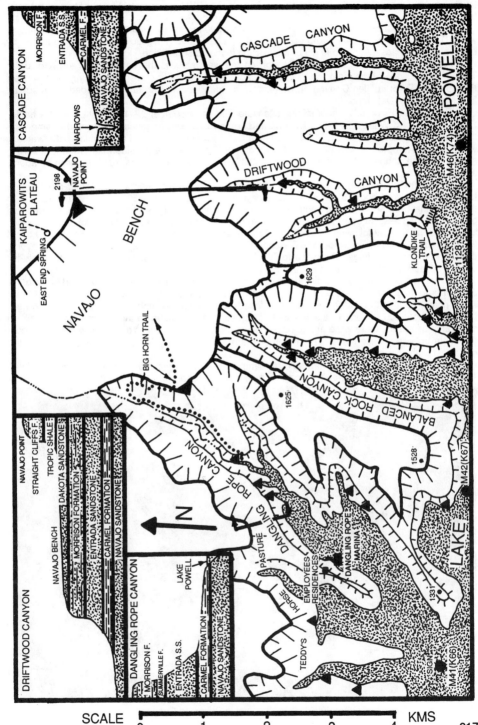

SCALE   0   1   2   3   4   KMS

217

the way; or you can get out and wade, pulling your boat up to the tiny sandy beach. Wading in the floating debris isn't as bad as it may first appear. By doing this you'll have a chance to camp right there on a three meter-wide beach(but not during times of bad weather). On the other hand, if the lake levels are low, the driftwood ends up *dry-docked* at the HWM, and you will just boat up to a sandy beach instead.

In Driftwood Canyon you can walk very easily for 200 meters in a slot that's one to three meters wide. Then there's a narrowing and you'll have to climb. Some energetic climbers can go further by using pressure holds. Above this minor obstruction it should be exciting.

Right at the mouth of Driftwood Canyon on the west side, is the beginning of the **Klondike Trail.** This was one of the main routes in and out of one of the major placer gold mining sand bars on the Colorado River in Glen Canyon. It was known as the Klondike Bar and it extended down stream from the mouth of Driftwood.

The first claims on this placer mining site were filed on December 22, 1897, by Louis M. Chaffin, Seth Laugee, and William B. Hay. They named it **Klondike Bar,** because it coincided in time with the Yukon Gold Rush. By 1899, these three men had sold their claims, but it was mined afterwards as well. When Crampton visited the place in the late 1950's, he saw a considerable amount of mining equipment and debris. There were gravel chutes, ditches, wooden tracks, ore cars, iron scrapers, and sluice flumes.

The Klondike Trail began at the head of the bar. It must have been a spectacular route before Lake Powell covered about 3/4 of it. In those days it wound its way for 250 meters up a steep wall to the top of the Carmel bench. In some places stakes were set in the slickrock, with rocks and brush piled on top of poles. In other places, steps were cut in solid sandstone. From the top of the Carmel bench, the trail closely followed the 1200 to 1250 meter contour lines. It went eastward into and out of the upper back ends of Driftwood and Cascade Canyons, as well as Navajo Valley(Twilight Canyon), then around one more finger of a mesa to Fifty Mile Point. From there it connected with the Hole-in-the-Rock Road, which led north to Escalante.

To find the beginning of this historic trail, boat to the mouth of Driftwood Canyon and just around the corner to the west side. Look closely in the area just above and below the HWM. You should see steps coming out of the water. There's no place to dock there, so boat around the corner toward Driftwood about 100 meters to a small inlet. Dock there and walk up on the slickrock to the trail. In all, Crampton states, there were at least 8 places where steps were cut. You can now see only about three. In between these steps are several cairns marking the way, as the trail runs up and to the northwest to the Carmel bench.

Balanced Rock Canyon has several campsites leading into the far end of its narrow inlet. This is still another very fine slot-type canyon hike, but it's a short one. The author made it only about

You may have to wade into the upper end of the inlet in Driftwood Canyon.

250 meters, but he had to use some pressure holds to get that far. Put your feet on one wall, and back against the other, to get over one chokestone. Tough climbers might get further than did the author.

Dangling Rope Canyon has a large bay with a sign at the entrance. However, one need not worry about finding this place, as there will be hundreds of boats going that way daily to fuel up at the **Dangling Rope Marina.** Originally this marina was located near Rainbow Bridge, but traffic there was so heavy and the inlet so narrow, they finally had to move it to its present location in about 1983. Waste disposal was another problem at the Bridge.

This canyon got it's name because in the days before Lake Powell, river runners found a rope dangling down over a cliff just up canyon from the river. There were also some old toe holds or steps cut in the wall. It is believed that the steps date back perhaps to the Anasazi days, and later used by Piutes or Navajos, but the rope was probably put there by white men, perhaps during the 1950's uranium boom days.

Today the floating marina juts out from a low bench in the middle of the bay. Just behind it on the bench is the employee housing. At this marina is a ranger office, but it's only open intermittently. There is gasoline, both regular and pre-mixed 50 to 1 gas, along with a repair garage. The fuel is brought out daily by a large Chevron owned boat. All other supplies arrive in containers on a barge from Wahweap. Garbage is hauled out in truck bed units which can then be towed to the local dump near Wahweap.

There is water, both for flushing and for drinking and garbage bins. The NPS hands out free garbage bags--please take one to use. It has a small store with the basic essentials and at prices about double what you pay in the lowest priced supermarkets in northern Utah(one of the cheapest areas in the nation). You can buy ice cream and ice, both very popular items in summer; and you can eat under a shaded picnic site nearby.

Even though this place is in the middle of a wilderness with boater access only, you can still make long distance telefone calls to the outside world via satellite. You can send letters or postcards from Dangling Rope, but they'll have a Page, Arizona postmark.

Because all their supplies come from Page and Wahweap, the marina uses Arizona time, which is *not* daylight saving time in the summer months. In summer, you can buy gasoline from 7 am until 7 pm, Arizona time. The store has these same hours, but the ice cream shop is open from 8 am until 5.30 pm(9 am to 6:30 pm Utah or daylight savings time). Dangling Rope Marina is open the year-round. The busy season is from Memorial Day until Labor Day, and on weekends in the spring(especially at Easter time) and fall.

There are some pretty good campsites in Dangling Rope Inlet and even better hiking or climbing. In the upper end of the inlet it narrows, and if the water is high, you'll pass through a very narrow place, then it opens a bit. At that point you can climb out of the narrows and onto the bench to the east. If

Driftwood at the HWM in Driftwood Canyon.

219

you go directly up the bottom of the canyon, you'll be stopped after only 100 meters or so by a chokestone and falls.

Once on the bench, walk along beside the narrows and north toward the head of the canyon. Higher up, it'll be easy to get back down into the dry creek bed for a short distance. Near the headwall, the creek bed will make a left turn to the west. At that point you will see a talus slope in front of you. Walk up this slope(north) which has signs of a big horn sheep trail. The author saw a ewe and a lamb in this section on one of his hikes.

As you climb this easy slope, you'll gradually veer to the right or east. At the top of the talus, scan the slope to the east and south of you for a route along the benches which are at the top of the Entrada Sandstone. You must then bench-walk to the south along one of these narrow terraces.

After walking about 200 meters south, turn up and to the east and climb a second talus slope. At the top of this, route-find up through one easy terrace, then up through a second bench. The big horns make it up some how and so can you, but there's a little climbing on all fours. Once on top of the second rock band, walk south while looking for an easy route up through the third cliff. Once through this one, continue south until you're at the corner, then make an abrupt turn to the left and walk up through some easy ledges to the northeast.

Energetic climbers or hikers can walk cross-country to the northeast and look for still another route to the top of the Kaiparowits Plateau(the author hasn't done this, but it looked possible). To do this would be a long and slightly challenging climb. From Navajo Point, you will have some great views to the south and east, especially if it's a clear day.

Hike Length and Time Needed The distance in Cascade, Driftwood and Balanced Rock Canyons is very short, so in half an hour or an hour you may do about all you can. You can see everything in a few minutes in the 200 meters of the Klondike Trail. From the lake in Dangling Rope Canyon, to the top of the Kaiparowits at Navajo Point, is 8 to 10 kms. This is a *slow and go* hike, so would be an all day affair. You can cut the distance in half if you stop at the top of the Morrison cliffs, which will give you the best view of Dangling Rope Inlet and Marina.

Boots or Shoes In Cascade, Driftwood or Balanced Rock Canyons, any kind of boot or shoe would be OK, but you may have to wade through some driftwood in the upper parts of the inlets to get your boat all the way in. To reach the top of the Kaiparowits, you'll need some rugged hiking boots of some kind.

Water There are no springs or water anywhere, except for some minor seeps or springs just under the top rim of the Kaiparowits. You may or may not find water at the East End Spring on top of the plateau. Take lots of water with you on that hike if it's a hot summer day!

Main Attractions The narrowest waterways on Lake Powell, some short but very tight canyon

Some of the best narrows around are in Driftwood Canyon.

hikes, a climb to the top of a very high lookout, a chance to see desert big horn sheep, and a place you can buy ice cream on a hot summer day.

Hiking Maps USGS or BLM maps Navajo Mountain and Smoky Mountain(1:100,000), or Navajo Mtn. and Cummings Mesa(1:62,500).

These steps cut in the sandstone are part of the Klondike Trail.

Balanced Rock Canyon also has some good, but short narrows.

A good view of Dangling Rope Bay and Marina from the top of the Morrison Cliffs and Big Horn Trail in Dangling Rope Canyon.

Dangling Rope Marina surrounded by soaring cliffs.

Boat garage at Dangling Rope Marina. Looking north into Dangling Rope Canyon and the Kaiparowits Plateau.

All supplies at Dangling Rope Marina are brought in by barge and container trailers like this.

Cathedral and Mountain Sheep Canyons

Location and Campsites These two canyons are located south of the main channel and drain part of the north side of Cummings Mesa. They are also about half way between the Dangling Rope Marina and Rainbow Bridge. One buoy marked M46(K74) is near the mouth of Cathedral Inlet, and another one marked M43(K69) is near Mountain Sheep Bay. Because of the position on the lake, there's lots of traffic out in the main channel.

The dominant rock formation at the HWM or at lake level in each inlet, is the ever present Navajo Sandstone. This means there's slickrock coming down to the water everywhere. But it also means, because of weathering of this sandstone, you will see a number of small sandy campsites. These are never large, but in the back end of some of the little coves, you can find some of the cleanest sand on the lake. There are also dozens of small hidden slickrock coves, so if you're equipped with the proper ropes and anchors, you can still have excellent slickrock campsites. Of the two inlets, Mountain Sheep has the most sites.

Routes or Trails There are no trails in either of these two drainages, and both appear to be box canyons. For the most part, **Cathedral Canyon** is a non-hiking area. The author went all the way into the back end of its main channel and found it pinched down to nothing. It would have been necessary to swim into a very constricted channel to *perhaps* find walking space above. He went no further however, but an ambitious person would likely find some interesting narrows up above. Lower water levels may allow for some hiking opportunities.

Mountain Sheep Canyon on the other hand has a slightly wider channel at the end which makes *the best* slot canyon hike in this book. As you head into this inlet, it may be necessary to get out of your boat and wade up-channel pulling your craft in. This is what the author did with his inflatable. He took it up to a point where it wedged into the walls, then walked another short distance in water to where the inlet finally ended. From there it was a mostly sandy walk for perhaps 1 1/2 kms.

Along the way, there were several small chokestones, but they were easy to get around. At the end of the author's walk, he found a large chokestone with slippery walls and a small deep pool below. This pool will likely always have some water or mud in it, so this is likely the end of hiking in Mountain Sheep Canyon. For the entire distance, the slot averages about 2 meters in width.

Hike Length and Time Needed No one knows what lies ahead for the adventurous hiker in Cathedral, but in Mountain Sheep Canyon, you can only walk 1 1/2 kms. This should take about 2 hours for a round-trip hike. Don't do this one during stormy conditions.

Boots or Shoes You'll need wading shoes in both canyons.

Water Take your own water.

Mountain Sheep Canyon is like this for a couple of kms.

MAP 32, CATHEDRAL & MTN. SHEEP CANYONS

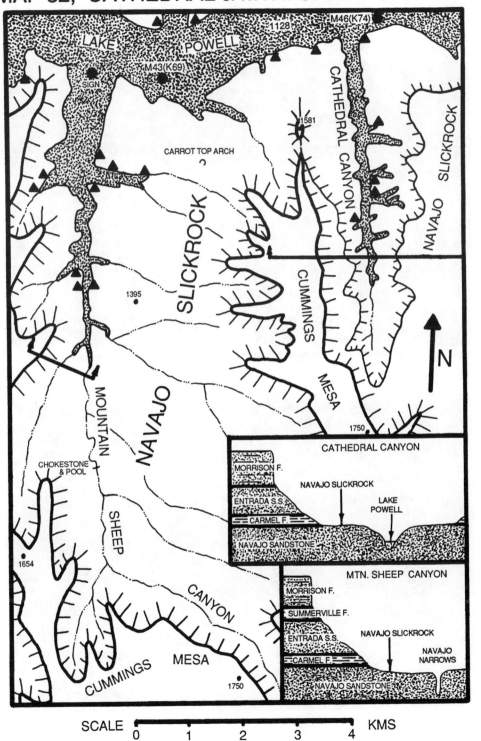

LAKE POWELL

M46(K74)

1128

M43(K69)

SIGN

1581

CATHEDRAL CANYON

NAVAJO SLICKROCK

CARROT TOP ARCH ?

SLICKROCK

1395

CUMMINGS MESA

N

MOUNTAIN

NAVAJO

CHOKESTONE & POOL

SHEEP

1654

CANYON

MESA

CUMMINGS

1750

1750

CATHEDRAL CANYON

MORRISON F.

NAVAJO SLICKROCK

ENTRADA S.S.

CARMEL F.

LAKE POWELL

NAVAJO SANDSTONE

MTN. SHEEP CANYON

MORRISON F.

SUMMERVILLE F.

ENTRADA S.S.

NAVAJO SLICKROCK

CARMEL F.

NAVAJO NARROWS

NAVAJO SANDSTONE

SCALE   0   1   2   3   4   KMS

Main Attractions Dozens of little hidden coves for camping, and the best slot canyon hike on Lake Powell.
Hiking Maps USGS or BLM map Smoky Mountain(1:100,000), or Cummings Mesa(1:62,500).

Mountain Sheep Canyon is another narrow inlet where you'll have to pull your boat in and wade.

Another scene in Mountain Sheep Canyon.

This is what is seen if you climb out of the narrows of Wetherill Canyon.

The darkest passage in Wetherill Canyon.

Wetherill and Dungeon Canyons

Location and Campsites On this map are a couple of the more interesting canyons and hikes in this book. Together they lie south and southwest of the Dangling Rope Canyon Marina, and are on the south side of the main channel. The buoy marked M39(K62), should be in the lake between the mouths of Wetherill and Dungeon Bays.

In this section of the lake, the rock formations are dipping slightly to the west. In Dungeon Bay, the geologic formation exposed at the shore line when the lake is at or near the HWM, is the bench forming Carmel Formation. The Carmel sits atop the Navajo(which is exposed at shore line in Wetherill Bay), which would be exposed in Dungeon Bay if the lake level were 20 or 30 meters below the HWM. As a result of the geology, you will find the shore line in Dungeon Bay having a gradual slope out of the water with many good campsites. Wetherill Bay has many little coves, some with tiny beaches.

Routes and Trails The upper end of the inlet in **Wetherill Canyon** is another narrow one, similar to those canyons to the east. The rock exposed is the Navajo. This has resulted in another very narrow slot-type canyon. You may have to get out of your boat and wade up to the end of the inlet because of shallow water. Then it's an easy walk for about a km in one of the better slot canyons on the lake.

After about half a km you will come to a talus slope on the right, coming down to the canyon bottom. You can exit at this place. Or you can walk to the left, staying in the canyon bottom, and walk about 100 meters more in one of the darkest holes anywhere. This section is slanted and overhung so much it's too dark to take fotos, even with high speed film. Just beyond this dark cavern is another exit to the right. This exit is connected with the first one mentioned. The slot at that point takes a strange twist!

If you were to continue up the slot, you could only walk another 200-300 meters, before coming to a small pool and a chokestone. You will need two people and maybe a rope to get up and around this obstacle, which will be the end of the hike for the average person or party.

If you exit the bottom, you can climb up the Navajo slickrock to the west and get upon the Carmel bench, where you'll find an old livestock trail heading up canyon. It's an easy walk once on this trail, which must have been heavily used before the coming of Lake Powell. The author walked from the exit to about the bottom of this map, and returned.

However, by looking at the topo maps carefully, it appears there is the possibility of a trail or route of some kind out the upper end of Wetherill about 7 kms beyond the bottom of this map(the livestock trail hints of an exit; or they could have gotten into this drainage via the stock trail in Dungeon Canyon). If you try it, make a left turn at the upper end of the canyon and look for a trail heading due south in the upper east fork. If you find a trail, please let the author know.

Small spring near the old ruins in Dungeon Canyon.

MAP 33, WETHERILL & DUNGEON CANYONS

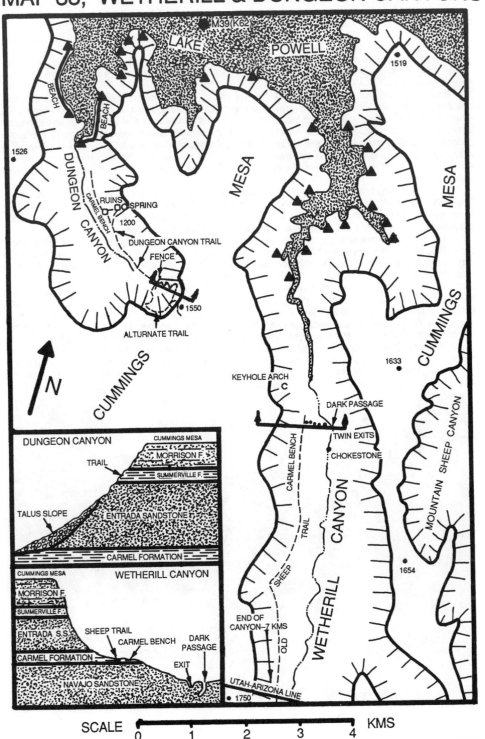

SCALE 0 1 2 3 4 KMS

If you can get out on top of Cummings Mesa, you could then walk southeast about 3 kms to the eastern rim, and descend to the east on another well built stock trail(probably constructed during the Depression of the 1930's). This trail drops into the middle section of Aztec Creek(Forbidding Canyon), then the author guesses it ascends the other side and comes out onto the Chaiyahi Rim, a couple of kms southwest of the old Rainbow Lodge site(the beginning point of the trail to Rainbow Bridge before Lake Powell times) just south of Navajo Mountain.

Dungeon Canyon is a little different than Wetherill. This one has no narrow slot canyon to cool off in. Instead there's an old **stock trail** to the top of Cummings Mesa, which makes for a different type of hike.

From the upper end of the bay, walk along the left, or east side of the drainage. Eventually you'll see several hiker and livestock trails gradually merge to form one good one higher up. About a km above the HWM, you will see to your left, or east, some old rock corrals and the ruins of an old hogan or some kind of shelter. From there walk to the east and into a shallow alcove where you'll see some greenery. Up near the cliff you'll see evidence of an old encampment or corrals. Just under the cliff is a tiny spring, dripping water from the wall. Someone has placed two kettles in the wettest places, which should be full when you arrive. In summer, one person can put away both kettles of clear, cool water at a time.

From the spring head back down to the main trail, which at that point is becoming easy to follow. The further up you go to the southeast, the better the trail becomes. Further up canyon, you will see a fence across the valley floor just as the trail begins to steepen. The fence has been decorated with old Navajo clothing. Pass over the fence and head up the steep talus slope.

The trail in this section has been built by the hands of man, very likely during the 1930's when the CCC crews built many stock trails on Navajo Nation lands. It zig zags up the talus about 2/3 of the way to the top, then veers to the right, or south, and contours along one of the terraces. You may lose the trail in this area, but just head right on the same level, which is likely to be along the Summerville bench. To the south a ways, you will find the trail again, then follow it zig zag fashion up to the rim. If you have time you might try walking to the east for a view down into Wetherill Canyon. It's a lot cooler on top than at the lake.

So as not to back-track, you can take another old trail to the bottom. Look this one over from the rim before heading down. When you get back down the trail to the Summerville bench(perhaps the top of the Entrada Sandstone?), head south instead of north, and follow the other trail as it contours south, then west, around the perimeter of the huge bowl. As the trail passes one minor ridge, it starts zig zagging down another talus slope. But about half way down, the trail disappears because of a washout. You can still get down easily, but you'll have to route-find, either out on the slickrock or

The upper end of Dungeon Canyon.

down on the steep talus. This was likely the first trail built up this canyon, but perhaps after a flood, it was rebuilt in the other location.

Hike Length and Time Needed In the bottom of Wetherill, you can hike about one km(one hour round-trip), but to get out and walk to the end of the canyon, one will walk closer to 9 or 10 kms. This would be an all day hike. To reach the top of the trail in Dungeon Canyon, you will be walking about 5 to 6 kms, one way. The author did this one in less than 3 hours, but you'll likely want 4 or 5 hours, round-trip.

Boots or Shoes Better use wading shoes in the bottom of Wetherill Canyon, but upon the Carmel bench and in Dungeon Canyon, you can use any kind of hiking boots or shoes.

Water None in Wetherill, but a nice little spring in Dungeon. There are sheep and goats in Dungeon Canyon at times, but the spring water should always be good(if you catch it falling from the little hanging garden).

Main Attractions Good narrows, wild and seldom visited canyons, good campsites, and a historic livestock trail with good views from the rim.

Hiking Maps USGS or BLM maps Smoky Mountain and Glen Canyon Dam(1:100,000), or Cummings Mesa and Navajo Creek(1:62,500).

The old stock trail up Dungeon Canyon goes up the talus slope near the center of the foto.

Dry and Middle Rock Creeks

Location and Campsites Dry and Middle Rock Creeks both drain into Rock Creek Bay, which is the first large bay or inlet to the west of Dangling Rope Canyon and Marina. At the mouth of Rock Creek Bay is buoy M35(K56).

At the entrance of Rock Creek Bay and the inlets of Dry and Middle Rock Creeks as well, you'll find the Entrada Sandstone rising abruptly out of the water with no campsites around. As you near the upper ends of both inlets, the formations are seen rising and finally the bench forming Carmel Formation is exposed. There you will find a number of sandy beaches and campsites under the towering Entrada-Morrison walls.

Routes or Trails **Dry Rock Creek** makes for one of the better hikes around. Boat into the narrow upper part of the inlet, which begins to cut into the top of the Navajo Sandstone. You'll immediately begin walking in a good narrows section, but which is very shallow. If it were deeper it would really be something. After about 5 or 6 kms, you'll come to a 3 meter high dry falls. Pass this on the left. A short rope at that point could help less experienced hikers get up or down. The author had no trouble alone.

Just beyond the falls, the creek bed turns to the west and a minor drainage enters from the north. Just after this junction, you turn to the right, or north, and walk up the steep talus slope in between(at that point, the canyon is filled with landslide and talus deposits. If you were to continue in the main creek, you would soon find a boulder-filled gorge with a small spring, and not far above that, a blocking falls. It was in the area of the spring, the author saw a young big horn ram). As you walk up the minor talus ridge, it gradually turns to the right, or east. In the upper part you will find a big horn sheep trail, and the ridge becomes a knife-edge. For about 100 meters, it'll be necessary to pay attention and walk carefully. This is a slightly risky part, but anyone should be able to make it OK.

Above the knife-edge ridge, is a broad bench covered with landslide debris, covering up the Dakota Sandstone and Tropic Shale. Walk due east. On this bench, you will notice stud piles(piles of manure from wild stallions) which indicate a herd of feral or semi-wild horses in the area. As you approach the second or final cliff making the top layer of the Kaiparowits Plateau, be looking for the best route up. You will see a small seep and greenery on the left, and another on the right in a slightly rounded shallow bowl. Head up slightly to the right near the southerly seep. You won't get water out of this one, but maybe the flow is better at the northern seep?

Route-find up through the cliffs. Once on top, rim-walk south. After about half a km, you'll come to a cattle trail heading down to a small spring just under the first rim rocks. If you're careful, you can build a small mud dam to obtain drinking water just out of reach of the cows. However, this minor seep could dry up at times, so don't depend on finding enough water there for a good drink.

Middle Rock Creek Canyon and talus slopes in the middle of the foto.

MAP 34, DRY AND MIDDLE ROCK CREEKS

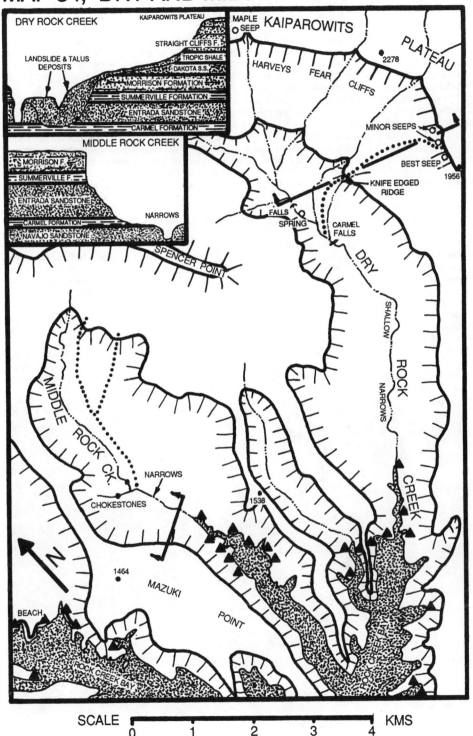

DRY ROCK CREEK

KAIPAROWITS PLATEAU

STRAIGHT CLIFFS F.

LANDSLIDE & TALUS DEPOSITS

TROPIC SHALE

DAKOTA S.S.

MORRISON FORMATION

SUMMERVILLE FORMATION

ENTRADA SANDSTONE

CARMEL FORMATION

MIDDLE ROCK CREEK

MORRISON F.

SUMMERVILLE F.

ENTRADA SANDSTONE

CARMEL FORMATION

NAVAJO SANDSTONE

NARROWS

MAPLE SEEP

KAIPAROWITS

PLATEAU

2278

HARVEYS

FEAR

CLIFFS

MINOR SEEPS

BEST SEEP

1956

KNIFE EDGED RIDGE

FALLS

SPRING

CARMEL FALLS

SPENCER POINT

DRY

SHALLOW

ROCK

NARROWS

MIDDLE ROCK CK.

NARROWS

CHOKESTONES

1538

CREEK

N

1464

MAZUKI

POINT

BEACH

ROCK CREEK BAY

ROCK CREEK BAY

SCALE

0   1   2   3   4   KMS

Again walk south from this seep and you'll come to the southern exposure of the Kaiparowits which is about 5 kms northwest of Navajo Point. This gives you a fine view of the lake, and in particular Dangling Rope Canyon. You can also see Navajo Mtn. to the east. This hike would be for the fit and adventurous hiker-climber.

As you boat into the upper end of **Middle Rock Creek Bay,** you will find it to be of the same appearance as Dry Rock Creek. Boat into the narrow end of the drainage, which again cuts into the upper part of the Navajo Sandstone. You will again walk up a narrow, shallow canyon. If you stay in the bottom of the drainage, you can only walk about two kms. then there are chokestones and falls in both tributaries shown. It's easy walking up to that point.

If you want to go further, regress from the junction of the two tributaries and climb a steep talus slope to the right, or east. This takes you out of the narrow gorge and onto the landslide or talus slope. Because of the late hour, the author didn't go further, but you can walk up canyon on the right side of the shallow gorge and onto one of two talus slopes covering up the Entrada-Morrison cliffs. Above these two landslides is the bench just below the final cliffs which form the top of the Kaiparowits or Fiftymile Mountain. With some route-finding you may find a way up to the very top.

Hike Length and Time Needed To walk up into the shallow Navajo narrows in Dry Rock Creek is to walk a few minutes, or an hour or two. But to walk to the top of the Kaiparowits is a long all day hike for anyone. The author walked the route described in 7 hours round-trip. Others may need as long as 9 or 10 hours. Doing this in cool weather would help.

In Middle Rock Creek, it'll only take a couple of hours to hike up to the chokestones and falls in the narrows. To get upon the first bench, it will likely take 4 to 5 hours for a round-trip hike; or longer if you try to get to the top of the Kaiparowits.

Boots or Shoes Any shoe will be fine if you stay in the narrow canyon bottoms but to hike to the rim, especially to the top of the Kaiparowits, you'll need a rugged hiking boot.

Water All seeps or springs on this map are small, and could dry up at times. So it's recommended you take all the water you'll need--which will be a lot on a hot summer day, especially if you attempt to reach the top of the Kaiparowits.

Main Attractions Good but shallow narrows, and some great views from the top of the Kaiparowits Plateau.

Hiking Maps USGS or BLM map Smoky Mountain(1:100,000), or Cummings Mesa(1:62,500).

History According to Crampton's studies of Glen Canyon in the University of Utah *Anthropological Paper #46,* he states there was an aboriginal route from the Colorado to the Kaiparowits Plateau somewhere within the Rock Creek Drainage. No mention is made as to which of the three canyons of Rock Creek was used. It's this author's opinion there were old Indian routes in and out of all three. In

Narrows in Middle Rock Creek Canyon.

1931, geologists Gregory and Moore, stated there was a stock trail from the Kaiparowits down to **Wild Horse Bar** at the mouth of Rock Creek on the Colorado River.

The author believes this is probably the present-day stock trail running up **Steer Canyon** to the top of the Kaiparowits, not far above or north of Woolsey Arch, in the upper end of the main Rock Creek Canyon. This Steer Canyon is the name shown on the *metric 1:100,000 scale Smoky Mountain map*. However, Leo Wilson of Escalante talked about a Pleasant Grove Canyon in the same area. This is likely the same canyon, but with two different names.

Before Lake Powell, there was a trail(Indian and miners) from Rock Creek down along the Colorado to the Ute Ford(usually known as the Crossing of the Fathers), located between Cane Creek and Gunsight Canyon.

A look down into Dry Rock Creek Inlet from the talus slope which can be climbed to reach the top of the Kaiparowits Plateau.

Rock Creek, Woolsey Arch and Steer Canyon

Location and Campsites The water shown on this map is the upper end of the main Rock Creek Bay. At the mouth of this bay should be a buoy marked M35(K56).

As you boat up the bay, you will find Entrada Sandstone walls rising abruptly out of the water with no campsites. But as you near the upper end, the rocks are uplifted to the north and northeast, exposing several sandy beaches which make fine campsites. These beaches are on the bench forming Carmel Formation. Above the Carmel is the Entrada, which contributes some of the sand. As you enter the very end of the inlet, it becomes narrow and you begin to see the top of the Navajo Sandstone. The Navajo is exposed in the middle of this large bowl, or valley, above the water line.

Routes or Trails Featured here is a hike to what is generally known as **Woolsey Arch.** You could walk up the valley on either side of the dry creek, but the best and easiest way is in the narrow creek bed. At about the HWM in the inlet, you will find a small seep of clear pure water coming out at the top of the Navajo. Above this seep, there is no more water in the canyon.

Rock Creek is shallow and narrow. On average it's about 10-15 meters deep and there are a number of places you can exit. After about 8 kms of easy walking you'll come to a minor dry fall, made up of a conglomerate member of the Carmel Formation. You can pass this fall easily on either side.

Immediately above the fall look to the right, or east, and you'll see some disturbed ground. Climb a 10 meter high slope and you'll see a small dam. Then look due north 100 meters, to see a 3 meter high metal pole in the middle of a clearing. This is an old oil well(dry) which has been capped. The dam was built to handle anything which may have escaped the well.

Due east of the capped well, **Woolsey Arch** can be seen in an exposed bluff of Entrada Sandstone. It's one of the more interesting arches you'll see. Underneath the arch is one cowboyglyph, reading *Burnham Bridge, 7/30/27.* It appears to be genuine, and is perhaps the original name for this arch.

The road leading to this capped well starts at Big Water west of Wahweap, near mile post 7 on Highway 89. There it's generally called the Warm Creek Road. It makes its way across Warm Creek, north of Last Chance Bay, and across Little Valley Canyon. From there it heads east to where you see it on this map. It then turns north to the base of the Kaiparowits Plateau, then south to end at Woolsey Arch. It's no longer usable beyond Little Valley Canyon.

Here's a hike the author didn't make, but which is just to the north of the map shown here. He was told about the possibility later by an old stockman from Escalante named Leo Wilson. From Woolsey Arch walk up the old road to the north to where it begins to make a loop south. At that point you'll be right at the base of the main cliff making up the top part of the Kaiparowits Plateau, and on an

The shallow narrows of Rock Creek.

MAP 35, ROCK CREEK AND WOOLSEY ARCH

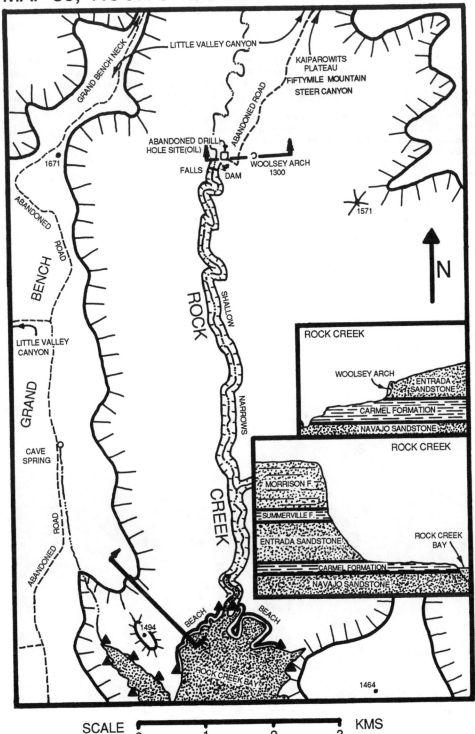

LITTLE VALLEY CANYON

GRAND BENCH NECK

KAIPAROWITS
PLATEAU
FIFTYMILE MOUNTAIN
STEER CANYON

ABANDONED ROAD

ABANDONED DRILL
HOLE SITE(OIL)

1671

ABANDONED ROAD

FALLS

DAM

WOOLSEY ARCH
1300

1571

BENCH

ROCK

SHALLOW

LITTLE VALLEY
CANYON

GRAND

NARROWS

CAVE
SPRING

N

ROCK CREEK

WOOLSEY ARCH

ENTRADA
SANDSTONE

CARMEL FORMATION

NAVAJO SANDSTONE

ROCK CREEK

MORRISON F.

SUMMERVILLE F.

ENTRADA SANDSTONE

ROCK CREEK
BAY

CARMEL FORMATION

NAVAJO SANDSTONE

ABANDONED ROAD

CREEK

1494

BEACH

BEACH

ROCK CREEK BAY

1464

SCALE 0   1   2   3   KMS

237

extension of the Grand Bench--or at least at that same level.

Then you walk due north into what the Smoky Mountain map calls **Steer Canyon.** There's a **cattle trail** up this short drainage to the top. Also, there's a spring on the right, or east side of the canyon near the rim. Since the spring is mentioned on the map, it likely has a year-round flow. Local cattlemen out of Escalante seem to be calling this same drainage Pleasant Grove Canyon. On top the altitude is about 2300 meters.

Hike Length and Time Needed From the HWM to Woolsey Arch is about 8 kms. The author did this one in less than 4 hours, but you may want 5-7 hours, round-trip. If you try the hike up to and through Steer Canyon to the top of the Kaiparowits, you will very likely need two days, with a camp at the spring mentioned above. Really strong hikers could do it in one day from the lake, but it would be a long day.

Boots or Shoes Any dry weather boots or shoes are OK.

Water Just one seep near the HWM, but take water from the source, because there are cattle in the area. One spring exists in upper Steer Canyon.

Main Attractions A long narrow slot canyon, soaring cliffs, Woolsey Arch, and the possibility of reaching the top of the Kaiparowits.

Hiking Maps USGS or BLM map Smoky Mountain(1:100,000), or Cummings Mesa(1:62,500).

Woolsey Arch set in an outcropping of Entrada Sandstone.

Here is a *cowboyglyph* underneath Woolsey Arch. Is this the rightful name for this arch?

Camping scene in upper Rock Creek Inlet.

West and Face Canyons

Location and Campsites These two canyons are located on the south side of the lake and south and southeast of Last Chance and Padre Bays, two of the largest open bodies of water on the lake. Most of the buoys in this part of the lake have letters on them instead of numbers. However, one buoy about half way between the mouths of Face and West, is numbered M24(K38).

The Utah-Arizona state line cuts across the area near the mouth of Face, and about mid-way along West Canyon Inlet(during times of high water). When the lake waters are high, this part of the lake will have many sandy campsites available. The reason is, the northern parts have the bench-forming rocks of the Carmel Formation exposed along the shore line. As you head up canyon in either drainage, the beds will be seen slowly rising from the water and the Navajo Sandstone, which underlies the Carmel, will be exposed. The Navajo is more prominent in West Canyon. This means sheer walls rising abruptly out of the water, with fewer and smaller campsites in little inlets.

Routes or Trails West Canyon offers one of the more exciting hikes in this book. As you near the upper end of the inlet, the Navajo walls will become higher and it becomes more narrow. From the HWM, you can walk up a very sandy canyon bottom with a small year-round stream. It's so sandy, many boaters hike this lower end in bare feet.

After nearly a km, you'll be in a very narrow little gorge. At one point you will walk under a log, brought down by a flash flood, jammed in the walls above you. Not far above this you come to a very narrow crack, which is a group of interconnected potholes, filled with water year-round. This 30 meter long swimming hole is the source of the water you walked in to arrive at that point. It's always shaded, therefore the water is very cold, even on hot summer days. You'll have to swim through this part. If you intend to hike for long distances above this swimming hole, you'll have to figure out a way to get your camera, watch, wallet and pack through it in a dry state. Any kind of float device; an inner tube, child's play pool, or plastic sack should do. Most boaters just swim through, without trying to take anything with them, and return down canyon.

If you prefer not to swim, or if you don't have a float device, you can still get into the canyon above. Regress from the swimming hole about 300 meters or so, and on your left, or south, will be an embankment choked with reeds. Fight your way up through these reeds to a break in the wall. Climb up and first head southeast up a short drainage, then veer to the right, or west, and walk the slickrock in a west, northwest direction. You will soon come to a large pothole with a couple of cottonwood trees growing in the bottom. Cross this short drainage and walk up the slickrock to the rim along the easiest route. From there you can see in all directions. Then walk in a south, southwest direction to a point about two bends in the canyon above the swimming hole. At that point, you will see a kind of talus-filled crack heading down to the canyon bottom. Route-find down this and you're back into the dry

The narrows of West Canyon. A log is lodged high above the stream bed.

MAP 36, WEST AND FACE CANYONS

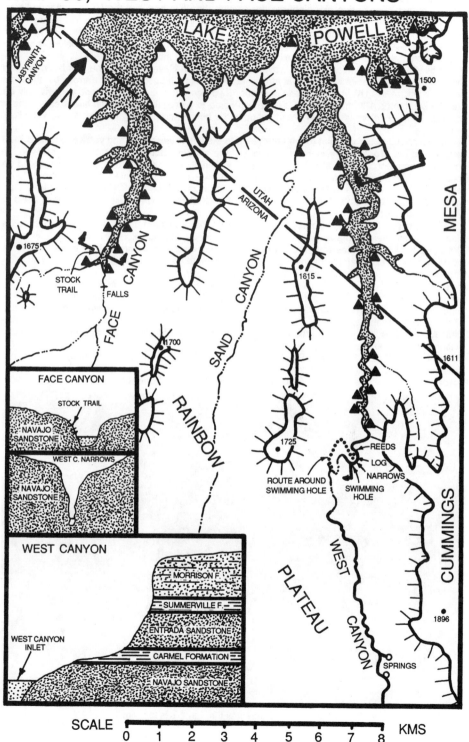

SCALE

0 1 2 3 4 5 6 7 8 KMS

241

creek bed. Just above this, there are some trees in the bottom indicating there is more water somewhere above.

The author hasn't been any higher in the canyon than this part, but the USGS maps indicate running water up canyon. This drainage goes on for many kms, but it likely doesn't get any more interesting than the part around the swimming hole. Stan Jones calls it one of the best long hikes on the lake. The part of this map showing the swimming hole and canyon just above and below, is slightly enlarged from the scale of the rest of the map, in order to show it more clearly.

Face Canyon is similar in some ways to West, but the Navajo Sandstone has been pushed down, so less of it is above water. Right at the end of the inlet, it becomes very narrow, but the walls barely rise above the HWM. At the end is a fork. If you go into the southeast fork, you will only be able to hike about a 100 meters or so, before you come to a dry fall. Energetic hikers can perhaps get around this, or return to the HWM and get upon the bench and possibly re-enter the very shallow gorge above.

As you head out of the inlet to the north, look to the left or west side, and you'll see just north of the forks, an old **stock trail** running up and out of the bottom. Someone cut or drilled holes in the slickrock, then placed oblong stones in the holes, and finally more stones and sand were placed on those. In other places, steps were cut in the slickrock. The trail is only visible for about 30-40 meters, then it disappears in the nearly flat sandy and slickrock bench. This trail was surely built during the Depression days of the mid-1930's by the CCC crews who built so many other trails in Navajo Nation lands.

Face Canyon is not that interesting for hikers, but the prominent buttes and mesas in the area rising to dramatic heights make an interesting backdrop for a camping trip.

Hike Length and Time Needed The walk up West Canyon to the swimming hole is about one km. You can do this in about an hour if that's as far as you want to go, or you can hike all day. In just a few minutes, you can see about all there is to see in Face Canyon.

Boots or Shoes Take wading shoes in West, but dry weather boots or shoes in Face Canyon.

Water None in Face Canyon, but you should be able to get a safe drink at the upper end of the swimming hole in the West Canyon narrows. The sandy stream below the swimming hole is often polluted with dog manure.

Main Attractions Towering buttes and mesas, a well built old stock trail, and one of the most exciting narrows hikes around.

Hiking Maps USGS or BLM maps Smoky Mountain and Glen Canyon Dam(1:100,000), or Cummings Mesa and Navajo Creek(1:62,500).

History During the Glen Canyon Gold Rush days which lasted from about 1884 until about 1900,

The *Swimming Hole* of West Canyon. The only way through this is to swim.

there was considerable activity in the canyon. Most of the action was north of the San Juan River, but there were a number of gravel bars prospected in this lower half as well. One of those places was **Mesken Bar**, located 2 or 3 kms up river from the mouth of Face Canyon, on the south side of the river.

Crampton states the bar was named after a German prospector and trapper from Denver, Edward Mesken. He located a placer claim there on September 18, 1889. Mesken was one of the earliest prospectors to work the lower Glen Canyon. He stayed there for many years. He would travel up and down the canyon in a small boat, accompanied by a dog, while trapping and prospecting. Apparently he made this bar his home, but no one mentions anything about any house or cabin.

The last claim locations were filed in 1932 during the Depression. Just before Lake Powell came to be, Crampton reported many signs of mining activity on the bar, including screens, a shaking machine, a wheelbarrow and camp debris. There were signs of horses recently grazing there and a trail from the head of the bar, up to the bench above, and evidently on up to the canyon rim.

Part of the stock trail leading down into the upper end of Face Canyon Inlet.

243

Above the *Swimming Hole,* West Canyon goes on for many kms.

Tourist cruise boat heading for Rainbow Bridge.

Tower Butte dominates the scene between Labyrinth and Navajo Canyons.

At the mouth of Last Chance Bay stands Gregory Butte.

Last Chance, Croton, Little Valley & Friendship Canyons and Last Chance Bay

Location and Campsites The three short canyons on this map are all at the upper or northern end of Last Chance Bay. Last Chance Bay is located between Padre Bay and the Dangling Rope Marina. Buoy number M23(K37) is found near the mouth, as is the unmistakable Gregory Butte. This is one of the longest and largest bays or inlets on Lake Powell. Friendship Cove is not on this map, but is discussed below.

There are not many campsites in Last Chance Bay. The reason is, in the lower or southern end the Entrada Sandstone walls rise abruptly from the water, and there are simply no beaches or talus slopes around. But as you head up the bay, the beds are gradually dipping to the north, and the walls aren't as high. At a point about 2/3 the way up the bay, things change and the top of the Entrada is right at the shore line. This is also where the Summerville Formation is exposed. At that point a minor bench is formed, thus a number of campsites can be found. Most of the campsites in Last Chance Bay are found in the Twitchell Canyon Inlet, as shown on the map. North and south of this section of the lake, there are very few places to camp.

The author once drove his VW Rabbit from Big Water and Highway 89, up along the Warm Creek Road. It's a good road especially in the beginning, but the further you go, the rougher it gets. Most cars driven with care, could make it to Croton Canyon crossing, but the last part of the road to the corral at the rim of Little Valley Canyon, is for high clearance vehicles only.

Routes or Trails Probably the most interesting place on this map for hikers, is **Little Valley Canyon.** It begins on the western slopes of the Kaiparowits Plateau and drains into the upper right hand fork of Last Chance Bay. There should always be some kind of campsite at the upper end of the inlet, regardless of lake levels.

As you walk up canyon, all the rocks visible will be those of the Morrison Formation. It's a rather confined canyon in the lower end, but higher up, it opens up into the Little Valley. In the lower end are several small seeps or springs. The one furthest up canyon will be the best to get a safe drink from. The canyon is used by cattle beginning in October, then they're taken out by June 15 each year.

About 5 kms up canyon from the HWM, you'll come to an old abandoned road. This used to be an extension of the Warm Creek Road. that begins at Big Water, on Highway 89 west of Wahweap(very near mile post 7). It's usable up to the corral on the west side of the canyon, then it's been blocked off and the rest now serves as a cow trail. This is the same road you see dead-ending at the drill hole site next to Woolsey Arch near the head of Rock Creek(Map 35). It was built and used by an oil company in about 1960. You can use this road to get out of the canyon bottom on either side. The corral is still used each year by an Escalante stockman.

At or very near where you begin hiking up Little Valley Canyon, you can also begin hiking up

Typical wall scene along Last Chance Bay.

246

MAP 37, LAST CHANCE CREEK AND CROTON & LITTLE VALLEY CANYONS

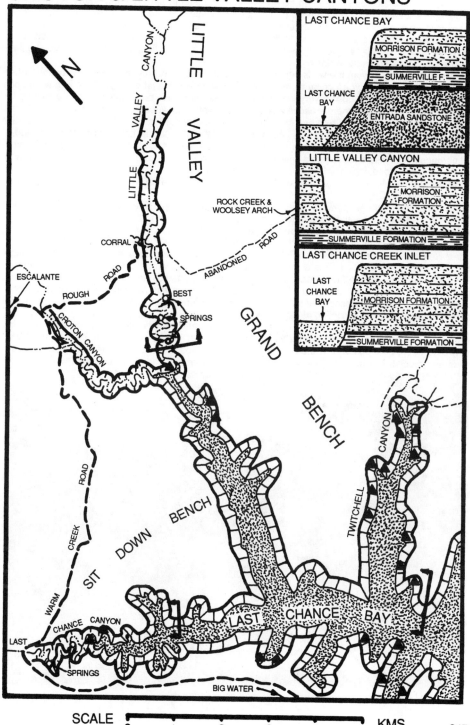

LITTLE VALLEY CANYON

LITTLE VALLEY

N

ROCK CREEK & WOOLSEY ARCH

CORRAL

ROAD

ESCALANTE

ROUGH

ROAD

BEST

SPRINGS

ABANDONED ROAD

CROTON CANYON

GRAND

BENCH

BENCH

SIT DOWN BENCH

CREEK ROAD

WARM

LAST

CHANCE CANYON

SPRINGS

TWITCHELL CANYON

LAST CHANCE BAY

BIG WATER

LAST CHANCE BAY

MORRISON FORMATION

SUMMERVILLE F.

LAST CHANCE BAY

ENTRADA SANDSTONE

LITTLE VALLEY CANYON

MORRISON FORMATION

SUMMERVILLE FORMATION

LAST CHANCE CREEK INLET

LAST CHANCE BAY

MORRISON FORMATION

SUMMERVILLE FORMATION

SCALE 0 1 2 3 4 5 KMS

another short drainage to the north called **Croton Canyon**. The author hasn't been into this one, because it didn't look so interesting on the map. It's deeper at it's lower end but becomes shallow higher up, where the Warm Creek Road crosses it.

The last hike included here is up from the end of the inlet in **Last Chance Canyon.** This may be the shortest hike of the three, and is in the same geologic formation, so it looks the same. There will always be some kind of campsite at the end of the inlet. As you walk up canyon, there will be running water part of the time in the main drainage. Part of this stream comes from a side canyon. If you head up this short drainage, there will be a short jump-up, which keeps cows out. Above the little waterfall, water looked safe to drink.

Continuing up canyon, the walls become lower and lower, until they become a low bench. After about 3 kms of walking you'll come to the Warm Creek Road. At that point you'll be in a wide open valley. You can continue up this very long canyon to the northwest, but it doesn't look interesting for hikers. Further up canyon there must be lots of running water, because the author saw several pieces of wood in the lower canyon which had been cut by beavers for dam construction.

Hike Length and Time Needed It's about 5 kms to the old road in Little Valley Canyon, and a round-trip hike there will take 3 or 4 hours. It's about the same distance to the road up Croton Canyon, but perhaps a little less time. There's only about 3 kms of walking up Last Chance Creek or Canyon to the Warm Creek Road, which will take only a couple of hours.

Boots or Shoes While there is some water in each canyon, there will be no wading, so any kind of boots or shoes are OK.

Water From the highest spring in Little Valley Canyon, or from the side canyon along Last Chance Creek. Be careful though, there are cattle in the area from October 1 until June 15 each year.

Main Attraction Short hikes in unknown canyons and solitude.

Hiking Maps USGS or BLM map Smoky Mountain(1:100,000), or Gunsight Butte(1:62,500).

Other Nearby Canyons In between Rock Creek and Last Chance Bays is another minor drainage called **Friendship Cove.** This is a rather short and open bay, with slickrock walls of the Entrada Sandstone coming down to the water. However, the author plotted 5 campsites on his map of the bay, the best of which are at the very end. This is a box type canyon with no exit at the upper end, nor is there any long drainage associated with the canyon. Evidently there wasn't much going on in this immediate area prior to the coming of Lake Powell.

Last Chance Bay is another very large body of water that doesn't seem to have a lot of history associated with it. In the area which is now under water, was a pasture for cattle in the early days of the 20th century. The big walls you see are made of the Entrada Sandstone; at least the lower and reddish-brown part of the wall. There aren't too many campsites available, but there are

Fences in Little Valley Canyon where an old road crosses the drainage.

several in the upper end, as shown on the map. The lower half of the bay is almost devoid of camping places for tents. Right at the mouth of this bay is Gregory Butte, standing tall out of the water in the middle of the main channel.

Stockman's camp and corrals on the lip of Little Valley Canyon.

Soaring buttes and mesas along the southern shore of Padre Bay.

Gunsight & Labyrinth Canyons and Padre Bay & The Crossing of the Fathers

Location and Campsites Gunsight Canyon drains from the north into what is known today as Padre Bay. Padre Bay is located about half way between Wahweap and Dangling Rope Marinas. The closest buoy in the main channel is numbered M19(K29). Gunsight Canyon is the most westerly of five canyons or inlets on the northern side of Padre Bay, perhaps the largest on the lake. On the southwest side of the bay is Labyrinth Canyon, which is to the east of Face Canyon. For a better look at the area, see the next map showing the Crossing of the Fathers.

The inlet or bay to Gunsight Canyon has some very fine campsites. There is one beach about 200-300 meters long, plus several other smaller sites. The shore line is composed of the Entrada Sandstone. In the upper end of Gunsight Bay, it forms a low bench, thus the many sandy beaches. Further out in Padre Bay the Carmel Formation is exposed, with even more sandy beaches. Upon the author's visit, it was a very busy and popular place. Labyrinth Canyon is discussed below.

Routes or Trails As you enter the upper part of the inlet to **Gunsight Canyon** it will become moderately narrow. As you hike up canyon, the walking is very easy. There is no running water; thus no willows, brush or trees. Nor are there any boulders or other obstructions to speak of. After 5 or 6 kms of fast walking, the walls begin to close in and the canyon becomes narrower. At about that point, you will come to the first of three minor dry falls spaced very close together. The author had no trouble getting around these but for some it might be best to take a short rope, to help less experienced hikers up. From the top of the third fall, you can only walk another 300 meters or so, then you'll come to a blocking dry fall.

Underneath the fall is Gunsight Spring. This is a tiny green hanging garden in the middle of the desert. The spring has been cemented up at the bottom of a dripping wall to form a drinking trough for cattle, but it appears cattle haven't been there for years. The water is clear and cool and safe to drink. Nearby is an old metal tank that hasn't been used recently either. This is a fine place to cool off in the shade, but the author remembers a few mosquitos even in the middle of the day!?

If you head back down canyon toward the falls about 200 meters(100 meters above the falls), and look to the right, or west, you will see just faintly visible the beginning of an old **cattle trail.** It runs along a bench at about the same elevation as Gunsight Spring. It is obviously man-made. It runs for about a km on the same bench, until it rounds the final bend to the right. Then it heads out to the mesa top called Alstrom Point and to an old road near the head of the canyon.

Hike Length and Time Needed From the HWM to Gunsight Spring is about 6 or 7 kms. The old cattle trail is about one km long. The author was out walking for 4 hours. You will need perhaps 5 hours to do the same hike.

At the upper end of Gunsight Canyon is the very green Gunsight Spring.

MAP 38, GUNSIGHT CANYON

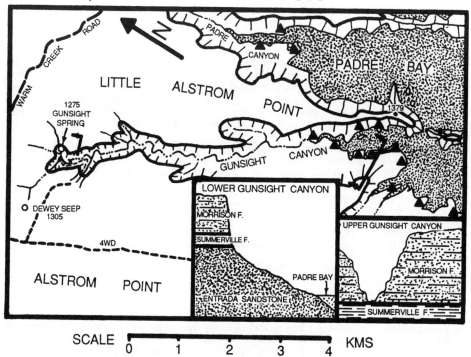

WARM CREEK ROAD

PADRE CANYON

PADRE BAY

LITTLE ALSTROM POINT

1379

1275 GUNSIGHT SPRING

GUNSIGHT CANYON

O DEWEY SEEP 1305

4WD

ALSTROM POINT

LOWER GUNSIGHT CANYON

MORRISON F.

SUMMERVILLE F.

PADRE BAY

ENTRADA SANDSTONE

UPPER GUNSIGHT CANYON

MORRISON F.

SUMMERVILLE F.

SCALE   0   1   2   3   4   KMS

Camping scene in Gunsight Canyon Inlet.

Boots or Shoes Any dry weather boots or shoes will do.

Water Gunsight Spring, one of the best around.

Main Attractions The upper canyon is interesting with the spring and old cattle trail. Nothing is left showing, but under Padre Bay is a historic site worth mentioning.

Hiking Maps USGS or BLM map Smoky Mountain(1:100,000), or Gunsight Butte(1:62,500).

Padre Bay & Crossing of the Fathers At the southern end of Padre Bay is a shallow inlet called **Labyrinth Canyon.** This is a very flat and open valley. It offers no real hiking, but there are plenty of good sandy campsites. Because it's open and shallow, you will have fine views of some of the more unique sites on the lake. One of these is **Tower Butte,** rising to 1610 meters--about 400 vertical meters above the lake. It's located due south of the inlet, has a square top and vertical sides, and is very visible. As you motor into Labyrinth Inlet, there are some grand buttes on the east as well. This scenery isn't the same as, for example, the Escalante River country, but in its own way just as majestic.

Below the waters of Padre Bay is one of the most famous historic sites associated with Lake Powell. This place was known as the **Crossing of the Fathers**. It was at that location on the Colorado River where the expedition known as the Dominguez and Escalante Party crossed on their return journey to Santa Fe, New Mexico, in November of 1776.

The story of their journey in this part of the country begins on the Colorado at the mouth of the Paria River, at the place we now call Lee's Ferry. They had camped on the lower Paria from October 26 through November 1, 1776, while looking for a way to cross. On November 2, they left the Paria about 5 kms upstream from the Colorado and made their way up the eastern canyon wall to the mesa top. That pass is still called Dominguez Pass(see Kelsey's book, *Hiking and Exploring the Paria River).*

From there they headed north and down into Wahweap Creek, at a location which is now under water. This was likely in the area due north of Wahweap Marina. The next morning they headed to the southeast down Wahweap Creek on a bench, but they found themselves 150 meters above the river. They then followed the river gorge up stream, in the area that is now the south shore of Antelope Island, and ended up camping just about opposite the mouth of Navajo Canyon.

During the day of November 4, they looked for a way down to the canyon bottom, and eventually found a route, which in 1960 was just a ravine for big game. Two of their party, Domingo and Muniz, crossed the river and entered Navajo Canyon. After some distance and not finding a route out of the canyon, they returned. Had they continued up Navajo Creek they would have saved themselves a lot of time. They camped the night of the 4th on a sand bar just above the river.

The next morning, they returned to the canyon rim via the same ravine, then went north to the lower end of Warm Creek. But it was entrenched in the lower end and they had to move north on the

Great beaches make great campsites around the shore of Padre Bay.

252

PADRE BAY--CROSSING OF THE FATHERS

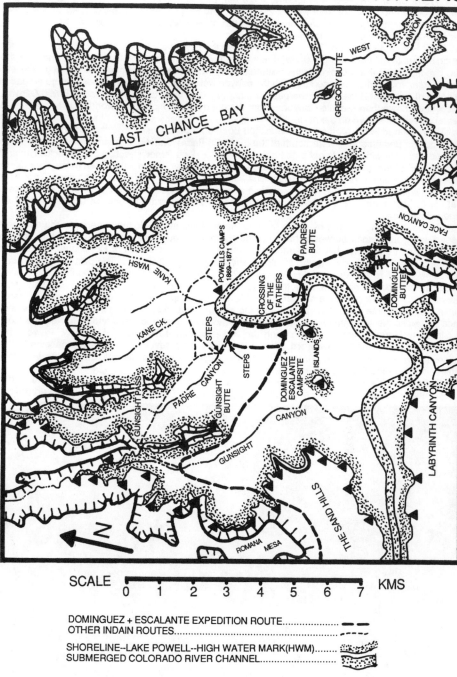

SCALE
0 1 2 3 4 5 6 7 KMS

DOMINGUEZ + ESCALANTE EXPEDITION ROUTE.................... ▬ ▬
OTHER INDAIN ROUTES... ▬ ▬ ▬
SHORELINE--LAKE POWELL--HIGH WATER MARK(HWM)........
SUBMERGED COLORADO RIVER CHANNEL..........................

west side of the slot. About 1 1/2 kms up canyon from the mouth, they found a way down into the gorge. Half a km further up stream they made an exit to the east side and got back above the Navajo Sandstone and onto the Carmel Bench.

They camped the night of November 5 near a spring which is now under the eastern bay of the larger Warm Creek Bay. On the morning of the 6th, they headed east around the southern end of Romana Mesa and on top of what we call today the Sand Hills. There is to this day, an old 4WD road on top of this bench. Before the lake came to be, this same road headed around the cliffs and ended near the Kane Creek boat landing(river rafts).

From Romana Mesa, they headed northeast into the bottom of Gunsight Canyon, then southeast around the south side of Gunsight Butte. From there it was again southeast to a point overlooking the river directly above the Crossing of the Fathers. They would have been better off had they used the normal Indian route which crossed through the canyon wall at Gunsight Pass, rather than go around to the south of Gunsight Butte. From the pass the normal route went to the east side of Padre Canyon, or as it was known then, Navajo Canyon. From there the normal Indian trail went down to the river in several places, as shown on the map.

They camped in the area south of Gunsight Butte on a bench just above the river on the night of November 6. Because they were south of the mouth of Padre Canyon, instead of north, they had to do some trail work with axes to get their horses down one steep 3 meter section of slickrock. The next morning, part of the group went down Padre Canyon to the river and to a point just below their camp. Part of their supplies were lowered over the cliff from their camp, directly down to the river. Then they crossed in waist-deep water. Everyone made it across to the east side that day, where they camped. That night, November 7, 1776, they celebrated and called the ford *La Purisima Concepcion de la Virgen Santissima.*

The next day they began by going north up some steep slickrock, then veered to the east and passed along the bench between the river and Padres Butte. Today, just the tip of this butte is showing. From there they headed almost due south passing to the east of Dominguez Butte, then south and over a low divide into the shallow Labyrinth Canyon drainage. The part of their old trail above the HWM is still there today(apparently?). From Labyrinth, the *well beaten trail* veers southeast, then south, and finally southwest to where it zig zags down into Navajo Canyon, very near where Chaol Canyon enters. See Map 39. On that map, the author calls this part the North Dominguez-Escalante Trail. That part of their trip was on November 11. Just into Chaol Canyon they made an exit on the southern part of the trail, then headed south to Hopi Land and on to New Mexico.

In early Mormon history, and during the two river exploration trips of John W. Powell, this crossing was known as the **Ute Ford.** Jacob Hamblin used it several times while preaching to the Indians south and east of the Colorado. This ford was used by Navajos as well, often times with stolen cattle taken from the Mormons.

Dellenbaugh's Diary mentions the events of Powell's second expedition when they landed in the vicinity of Crossing of the Fathers in early October, 1871. Evidently they were very low on

Another beach camp on Padre Bay.

supplies as they neared the area, because he states; *The Major contemplated stopping long enough for a climb to the top[of Navajo Mtn.] but on appealing to Andy for information as to the state of the supplies he found we were near the last crust and he decided that we had better pull on as steadily as possible towards El Vado[Crossing of the Fathers].* That morning started at Music Temple Canyon.

The next morning, *Friday, October 6th, we got away as quickly as we could and pulled down the river hoping that El Vado was not far ahead and feeling somewhat as Escalante must have felt a century before when he was trying to find it. He had the advantage of having horses which could be eaten from time to time. Of course we knew from the position of the San Juan and of Navajo Mountain, that we could reach El Vado in at most two days, but the question was, "would we find any one there with rations?"*

Later on that afternoon they found a place where some brush had been burned, and the tracks of shod horses and two men. They went on about 5 kms more and *caught a glimpse of a stick with a white rag dangling from it stuck out from the right bank, and at the same moment heard a shot. On landing and mounting the bank we found Captain Pardyn Dodds and two prospectors, George Riley and John Bonnemort, encamped beside a large pile of rations.*

The party camped at that location for about a week, taking observations, and eating lots of food. They were also doing their best to recover from various illnesses. One member named Steward, was very ill. On October 13, and as they were contemplating moving on, two Navajos arrived in camp. Dellenbaugh stated, *We saw by their dress, so different from the Ute(red turbans, loose unbleached cotton shirts, native woven sashes at the waist, wide unbleached cotton trousers reaching to a little below the knee and there slashed up on the outer side for seven or eight inches[18 to 20 cms], bright woven garters twisted around their red buckskin leggins below the knee, and red moccasins with turned up soles and silver buttons), that they were Navajos.*

An hour later, seven more Navajos arrived in their camp, on their way to the Mormon settlements on a trading mission. None of the whites spoke Navajo and none of the Navajos spoke English, so after a while and after the rivermen discovered one of the visitors had sticky fingers, they decided to move their camp down river a ways. *Just below was El Vado de los Padres by which these Navajos had now come across. It was also sometimes called the Ute Ford. The necessary route was indicated by a line of small piles of stones showing above water. It was not an easy crossing, feasible only at low water, and quite impossible for waggons, even had there been a road to it. A shoal was followed up the middle of the river half a mile[700 meters] with deep channels cutting through it, reached from the south over a steep slope of bare sandstone and from the north through a very narrow, small canyon, not over ten feet[3 meters] wide.*

This crossing was the main route across the Colorado River for about a century, or until January 11, 1873. That's the day John D. Lee made the first trip across the river in his newly built ferry boat.

In the southwest corner of Padre Bay can be seen the unmistakable Tower Butte.

Lee's Ferry at the mouth of the Paria River, was then the normal route across the Colorado until 1929, when the Navajo Bridge was finished across the upper part of Marble Canyon.

From then on, the Crossing of the Fathers was lost in history, with the possible exception of cattlemen and prospectors who roamed the canyon. It was finally rediscovered in 1936 by a

Typical scene in the area south of Padre Bay near Face Canyon.

Semi-wild Navajo Donkeys grazing along the Face Canyon Inlet.

prospector named Byron Davies. He told historian Russell G. Frazier about it and in 1938, a party of several people rafted down the Colorado and erected a copper plaque right at the mouth of Padre Canyon, commemorating the spot.

This is the bottom part of the First Navajo Trail in Navajo Canyon Inlet.

Looking at the First Navajo Trail from the lake.

Navajo Creek, Chaol Canyon, and the Dominguez and Escalante Trail

Location and Campsites To get to the hikes on the two maps shown here, you first have to head for Navajo Canyon, which is the first major drainage east of Glen Canyon Dam and Wahweap Marina heading in a southerly direction. The inlet begins just east of Antelope Island and about 14 kms above the dam. Navajo Canyon Inlet is one of the longer tributaries on Lake Powell, about 25 kms. It's a very straight canyon until it reaches the junction seen on the maps. At that point Navajo Creek or Canyon heads east for a long distance, while Chaol Canyon or Kaibito Creek runs south for many kms.

Because of the north-south nature of Navajo Canyon and the prevailing southerly winds, expect to find lots of driftwood in the southern half or third of this inlet. The author managed to catch a small piece of driftwood in his propellor and broke a sheer pin(which he replaced easily in 10 minutes). So best to slow down as you enter the *driftwood-slicks,* otherwise some of the floaters can do serious damage. With care and a little more time, you can get through these obstacles OK. Above the end of the lake is one of the more interesting canyons discussed in this book.

There are very few campsites along Navajo Canyon Inlet, but several do exist at about the halfway mark. One of the better ones is labeled Sand Dome. It's right across the bay from the first of the old Navajo trails. You'll also find good campsites on either side of the Yazzie Trail, and another one at the very end of the inlet. However, there may be lots of driftwood in that area. It seems this driftwood stays in an area about a km north of the junction of Chaol and Navajo Canyons.

At the time of the author's first visit, he thought the water level was about 2 meters below the HWM. He camped at the end of the water line, which at that moment was 250 meters down stream from the junction of Navajo and Chaol Canyons. However, the USGS map shows lake water going up Navajo Creek for about 5 more kms! Surely a mistake, but it does tell you that the upper end of the lake has a very low gradient and the campsites will surely be in different places than shown on the map of Navajo Creek and Chaol Canyon.

One park employee told the author Navajo Canyon Inlet is silting up quicker than most others. The reason for this is the entire drainage is very sandy, and there are lots of Navajo livestock being grazed up stream. With this constant sedimentation, the upper end of the inlet and the campsite locations will change with every big storm.

Route or Trails In about the middle of the map showing **Navajo Canyon Inlet,** is the **First Navajo Trail** from the lake to the rim. You can find the lower end of it on the south side of a small peninsula just across the water from the *sandslide* on the map. At the beginning of the trail you'll see a number of finely cut steps in the slickrock as the trail emerges from the water and zig zags up to the

On the Yazzie Trail just above the lake is this old wooden storage box.

MAP 39, NAVAJO CANYON INLET & NAVAJO TRAILS

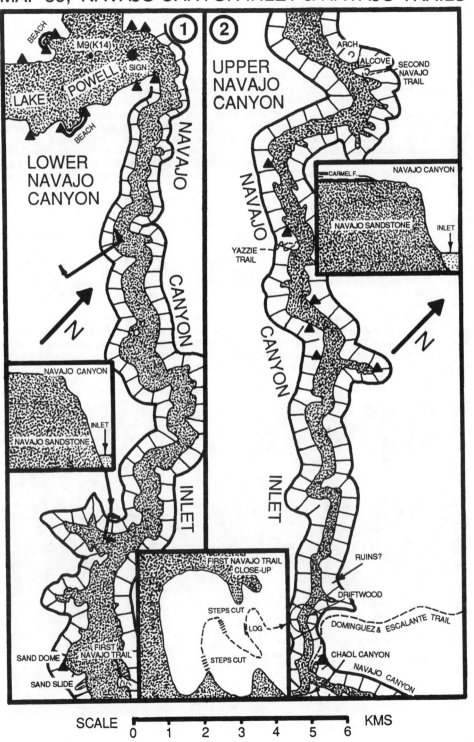

SCALE 0 1 2 3 4 5 6 KMS

rim on the east side.   Most of the cut steps are in the lower parts, while up higher, there are stone cairns marking the way. On top you'll have fine views of the canyon inlet.

This first trail was surely an old Indian route in the beginning, but what you see there today was upgraded by a government Civilian Conservation Corps(CCC) work crew during the Depression year of 1936. This information comes from Navajo patriarch Owen Yazzie, who lives with his family of about four generations, just southeast of the butte called Leche-E Rock, which is about 16 kms southeast of Page.

Yazzie was born in 1909, in the bottom of Navajo Canyon, about half way between the Colorado River and the lower part of Kaibito Creek. He couldn't place the spot on a map, but his family lived there until the waters of Lake Powell drove them out in about 1964. Their canyon home must have been northeast of Leche-E Rock and close to the *sand dome* shown on the map. His family was the only one in that section of the canyon and they had peach, apricot, and apple trees, plus a vineyard. They grew corn, squash and all the other vegetables so common to this part of the country.

Yazzie had a hard time remembering dates so long ago, but he did recall working for at least two summer seasons for the CCC work crews. He said the crews were typically of 15 to 20 men. The tools were almost exclusively picks and shovels, but they did use dynamite in places. They got around mostly on horseback.

The work began in the spring of the year, and finished not long before Christmas. There were many crews on the Navajo Nation, but he only worked in the area of Navajo Canyon. The one summer he does remember was 1936. They spent the entire warm season building trails in and out of the canyon. There were many trails. At the bottom of one, now under water, he said someone cut the numbers *1936*, indicating the year it was built.

Going southeast now. About 1 1/2 kms from the first Navajo trail, you'll see high on the rim to the left, or northeast, a small arch. About 300 meters further to the southeast of the arch, along the eastern shore, you will see some steps cut in the slickrock. On the map, this is called the **Second Navajo Trail**. These steps are found half way in between two little short inlets. This was surely another project of the CCC's.

Boat south from this second Navajo trail about 5 or 6 kms. Look to the right, or west side of the inlet. On a small terrace at the bottom of a minor ridge, look for a stone cairn right at the HWM. This is the beginning of what the author is calling the **Yazzie Trail**. This is the only trail the author found in the area on the west side fitting the description given to him by Owen Yazzie. This surely was the trail the Yazzie family used when they had to abandon their home in the canyon.

To use this trail, you'll first walk north a few meters on a minor terrace, finally turning south. About 100 meters from the water, you'll come to an old wooden storage box, perhaps a left-over from

Part of the Second Navajo Trail. Steps appear to have been notched out with an ordinary miners pick.

NAVAJO CREEK & CHAOL CANYON AND THE
DOMINGUEZ & ESCALANTE TRAIL

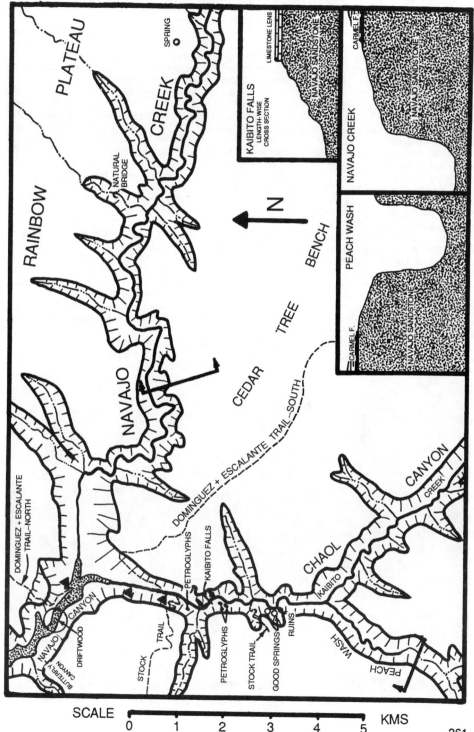

the CCC work crew days? From there, the trail heads west. One branch goes straight up the slickrock to another bench; while a second part veers to the left, around a bluff, and finally cuts back to the north up a gully, where it meets the first part just mentioned. At this second terrace, it zig zags a couple of times to the west before disappearing on the more gentle slope near the rim. This is another constructed trail for people and livestock, but it hasn't been used in years.

Right at the junction of Navajo and Chaol Canyons and on the north side, you will see a man-made trail zig zagging up to a low bench. This is another old Indian trail, and as the story goes, it was used by the **Dominguez and Escalante Party,** after they crossed the Colorado River on November 7, 1776. At that time, they had failed to find a suitable route to California and were low on supplies, so they were trying to return to Santa Fe, New Mexico, before winter set in.

The north branch of this trail runs along a bench parallel to Navajo Canyon for a ways, then it turns to the northeast and after about 1 1/2 kms tops out on the mesa. The trail you see today is not the same as it was in 1776. It has since been worked over in many places, surely by the CCC crew Owen Yazzie was with in 1936. They used lots of dynamite to build this one, and it's still used today by Navajo herdsmen.

If you decide to walk up **Navajo Creek,** you'll find a broad open canyon in the lower parts. This is where the lake covers the bottom during times of high water. Above the HWM, the canyon tightens up and becomes more narrow. It has a year-round stream flowing, which has its beginnings in the area near Inscription House, far to the east. This entire drainage is prime grazing country for Navajo livestock. About 15 kms up canyon and in a side drainage coming down from the north, is a natural bridge. The author found no Anasazi ruins in this canyon, but given the amount of available water, there could be some(but far up canyon?).

If you walk up **Chaol Canyon** about 1 1/2 kms from Navajo Creek, you'll find the second, or south half, of the **Dominguez and Escalante Trail.** It will be on your left, heading north northeast as it leaves the canyon bottom on a little minor ridge. It's found just to the side of a little alcove where cattails are growing. Once you get on this trail it's easy to follow, as it runs along a little valley to a point overlooking the junction of Navajo and Chaol Canyons. Then it turns south and southeast, and heads for Cedar Tree Bench and beyond. Like the north part of this trail, it tends to disappear on the mesa top. Along some parts, especially as it heads up the slickrock or steeper sections, it has steps cut out and stones piled up. But it's not had the heavy blasting and construction as the northern part of the trail.

About 300 meters above the South Dominguez and Escalante Trail on the right, or west side, is another very well built **stock trail.** It begins very near the HWM, and is marked by a couple of dead trees. This one is easy to find and follow and the CCC crew spent a lot of time on it. It zig zags up

The lower end of the Dominguez and Escalante Trail(north) as it rises above the canyon floor.

through the different layers of Navajo Sandstone until it reaches the mesa top. Of the three trails the author found leading down into lower Chaol Canyon, this one sees by far the most hoof traffic. By observing animal tracks, it's clear that horses, cattle, sheep, goats and probably donkeys use this trail to gain access to Kaibito Creek and drinking water.

About 200 meters above the stock trail on the right, or west, is a set of **petroglyphs** mostly hidden behind some cattails. Wade through the cattails and you'll see some etchings of big horn sheep, both high and low on the east facing wall.

Continue up **Kaibito Creek.** It begins many kms to the south and beyond Highway 98, the main link between Page and Kayenta. This is a year-round stream and one of the larger of the small creeks(combined with Navajo Creek) entering Lake Powell.

About a km above the first petroglyphs is **Kaibito Falls,** which is perhaps the most fotogenic waterfalls within walking distance of the lake. These falls have been created because of a thin limestone lens within the Navajo Sandstone. This lens is more resistant to erosion than the surrounding sandstone. The water first cascades over the limestone, then has cut interesting erosional features in the sandstone beneath. The falls, or perhaps it's best to call them *cascades,* are only about 5 meters high. See the length-wise cross-section on the map, to get an idea of the shape of Kaibito Falls.

Above the waterfalls about 300-400 meters and on the right, or west, are two panels of very good **petroglyphs.** Most of the figures are big horn sheep. These are among the best preserved the author has ever seen.

Continuing up canyon. Walk another 400 meters or so and again on the right, or west, is another old **stock trail.** This one is the steepest of all the trails in the Navajo and Chaol Canyon area. This one is also built up in places and is easy to find and follow. It's located just across the canyon from a major drainage coming in from the east.

Another 400 meters up canyon from the last stock trail, and within an area of about 60-70 meters, are three springs. Each comes out of a crack in the rock and the water should be safe to drink. The third or upper-most spring is interesting. It drains out of a crack about two meters above the creek bed, and is surrounded by a small hanging garden. Upon the author's visit, there was a log standing against the wall right at this spring. At the top of the log, about 3 meters up, were several very old and eroded steps cut in the wall. The author followed these up to **Anasazi ruins** just to the left. A word of caution: it's likely that log will have been washed away when you arrive, but regardless if it's there or not, it's recommended you forget trying to climb up. The author went up to find nothing of interest at the ruins, then was lucky to have gotten back down without falling or being injured. The old steps are about worn out, and it's all steep slickrock. Your best view of the ruins is from the creek bed.

This foto shows the first Stock Trail in lower Chaol Canyon(looking north).

The author went up to and into **Peach Wash** a ways, then returned. Peach Wash is short and deep, and appears to be a box canyon. If you continue on up Kaibito Creek, you will find good narrows for about 25 kms. Somewhere in the upper end there is one or more waterfalls to impede traffic. Rumors say there is a waterfall and some really good narrows above that, but the author guesses it'll be hard to get into the upper section of the canyon. To do any serious hiking in Chaol Canyon above Peach Wash, you'd need to take a pack and spend two or three days exploring. No telling what you might find.

Hike Length and Time Needed It's about 15 kms from the canyon forks up to the natural bridge in Navajo Canyon, which will be a long all day hike. The three trails in lower Chaol Canyon, including the Dominguez and Escalante, are all within about 2 kms of the canyon forks, and can all be visited easily in maybe 3 hours. It's about 7 kms up to the three springs and the ruins. This trip to see the ruins, petroglyphs, falls and trails in Chaol Canyon, will likely be most of a day, depending on how fast you walk and how long you observe the sights. The author considers this to be one of the most interesting hikes in this book.

Boots or Shoes Wading boots or shoes in either canyon, but any kind of shoes on the trails leading out of Navajo Canyon Inlet.

Water With all the livestock in the canyon, drink only from the springs near the ruins. Peach Wash had a small stream and the author saw no fresh sign of livestock, so it may be good to drink, especially if you walk up canyon a ways.

Main Attractions Ruins, petroglyphs, old historic stock trails, one of the prettiest waterfalls around, and very few other campers. You may also meet Navajo children herding flocks of sheep and goats. The driftwood in the upper end of Navajo Canyon Inlet, seems to scare away visitors to this area. But the author went through it twice, and really had no problems.

Hiking Maps USGS or BLM map Glen Canyon Dam(1:100,000), or Navajo Creek(1:62,500).

The very interesting Kaibito Falls showing the limestone lens above and the sandstone below.

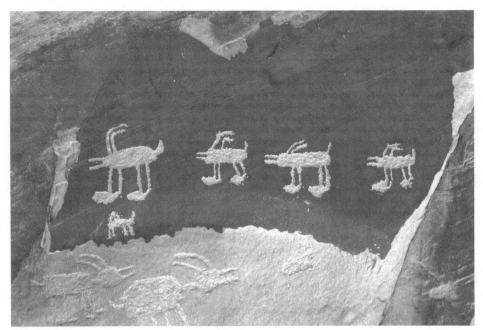

Petroglyphs along Chaol Canyon above Kaibito Falls.

Above this spring is a small Anasazi ruin which is very difficult to reach.

Warm Creek Bay, Crosby Canyon and the Spencer Coal Mines

Location and Campsites The historic Spencer Coal Mines are located in a little known side drainage entering Warm Creek Bay. The site is in Crosby Canyon, only about 200 meters from where the Warm Creek Road crosses the dry creek bed. You can drive to these old mines, or you can get there by hiking a short distance from the lake.

Warm Creek Bay is located just east of Wahweap Bay, which is where Wahweap Marina is found. Because it's so close to Wahweap, it's a very popular place in summer, both for camping and water skiing. This bay, most of which is shown on this map, probably has more good campsites and beaches per km than any other section of the lake. It's almost wall to wall beach. The reason for so many good sandy beaches, is that much of the shore line(at or near the HWM) makes contact with the Carmel Formation, which is just below the Entrada Sandstone walls. Little if any of the Carmel is actually exposed, as it is covered with eolian deposits--mostly sand from the Entrada Sandstone. Even at low water levels, there still should be plenty of campsites.

Routes or Trails The easiest way to get to the Spencer Mines is to drive along the Warm Creek Road which begins near mile post 7 on Highway 89, at Big Water, Utah. However, when it rains the clay-based road is impassable. Besides it's a short and easy hike from the lake anyway.

At the upper end of Crosby Canyon Inlet on either side, you'll see vehicle tracks. Dock where you can, and start up-canyon. Once you get above the HWM, you'll be on a road that's been graded by the National Park Service. They also seem to patrol it on a regular basis. This road has been graded along the bottom of the dry creek bed and any car can be driven down it. Floods will surely come down this canyon on occasions making changes for auto traffic. But the drainage is short, so the road should remain good for long periods of time after grading.

This is what you will find at the Spencer Coal Mines today. When you get to within 200 meters of the Warm Creek Road, look to the north against the south facing 10 meter-high canyon wall, and you'll notice a gray horizontal seam. This is the coal bed, about one meter thick. The outside surface exposed to weathering, looks more like gray shale than coal. Inside the tunnels, it looks more like real coal.

Just above the level of the dry creek bed will be seen the entrance to six tunnels. Of the six, two are almost completely buried by cave-ins, and a third is barely noticeable. Only three short tunnels are clearly visible. Upon inspection, the author found two of the six still had the wooden braces in place after all these years. They were mined in 1910 or 1911. You can see the end of each tunnel from the entrance--without going inside.

The junction of Warm Creek and Crosby Canyon Roads. About 200 meters to the right are the Spencer Coal Mines.

MAP 40, WARM CREEK BAY, CROSBY CANYON & THE SPENCER COAL MINES

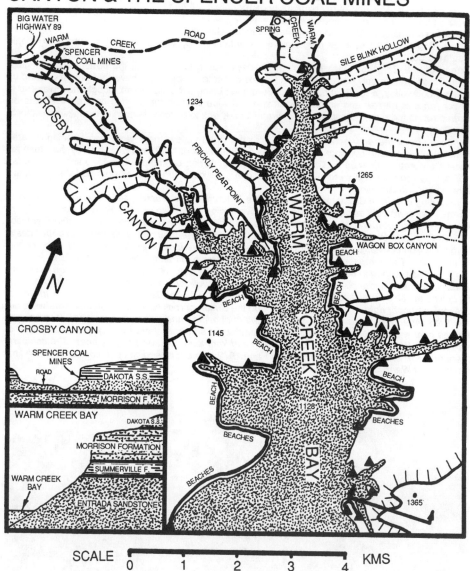

BIG WATER
HIGHWAY 89

WARM   CREEK   ROAD   SPRING   WARM CREEK

SPENCER
COAL MINES

SILE BLINK HOLLOW

CROSBY

1234

PRICKLY PEAR POINT

CANYON

1265

N

BEACH

WAGON BOX CANYON
BEACH

WARM

BEACH

CREEK

BEACH

1145

BEACH

BEACH

BEACH

CROSBY CANYON

SPENCER COAL
MINES

ROAD

DAKOTA S.S.

MORRISON F.

WARM CREEK BAY

DAKOTA S.S.

MORRISON FORMATION

SUMMERVILLE F.

WARM CREEK
BAY

ENTRADA SANDSTONE

BEACH

1128

BEACHES

BEACHES

BAY

BEACH

BEACHES

1365

SCALE
0   1   2   3   4   KMS

Hike Length and Time Needed From the HWM to the mines is about 5 kms along a good roadway. The time it will take for most people to see the mines and return to the lake will be less than 3 hours. The author drove up the road from the lake in 8 minutes in his VW Rabbit, so it's not far.
Boots or Shoes Any kind of dry weather boots or shoes will be fine.
Water There are no springs around, so take your own water.
Main Attractions Lots of good campsites and some historic coal mines.
Hiking Maps USGS or BLM map Smoky Mountain(1:100,000), or Gunsight Butte and Nipple Butte(1:62,500).
History of the Spencer Coal Mines In the days before Lake Powell, the bottom 6 or 7 kms of Warm Creek was deeply entrenched in a Navajo Sandstone canyon. Above that part, it opened up into an broad valley, a result of the Carmel Formation being exposed. Even though the lower end of the canyon was narrow and entrenched, it was still wide enough for wagons or even 4WD's to be driven down to the river. Because of this, Warm Creek was to become famous in the mining history of Glen Canyon.

Just above the entrenched part and into the open valley, there were before being covered by the lake, eight stone buildings. Their origins date from about 1910, and were built by the American Placer Corporation, headed by **Charles H. Spencer.** When Crampton visited the scene in the late 1950's, only two buildings were still standing and in good condition. The others had fallen down and were in very bad condition.

Quoting now from Crampton's writings in the Anthropological Papers, #46. *The rock buildings at Warm Creek were built as one part of an extensive mining enterprise at Lee's Ferry undertaken by the American Placer Corporation, a company formed in Chicago. Gold prospects in the Chinle Formation at Lee's Ferry and in the gravels at the mouth of the Paria River, and on the platforms on both sides of Marble Canyon downstream for several miles from there, were located in 1910 and 1911 by officers of the company. The company also staked some near the town of Paria[Pahreah] on the Paria River.*

It was planned to begin mining operations at Lee's Ferry. Steam boilers were to be used as a power source to operate pumps to provide water for hydraulicking and placering. In order to operate the boilers at Lee's Ferry, two coal mines were developed in Tibbet Canyon[they are actually in Crosby Canyon], an upper right fork of Warm Creek, and the cluster of rock buildings described here were built about this time to serve as headquarters for the coal mining and transport operation. It is believed that the coal was hauled down to this site by pack train and from there by wagon, probably with ox teams, down Warm Creek Canyon to the mouth and from there to Lee's Ferry by boat. The company operated a few months at Lee's Ferry in 1911 and 1912 before suspending operations after which time the cabins at Warm Creek must have been abandoned.

Spencer Coal Mines at the head of Crosby Canyon.

Spencer first thought coal could be brought directly to Lee's Ferry by mule, using an old trail called the Ute or Dominguez Trail, which was about 5 kms up the Paria River Canyon from the Ferry. Because of that extra distance, it was decided to make a shortcut route directly above the operation on the Colorado. So in the fall of 1910, Spencer and his men constructed the Spencer Trail from the river to the top of the cliffs. From there it was hoped they could head out to the northeast with mules for the Warm Creek Coal Fields. But the trail was never used to bring in coal. Instead it was more of a promotional scheme than anything else.

The next job was to build a wagon road right down the dry creek bed of Warm Creek to the Colorado River. While workers were building the road, others were building a barge on the banks of the river. This all went well--they brought coal down the canyon, loaded it onto the barge, then floated it down to the Ferry. But then the problem was to get the barge back up stream again.

This problem it was thought, could be solved by a tugboat of some kind. So with investor's money a 9 meter long tug boat called the *Violet Louise*, was purchased and brought to the Ferry. As it turned out, it was far underpowered to push a large barge upstream against the current. The current wasn't that fast, but pushing a barge wasn't easy.

While Spencer worked on problems at the Ferry, the managers of the Chicago company he worked for ordered a steam powered boat from San Francisco. The boat was built in 1911, dismantled, and shipped by train to Marysvale, Utah, the end of the railway line. It was then put onto large wagons for the rest of the 320 km trip to the mouth of Warm Creek. There it was reassembled in the spring of 1912. It was the biggest thing to sail the Colorado River above the Grand Canyon, with the exception of the Stanton Dredge up near Bullfrog. It measured 28 x 8 meters, was powered by a coal boiler, and had a 4 meter wide stern paddlewheel. Even though this part of the project wasn't one of Spencer's big ideas, the boat was named the *Charles H. Spencer.*

The next problem was to find a crew for the boat. This wasn't easy in the middle of the desert, but they found a crew anyway. A fellow by the name of Pete Hanna was at the helm, the only crew member who had any experience with boats. They loaded the deck full of coal for the trial run. But almost immediately they hit a sandbar. Then another. Finally, Hanna turned the boat around and allowed it to sail down the river backwards, which gave it better maneuverability. They spent one night in the canyon, then next morning finished the 45 km run to the Ferry.

They then had to figure out how to get the *Spencer* back up stream against the current, which was stronger than anyone had expected. Hanna decided to keep most of the coal which had been brought down on board, to insure passage back up to Warm Creek. This was a good move, because they barely made it back up stream. They again loaded the boat as full as possible and returned to the Ferry, where it sat for a couple of months. All this while the chemists and the workers figured out

Another closer look at the Spencer Coal Mines.

269

what to do about separating the gold from the Chinle clays.

Finally it was decided to try something different. They ended up towing the original barge upstream with the *Spencer*. This worked fine. Next, they loaded up both the barge and the steamer with coal. The barge was then allowed to drift down stream with several workers guiding it around the sandbars, with the *Spencer* following. This worked fine too, and it appeared they had this part of the gold mining problem solved. The only thing left to do, was to find a successful way to get the gold out of the clay. This Spencer was never able to do, and the steamboat had made its last run.

Spencer left the Ferry later in 1912, bound for the nearly abandoned settlement of Pahreah. Meanwhile, the steamship *Charles H. Spencer* sat on the river tied to the bank. In 1915 the combination of high water and piles of drift wood, put the boat on its side and it sank in a meter of water. Later, parts were stripped off and taken away and some of the lumber from its decks was used for various other projects. Today, you can just barely see the sunken remains of the boat just up stream from Lee's Fort and at the bottom end of the Spencer Trail. Nearby is the boiler and parts of the stern paddlewheel(see Kelsey's book, *Hiking and Exploring the Paria River*).

About 5 kms down stream from the mouth of Warm Creek was a sand bar, exposed only at low water. This was called the **Wright Bar,** after two brothers L. C. and G. W. Wright. They were the first to file claims to it on November 15, 1892. This site was unique, because it was one of the few places in the canyon where placer mining was done on a low-water sand bar. It's not known how extensive the mining operation was on the bar, but it's likely not too much.

For the most part, Glen Canyon was abandoned by miners after about 1900, with only sporadic prospecting thereafter. But when the American Placer Corporation began to stake out the countryside around Lee's Ferry, there was renewed interest in Glen Canyon. This sparked a mini gold rush. According to Crampton's report, in 1909 there were four men from Searchlight, Nevada, seen heading up stream to Wrights Bar, which appears to have been the last significant mining site in Glen Canyon above Lee's Ferry.

This mine tunnel still contains roof supports after nearly a century of inactivity.

Crampton's group took this foto of one of the stone building in Warm Creek Canyon just before the lake covered it.

Beneath this narrow cleft in the sandstone is the Antelope Canyon Narrows.

Antelope Canyon

Location and Campsites Antelope Canyon begins many kms to the south and runs north to the lake, passing between the Navajo Power Station east of Page and the town of Page itself. Antelope is the first canyon entering the lake east of the dam. In recent years this canyon has become famous because of post card fotos showing its narrows. Part of this same drainage south of Highway 98 is sometimes called **Corkscrew Canyon.** That part is very narrow, winding, and has very intricate patterns eroded in the Navajo Sandstone. In the summer of 1988, the Navajo Nation closed the road and a fee charged for a visit to that section. To quote an un-named NPS employee, *this is a political hot potato!* Get the latest information on entry problems to Corkscrew Canyon at the visitor center in Page.

However, there is another section of Antelope which may be just as interesting. This is between Highway 98 and the lake, and can be visited from the lake or road. To get there by boat, head south from Wahweap and into the old Colorado River channel south of Antelope Island. Near buoy M4(K6) is the beginning of Antelope Inlet. Just inside the inlet are a couple of fine campsites. There are also many good beaches just north of this mapped section in the main channel.

Routes or Trails From the end of the inlet walk up **Antelope Canyon.** It's an easy walk and in moderately good narrows. About 3/4 of the way from the HWM to the highway, you'll come to a blocking falls about 6 or 7 meters high. This may stop you, but when the author passed that way in the summer of 1988, there was a rope bolted to the wall above, and steps cut. If the rope remains there, you're in business.

About a km above this dry fall, be alert to the left side of the canyon, which then is becoming more shallow and open. You will almost miss what appears to be just a little side drainage. It's nothing more than a slit in the wall. This is actually the main drainage, but the part of the canyon heading due south is much larger and it appears to be the main canyon. This larger part almost dead-ends at the highway, which you can climb out to easily.

Back to the slit on the left. Just inside is a chamber with steps cut heading up a dry falls. In 1988, someone had bolted a rope to the rock above, allowing hikers to climb up easily. Inside the second chamber, you can walk a short distance more. It looks something like the geology cross section. At the back of this section, is another falls and steps. At one time, someone had rigged a rope down this one too, but it was gone in the summer of 1988. That was the end of hiking for the author, but there's more above.

You will find and can enter this same narrow slot further up canyon, if you head up to the highway and come down from the bridge just east of mile post 299, which is about 2 kms east of Page. If you do come down from the upper end, consider taking a rope so you can get down into the

Antelope Canyon Narrows as it runs underneath the highway bridge.

272

MAP 41, ANTELOPE CANYON

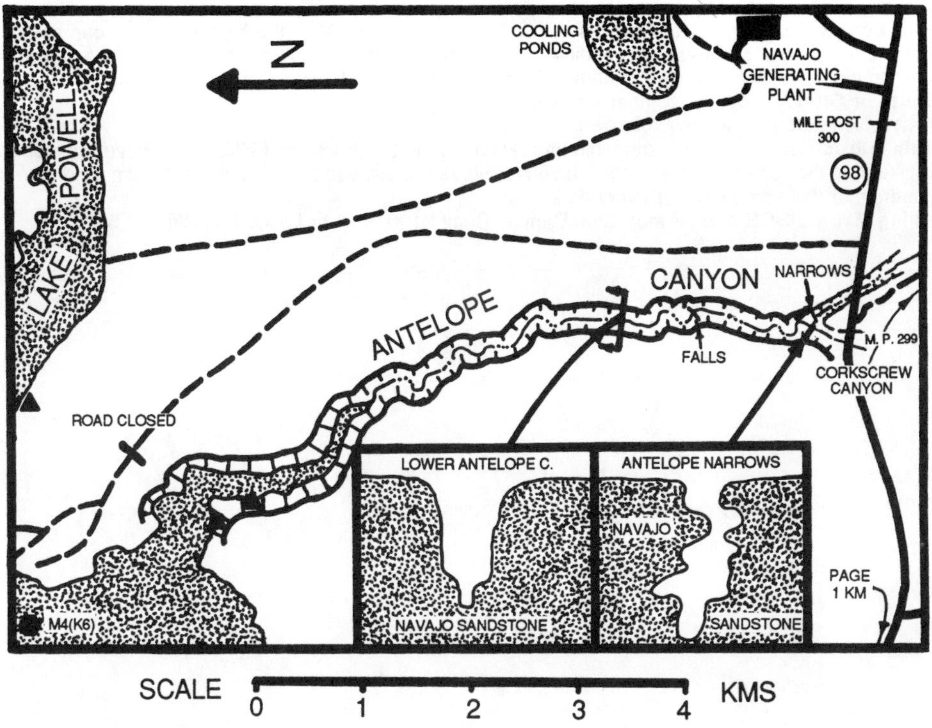

N
COOLING PONDS
NAVAJO GENERATING PLANT
MILE POST 300
98
LAKE POWELL
CANYON
NARROWS
ANTELOPE
FALLS
M. P. 299
CORKSCREW CANYON
ROAD CLOSED
LOWER ANTELOPE C.
NAVAJO SANDSTONE
ANTELOPE NARROWS
NAVAJO
SANDSTONE
PAGE 1 KM
M4(K6)
SCALE
0
1
2
3
4
KMS

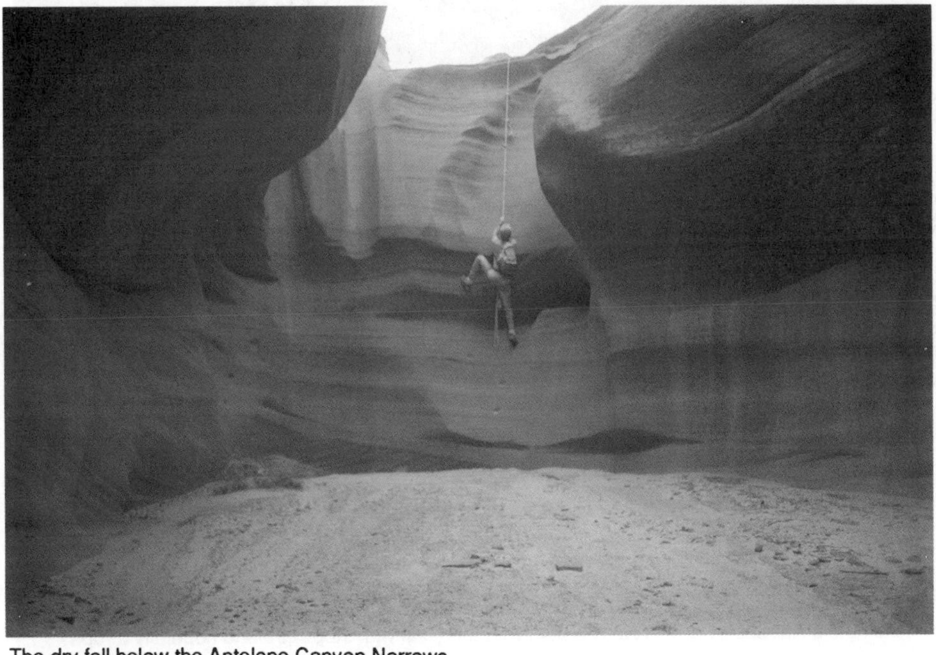

The dry fall below the Antelope Canyon Narrows.

middle parts of this 300 meter section. This is probably the most fotogenic little canyon the author has ever seen. You can get to it by boat, if the rope is still there in the middle of the main canyon, but it's more easily reached by car.

Hike Length and Time Needed It's 5 or 6 kms from the HWM to the highway. You can do this one in 3 to 5 hours, round-trip, depending on how much exploring you want to do. From the highway down to the really good narrows, is about 500 meters or less, and only a few minutes walk.

Boots or Shoes Any dry weather boots or shoes.

Water None around, so take your own.

Main Attractions The most fotogenic narrow canyon in this book and it likely will never be closed to hikers as the upper part has been. If you're a fotographer, use fast or high speed film and take a camera stand of some kind. It's very dark inside.

Hiking Maps USGS or BLM map Glen Canyon Dam(1:100,000), or Leche-E Rock(1:62,500).

Just inside the Antelope Canyon Narrows is this big dry fall with steps cut, and hopefully a rope?

This is inside the lower end of the Antelope Canyon Narrows.

Wiregrass Canyon and Wahweap Bay

Location and Campsites Wiregrass Canyon is located in the upper or west end of Wahweap Bay. It drains into the lake just northwest of Lone Rock. This is virtually an unknown canyon, but its two bridges are among the newest and most interesting around. More on this below.

Wahweap Bay which is the open body of water just to the west of Wahweap Marina, is one of the best areas on the lake for camping, as much of its shore line has sandy beaches. The reason for all the beaches are the white Entrada Sandstone cliffs which circle the bay. As they erode, the sands are left on or near the shore.

One of the best camping sites on the lake is Lone Rock Beach. This one you can drive to, and launch from. Leave Highway 89 about half a km northwest of the Utah-Arizona state line, and drive north to the lake. The beach has several pit toilets but no water. ORV's are allowed, so if you're looking for a quiet place to rest, better look somewhere else. This is the only place in the GCNRA where the National Park Service allows ORV's to be used.

Routes or Trails If you're interested in a short and easy hike, boat along the north shore of Wahweap Bay, not far to the northwest of Lone Rock and the Lone Rock Beach. The entrance to **Wiregrass Canyon Inlet** is a little difficult to find, so be observant. The waterway or inlet is narrow, and the Entrada walls aren't too high. As you near the upper end, you will once again have to watch carefully for the first of **two natural bridges** in the canyon. The **first bridge** is about 200 meters below the HWM on the left(going up). If the lake is full, you may have trouble seeing it, because it'll be tucked in under an overhang. The water then would be at the bottom of this small two meter square opening and you may not be able to boat under the overhang. If this is the case, boat on up a ways and walk into the canyon, where you can see it from above.

This bridge has been created recently by flood waters, which have eroded through one wall of a gooseneck and have dropped down and out the other side. The exit side is lower, thus creating a waterfall when floodwaters pour down the drainage. The author was there with the lake about 2 meters below the HWM. He climbed from his boat right up into and through the bridge opening.

As you walk up canyon, the walls become lower and more confined and the scenery isn't as interesting. But about 2/3 the way up, you'll pass a side canyon coming in from the right, or east. About 300 meters beyond that and again on the right, will be another hole in the wall. This is the **second bridge.** The tributary you just passed, has cut a hole in the wall of the main canyon where they once came just close together. This is a classic example of stream capture. There are now no more flood waters in the last 300 meters of the tributary canyon. If you continue up the drainage about another two kms you'll come to the Warm Creek Road, which begins at Big Water on Highway 89.

This is the first bridge in lower Wiregrass Canyon. It's just big enough to climb through.

MAP 42, WIREGRASS CANYON

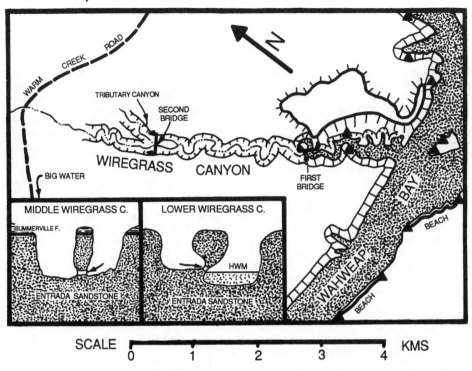

SCALE
0   1   2   3   4   KMS

Further up Wiregrass Canyon is the second bridge, and an excellent example of *stream capture*.

For those who would like to explore, you might try another drainage which is almost a twin to Wiregrass. It's called **Lone Rock Canyon,** which is due north of Lone Rock and just east of Wiregrass. It didn't look interesting to the author, so he only went up canyon a km or less. Paul Zaenger of the NPS, says there are several dry falls which keep hikers from reaching the Warm Creek Road.

If the lake is at or near the HWM and if you boat all the way to the upper end of the Wahweap Bay, you will have a chance to hike into some very short side canyons just to the south of Wiregrass Spring. One of the larger ones is called **Blue Pool Wash.** You can walk up this drainage only 300 meters or so from the dry Wahweap Creek, before being stopped by a dry fall. Or you can hike down into it from the highway. There are one or more falls about half way up, and some pretty good narrows. It passes under Highway 89, about half way between mile posts 3 and 4.

Hike Length and Time Needed From the first bridge or the HWM, to the second bridge, is about 3 kms. From the second bridge to the road, about another 2 kms. Visiting the bridges and going up to the road, will take 2, maybe 3 hours at the most, for the round-trip hike.

Boots or Shoes Any dry weather boots or shoes will do.

Water These are all dry canyons so take your own water.

Main Attractions Two recently made natural bridges, one great beach you can drive to, and many good beaches and campsites with boater access only.

Hiking Maps USGS or BLM map Smoky Mountain(1:100,000), or Nipple Butte(1:62,500).

Wahweap Bay and History Before Lake Powell came to be, the very first stream to enter the Colorado River above the dam site was **Wahweap Creek.** That distance was only about 2 1/2 kms. The bottom end of this canyon was very much intrenched in the Navajo Sandstone, but up stream about 6 or 7 kms, it opened up dramatically with the Carmel Formation exposed.

Dellenbaugh's Diary of 1871, has some interesting statements about what they found at the mouth of Wahweap Creek. It states, *the following morning, October 18th, we had not gone more than a mile[1 1/2 kms] when we came to a singular freak of erosion, a lone sandstone pinnacle on the right, three hundred or four hundred feet[100-125 meters] high, the river running on one side and a beautiful creek eight feet[2 1/2 meters] wide on the other. We named these Sentinel Rock and Sentinel Creek and camped there for Beaman to get some photographs. Prof. and I went up the creek and tried to climb out for observations, but though we made three separate attempts we had to give it up.* All this is now covered by about 150 meters of water.

There seems to have been very little mining activity in or along this canyon, but there were some claims staked out 6 or 7 kms up canyon. Crampton in 1959, reported seeing an abandoned automobile, about a 1936 model, at the mouth of the canyon. This could only have come down

The lower end of Blue Pool Wash. Get to this from Wahweap Bay.

WAHWEAP BAY

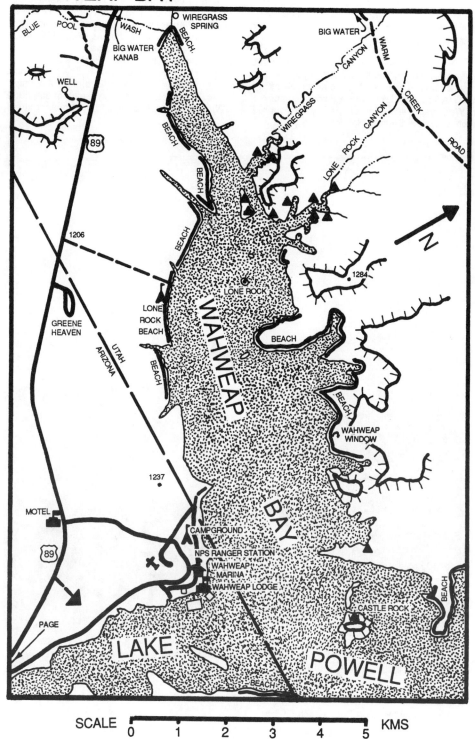

SCALE

0 1 2 3 4 5 KMS

Wahweap Creek.

In the time since the white man has been in this part of the country this canyon drainage has been known by several names; Sentinel Creek, Sentinel Rock Creek, and Warm Creek. However, Wahweap which is a Piute word, is likely the best name. Wahweap means something close to *alkaline seeps* or *salt licks,* or it may mean *little hollows containing stagnant pools of brackish water.* With the thick beds of Tropic Shale up canyon, this certainly is an appropriate name.

Wahweap Bay is one of the largest open bodies of water on Lake Powell. Besides all the good campsites already mentioned, it's a popular water skiing and day-use area as well. There are some scenic sites in the bay too. **Castle Rock,** northeast of Wahweap Marina, is one of the major landmarks on the lake. **Lone Rock,** just north of Lone Rock Beach is another site. Almost due north of Wahweap Marina and on the northern shore line is **Wahweap Window**, an 11 by 13 meter natural arch, set in the Entrada Sandstone.

The very crowded Lone Rock Beach.

Lone Rock is just out in the bay from Lone Rock Beach.

Just north of Wahweap Marina is what locals call Wahweap Window or Windows.

Castle Rock has one campsite on its western side.

Navajo Creek just above where it meets Chaol Canyon.

The lower part of the narrows in Antelope Canyon.

Part of the Dominguez and Escalante Trail(north).

This foto was taken from the end of the 4WD road part of the Hole-in-the-Rock Trail at the head of Cottonwood Canyon. It shows Cottonwood Canyon, the lake and the cleft in the canyon wall on the other side of the lake.

Looking northeast from the top of the Rincon Butte.

Petrified wood in Mikes Canyon, which is just west of the San Juan Marina.

Part of the Schock Trail which was blasted out of the Navajo Slickrock.

Further Reading

Archaeology of Glen Canyon

Archaeology of Eastern Utah,(Emphasis on the Fremont Culture), J. Eldon Dorman, College of Eastern Utah, Prehistoric Museum, Price, Utah.

Anthropological Papers, University of Utah, #104, 1980, *Cowboy Cave*, Jesse D. Jennings.

Anthropological Papers, University of Utah, #57, 1962, *Upper White Canyon and Palmer and Upper Gypsum(Fable Valley) Canyon,* Sharrock and others(Carnegie Museum).

Anthropological Papers, University of Utah, #52, 1961, *Lake Canyon,* Fowler and others.

Anthropological Papers, University of Utah, #49, 1960, *The Rincon, Iceberg, Moqui and Forgotten Canyons,* Lipe and others.

Anthropological Papers, University of Utah, #73, 1964, *Slickrock Canyon, Castle Wash, Steer Pasture Canyons,* Sharrock and others.

Anthropological Papers, University of Utah, #39, 1959, *Kaiparowits Plateau,* Fowler and others.

Anthropological Papers, University of Utah, #63, 1963, *Moqui Canyon and Castle Wash,* Sharrock and others.

Anthropological Papers, University of Utah, #71, 1964, *Kaiparowits Plateau and Glen Canyon Prehistory,* Lister.

Annals of the Carnegie Museum, Special Publication #8, Pittsburg, 1984, *The Pleistocene Dung Blanket of Bechan Cave, Utah,* (Bowns Canyon), Davis and others.

Museum of Northern Arizona, Bulletin 31, W. Y. and N. K. Adams, *Inventory of Prehistoric Sites on the Lower San Juan River, Utah,* 1959.

The Quarterly of the Museum of Northern Arizona--Plateau, Stephen C. Jett, *Testimony of the Sacredness of Rainbow Natural Bridge to Puebloans, Navajos, and Paiutes,* Spring, 1973.

History of the Glen Canyon Region

Boulder Country and its People, Lenora Hall Lefevre(Boulder, Utah), Art City Publishing, Springville, Utah, 1973

Desert River Crossing--Historic Lee's Ferry on the Colorado River, W. L. Rusho and C. Gregory Crampton, 1981, Peregrine Smith, Inc. Salt Lake City, Utah.

Ghosts of Glen Canyon-History Beneath Lake Powell, C. Gregory Crampton, Publishers Place, Inc., St. George, Utah.

Glen Canyon Dam and Steel-arch Bridge, Stan Jones, 1984, Sun Country Publications, Page, Arizona.

Hiking the Escalante, Rudi Lambrechtse, 1985, Wasatch Publishers, Inc., 4647 Idlewild Road, Salt Lake City, Utah.

Hiking and Exploring the Paria River, including the Story of John D. Lee, Mountain Meadows Massacre and Lee's Ferry, Kelsey, Kelsey Publishing, 456 E. 100 N., Provo, Utah.

Hiking and Exploring Utah's Henry Mountains and Robbers Roost, Including the Life and Legend and Butch Cassidy, Michael R. Kelsey, 1987, Kelsey Publishing, 456 E. 100 N., Provo, Utah.

History and Settlement of Northern San Juan County, Frank Silvey.

History of San Juan County, 1879-1917, Albert R. Lyman, unpublished manuscript.

Incredible Passage, Through the Hole-in-the-Rock, Lee Reay, 1980, Meadow Lane Publications, Provo, Utah.

J. A. Scorup: A Utah Cattleman, Stena Scorup, Self Published, 1946?

John W. Redd--Oral History, Charles Redd Center for Western Studies, BYU, Provo, Utah, CRC-C32, 1973.

Lee's Ferry, A Crossing of the Colorado River, Measeles, Pruett Publishing, Denver, Colorado.

Lemuel Hardison Redd, Jr., 1856-1923, Amasa J. Redd, 1967.

One Man's West, David Lavender, Doubleday & Company, Inc. Garden City, New York, 1956.

The Outlaw of Navajo Mountain, Albert R. Lyman, Deseret Book Company, Salt Lake City, Utah, 1963

San Juan In Controversy: American Livestock Frontier vs. Mormon Cattle Pool, Charles S. Peterson, Charles Redd Monographs of Western History, #3, BYU, 1974.

Standing Up Country, The Canyonlands of Utah and Arizona, C. Gregory Crampton, Peregrine Smith Books, Salt Lake City, Utah.

The Exploration of the Colorado River and its Canyons, John Wesley Powell, republished

by Dover Publications, Inc., New York, 1961.
The Cattle Industry of San Juan County, Utah, 1875-1900, Franklin D. Day, *Thesis,* Brigham Young University, 1958.
Utah Historical Quarterly, Neal Lambert, *Al Scorup, Cattleman of the Canyons,* 1964
A Canyon Voyage, Frederick S. Dellenbaugh, 1926, Yale University Press.
Anthropological Papers, University of Utah, #42, 1959, *Outline History of the Glen Canyon Region, 1776-1922,* C.Gregory Crampton.
Anthropological Papers, University of Utah, #72, 1964, *Historical Sites in Cataract and Narrow Canyons, and in Glen Canyon to California Bar,* C. Gregory Crampton.
Anthropological Papers, University of Utah, #61, 1962, *Historical Sites in Glen Canyon--Mouth of Hansen Creek to Mouth of San Juan River,* C. Gregory Crampton.
Anthropological Papers, University of Utah, #54, 1961, *The Hoskaninni Papers, Mining in Glen Canyon, 1897-1902,* Robert B. Stanton.
Anthropological Papers, University of Utah, #70, 1964, *The San Juan Canyon Historical Sites,* C. Gregory Crampton.
Anthropological Papers, University of Utah, #46, 1960, *Historical Sites in Glen Canyon, Mouth of San Juan River to Lee's Ferry,* C. Gregory Crampton.

Geology of Glen Canyon

Glen Canyon Geology(hand out), GCNRA, National Park Service, Page, Arizona.
Geologic History of Utah, Lehi F. Hintze, BYU Geology Studies, Vol. 20, Pt. 3, Provo, Utah.
Geology Map of Canyonlands National Park and Vicinity, Utah, Huntoon, Billingsley, Breed, Canyonlands Natural History Association and USGS. Moab, Utah.
Geology, Structure, and Uranium Deposits of the Escalante Quadrangle, Utah, and Arizona, Hackman and Wyant, 1973-79, USGS Map I-744.
Geology, Structure, and Uranium Deposits of the Marble Canyon Quadrangle, Arizona, Haynes and Hackman, 1978, USGS Map I-1003.
Geology of the Salina Quadrangle, Utah, Williams and Hackman, 1971-83, USGS Map I-591-A
River Runners Guide to Canyonlands National Park and Vicinity, with Emphasis on Geologic Features(and some history), Feli, E. Mutschler, Powell Society Ltd., Denver, Colorado.

Other Sources

Glen Canyon Camping(handout), National Park Service, 1988
Letter on Lake Powell Water Quality, John O. Lancaster, Superintendent, GCNRA, September 26, 1988
Stan Jones' Boating and Exploring Map of Lake Powell, Stan Jones, Sun Country Publication, Page, Arizona
Personel Communication, Edith Clinger, Orem, Utah, November 6 & 7, 1988
Personel Communication, Carl Mahon, Monticello, Utah, September 15, 1988
Personel Communication, Clarence Rogers, Blanding, Utah, November 24, 1988
Personel Communication, John Scorup, Monticello, Utah, November 6 & 7, 1988
Personel Communication, Kee B. Tso, Kaibito, Navajo Nation, September 14, 1988
Personel Communication, John Redd, Blanding, Utah, November 22, 1988
Personel Communication, Leo Wilson, Escalante, Utah, September 13, 1988
Personel Communication, Melvin Dalton, Monticello, Utah, October 29, November 6 & 22, 1988
Personel Communication, Owen Yazzie, Leche-e Rock, Navajo Nation, October 1, 1988
Personel Communication, Riter Ekker, Hanksville, Utah, September 12, 1988
Personel Communication, Vernon Griffin, Escalante, Utah, September 13, 1988.

Other Guide Books by the Author

Climbers and Hikers Guide to the Worlds Mountains(2nd Ed.), Kelsey, 800 pages, 377 maps, 380 fotos, waterproof cover, 14cm x 21cm(5 1/2" x 8" x 1 1/2"), ISBN 0-9605824-2-8. **US $19.95** (Mail orders US $20.95). **(Out of stock--3rd Edition coming in 1990-91?)**
Utah Mountaineering Guide, and the Best Canyon Hikes(2nd Ed.), Kelsey, 192 pages, 105 fotos, ISBN 0-9605824-5-2. **US $7.95** (Mail orders US $9.00).
Canyon Hiking Guide to the Colorado Plateau(2nd Printing), Kelsey, 256 pages, 117 hikes and maps, 130 fotos, ISBN 0-9605824-1-5. **US $9.95** (Mail orders US $11.00).
Hiking Utah's San Rafael Swell, Kelsey, 144 pages, 30 mapped hikes, plus lots of history, 104 fotos, ISBN 0-9605824-4-4. **US $7.95** (Mail orders US $9.00).
Hiking and Exploring Utah's Henry Mountains and Robbers Roost, Kelsey, 224 pages, 38 hikes or climbs, 163 fotos, including The Life and Legend of Butch Cassidy, ISBN 0-9605824-6-0. **US $8.95** (Mail orders US $10.00).
Hiking and Exploring the Paria River, Kelsey, 208 pages, 30 different hikes from Bryce Canyon to Lee's Ferry, including the Story of John D. Lee, Mountain Meadows Massacre and Lee's Ferry, 155 fotos, ISBN 0-9605824-7-9. **US $8.95**(Mail Orders US $10,00).
Hiking and Exploring in the Great Basin National Park--A Guide to Nevada's Wheeler Peak, Mt. Moriah, and the Snake Range, Kelsey, 192 pages, 47 hikes or climbs, 125 fotos, ISBN 0-9605824-8-7. **US $8.95**(Mail Orders $10.00).
China on Your Own, and The Hiking Guide to China's Nine Sacred Mountains(3rd and Revised Ed.), Jennings/Kelsey, 240 pages, 110 maps, 16 hikes or climbs, ISBN 0-9691363-1-5. **US $9.95**(Mail Orders US$11.00)(Please order this book from **Milestone Publications, P.O. Box 35548, Station E, Vancouver, B.C., Canada, V6M 4G8**).

Distributors for Kelsey Publishing

Please write to one of these companies when ordering any of Mike Kelsey's guide books.

Primary Distributor

Wasatch Publishers, Inc., 4647 Idlewild Road, Salt Lake City, Utah, USA, 84124, Tele. 801-278-3174.

Alpenbooks, P.O. Box 27344, Seattle, Washington, 98125, Tele. 206-672-9316
Bookpeople, 2929 Fifth Street, Berkeley, California, 94710, Tele. 227-1516
Canyon Country Publications, P. O. Box 963, Moab, Utah, 84532, Tele. 801-259-6700
Gordon's Books, 2323 Delgany, Denver, Colorado, 80216, Tele. 303-296-1830
Many Feathers, 2626 West, Indian School Road, Phoenix, Arizona, 85012, Tele. 602-266-1043
Nevada Publications, 4135 Badger Circle, Reno, Nevada, 89509, Tele. 702-747-0800
Pacific Pipeline, Inc., 19215 66th Avenue S., Kent, Washington, 98032-1171, Tele. 206-872-5523
Quality Books(Library Distributor), 918 Sherwood Drive, Lake Bluff, Illinois, 60044, Tele.
Mountain 'n Air Books, 3704 1/2 Foothill Blvd., La Crescenta, California, 91214, Tele. 818-957-5338
Recreational Equipment, Inc.(R.E.I.), P.O. Box C-88126, Seattle, Washington, 98188, Tele. 800-426-4840(or check at any of their local stores).

For the **UK** and **Europe**, and the rest of the world contact:
CORDEE, 3a De Montfort Street, Leicester, England, UK, LE1 7HD, Tele. 0533-54379